Long-Term Care

Options in an Expanding Market

Susan L. Hughes

DOW JONES-IRWIN
Homewood, Illinois 60430

*To E. F. X., Ed, John Patrick,
and Dempsey Lane*

This publication is designed to provide accurate and
authoritative information in regard to the subject matter
covered. It is sold with the understanding that the
publisher is not engaged in rendering legal, accounting, or
other professional service. If legal advice or other expert
assistance is required, the services of a competent
professional person should be sought.

*From a Declaration of Principles jointly adopted by a Committee
of the American Bar Association and a Committee of Publishers.*

ISBN 0-87094-497-5

Library of Congress Catalog Card No. 86–71440

Printed in the United States of America

1 2 3 4 5 6 7 8 9 0 K 3 2 1 0 9 8 7 6

PREFACE

The adequate financing of long-term care, now approximately a $40 billion industry, is one of the most pressing challenges facing the United States. There are two major problems with our current financing system. First, under the current system, the elderly are encouraged to divest themselves of a lifetime's accumulated assets in order to become eligible for public assistance from Medicaid to finance lengthy nursing home stays. Second, public funding for institutional care exceeds that for community care by a ratio of three to one.

Meanwhile, the elderly as a group understand very little about the paucity of their Medicare long-term care benefits and often purchase multiple medigap policies in the mistaken belief that this will protect them from the catastrophic cost of long-term care. The problems created by this lamentable financing system are only expected to become more acute in the future as the number of individuals surviving into their 80s and 90s increases.

Changes are afoot, however, which suggest that the cost of long-term care can be managed in the future. This book seeks to acquaint persons new to the long-term care field with the diversity and complexity of the critical long-term care actors including the consumers, payors, regulators, and providers. Using a framework of five critical policy concerns, the book analyzes the current organization, regulation, and financing of care and attempts to discern what we have learned from our experience over the last 20 years that can be used to build a better system for the future.

Finally, the book concludes that we face a critical juncture at present, with important choices that must be made during the next 5 to 10 years. Specifically, we now have the opportunity to develop new, private, risk-sharing financing options for long-term care which have the potential to empower future users and/or their families to become informed consumers of care. The improved ability to anticipate need for care is seen as a critical first step in arranging to finance it adequately. The high death rates of the early 1900s and the rising use and cost of hospital care during the 1930s spurred the development of the life insurance and hospital insurance products that are taken for granted today. In similar fashion today, as a nation, we are beginning to come to grips with the results of our successes. As a result of increased literacy, sanitation, immunization, and medical technology, to name but a few of the many advances experienced during the 20th century, record numbers of us are surviving as low birth-weight infants, trauma victims, and frail elderly needing assistance with everyday living tasks like eating, dressing, and bathing.

A humane society plans for and invests in the care of its frail or incapacitated members and does not leave their future to chance, under the theory that these accidents of nature could happen to any of us, that we are all at risk, and that while costs for an individual may be catastrophic, spread across a group these costs are affordable. If we continue to ignore the problem of financing long-term care it will only increase in size. Rather, we can seize the opportunity that exists today to reshape the financing of care and develop a competitive approach to the reimbursement of catastrophic care. In so doing, we can increase the quality, continuity, and access to care while simultaneously making the cost of care for the individual consumer more affordable. As a result of the numerous demonstrations, evaluations, and other research conducted during the last 20 years, we now have a body of knowledge that allows us to select from available options with some degree of confidence. If we continue this type of investment in the future and use this type of knowledge as it becomes available, we can transform the long-term care "crisis" into an opportunity to lay the groundwork for meaningful catastrophic insurance for all.

ACKNOWLEDGMENTS

I am indebted to many individuals for their generous gifts of time and help during the development of this book. First, many thanks to colleagues Barry Friedman, Steve Shortell, Larry Manheim, Perry Edelman, Sandy Sherman, and Diane Cowper at Northwestern University's Center for Health Services and Policy Research for their advice and encouragement on earlier drafts of the manuscript and to the chairman of my department in the medical school, Jeremiah Stamler, and David Mintzer, vice president for research, for their support of this activity. Randi Claassen, Paula Pfankuch, and Sandra Collins did a superb job typing and organizing the manuscript, and many kind friends including Mark Meiners, Dennis Kodner, David Kannell, Helen Raisz, Don Schneider, Greg Arling, Saul Spivack, and Larry Branch provided critical insights and/or late-breaking statistics from their respective areas of expertise. Bill Cabin from the National Association for Home Care, Al Sirrocco at the National Center for Health Statistics, Greg Adler at the Health Care Financing Administration, Dick Merrill of the Inter-Governmental Health Policy Project, and Betty Ransom from the National Institute for Adult Day Care never refused a request for an elusive statistic and are also gratefully acknowledged. Many thanks also to the staff at the Falmouth and Vail public libraries who cheerfully provided Scotch tape, paper clips, change for Xerox machines, and other necessary accoutrements of working vacations.

Finally, I'd like to thank my family for their support during a sometimes harrowing two years and promise them that the next time around, it will be an edited volume.

Susan Lane Hughes
Northwestern University
Center for Health Services
and Policy Research

"The trouble with our times," it has been said, "is that the future isn't what it used to be." Robert Butler, former Director, the National Institute on Aging, NIH.

CONTENTS

LIST OF FIGURES

LIST OF TABLES

PART ONE

Overview, Development, and Cost of Long-Term Care

CHAPTER ONE

Long-Term Care: An Overview

- Long-term care is undergoing an era of unprecedented ferment and growth, simultaneously challenging the limits of public financing and regulation and providing important new market opportunities for health care providers.
- Five essential attributes of long-term care that must be considered in choosing regulatory versus competitive approaches to reforming our system of care include:
  Access.
  Equity.
  Affordability.
  Quality.
  Continuity.

These concepts are discussed and constitute a framework for the analysis of alternative long-term care policy options for the future.

Choice and change are the two bywords that best characterize long-term care today. In an era marked by declining demand for acute hospital care, long-term care of the chronically ill is beginning to be recognized as a fundamental concern of health care providers. We are beginning to realize the difference between discretionary and nondiscretionary need for and use of health care services as well as the true dimensions and significance of catastrophic care needs and costs. This book seeks to acquaint students of hospital and health services administration, health care providers, and policy analysts who may be new to the long-term care field with the necessary background information and insights that this very complex system of services requires. The book also synthesizes relevant research findings that will be useful to those already practicing in this field.

Some analysts have characterized long-term care as a crisis. This book presents it as a very important new market opportunity for health care providers. It argues that the development of new financing mechanisms can greatly assist in attaining the policy goals of increased access to and equity, quality, affordability, and continuity of long-term care services.

Part 1 (Chapters 1, 2, and 3) presents background information on the development and cost of long-term care. Part 2 (Chapters 4, 5, and 6) concentrates on several important dimensions of the long-term care marketplace; namely, overviews of the consumers, the supply, and the organization of services both at present and as projected into the future. Part 3 (Chapters 7 and 8) synthesizes the important lessons we have learned and gains we have made in the past decade in quality assurance and public reimbursement for long-term care. Finally, Part 4 (Chapters 9 and 10) describes the range of new financing mechanisms and revenue sources needed to ensure that our funding supply is adequate to accommodate the projected increase in demand for long-term care services. It also analyzes the impact of private insurance on key policy attributes of long-term care.

OVERVIEW

Long-term care is simultaneously the health care crisis and the health care opportunity of the 80s. The turmoil currently surrounding the provision of this care reflects profound changes in our society. These changes range from increased levels of literacy and public sanitation on the social side to increasingly sophisticated use of technology on the medical side. The net result of a century of remarkable social and medical progress has been increased probability of living a normal life span, accompanied by a shift in focus from acute to chronic disease. More of us are surviving with good health to our 80s and 90s than ever before. Unfortunately, however, for many survival is accompanied by increased frailty and the presence of multiple chronic debilitating conditions. Increased medical technology has also made possible the survival of congenitally impaired newborns, medically fragile children, and young trauma victims to an extent not previously anticipated. Growing awareness of the increased prevalence of chronic impairments and of the increased cost of care for individuals suffering from them has sparked a critical reexamination of the organization of long-term care in the United States.

In 1984, combined public and private outlays for institution-based long-term care amounted to $30 billion.[1] Between 1975 and 1981, the number of acute care hospital beds increased by 10.6 percent. Under Medicare prospective payment, hospitals are now "downsizing" or closing beds, and the average hospital length of stay has declined from 9.5 to 7.5 days. In contrast, between 1975 and 1981 skilled nursing facility beds and home care agencies grew by 59.2 and 38.7 percent, respectively, and now constitute the fastest growing segments of the health care industry.[2] Experts in this field disagree about the specific rate of growth in the long-term care market over the next 50 to 60 years; however, all agree that substantial growth is bound to occur.

At present, 50 percent of institutional long-term care services are paid for by public funds. In view of projected increases in demand for care, we appear to have reached a crossroad in the delivery and financing of care for the chronically ill and may be facing the limits of public expenditures and regulation. Although public financing of long-term care may represent a health care crisis, this same crisis may be the private sector's opportunity. Specifically, as government expenditures become more constrained over time, a new market for private long-term care insurance is developing, spurred by consumers' desires to exercise choice over the locus of long-term care provision and by health care organizations seeking to diversify into the provision of chronic care. This type of diversification promotes vertical integration, increased control over patient flow, and increased stability for health care organizations coping with a turbulent external economic environment.

The forces described above have convinced many that an overhaul of the delivery and funding of long-term care services is clearly needed. This overhaul in our long-term care system is, in fact, already taking place. However, the ultimate goals of this overhaul and the specific steps to be taken to achieve an improved system of care are less clear. This book first explains why we are dealing with a long-term care crisis today; second, describes the dimensions of the problem; and third, systematically examines possible options for change.

For the purpose of this book, long-term care is defined as a continuum of health and social services provided to individuals of any age who are chronically impaired in their ability to perform necessary activities of daily living (ADL) such as eating, toileting, bathing, shopping, and food preparation. At present it is estimated that close to 6 million physically or mentally impaired individuals living in the community need help of this kind, and another 1.3 million individuals currently receive this assistance in institutional settings.[3] Although people with limitations in activities are estimated to constitute 10 percent of the population nationally, recent research indicates they are responsible for one third of health care costs. They have three times as many hospital admissions as functionally independent people, and their hospital stays are four days longer.[4] The federal cost of institutional long-term care alone is anticipated to exceed $48 billion (in constant 1980 dollars) by 2040.[5] Both the number of individuals requiring long-term care services and the cost of this care are currently anticipated to increase sharply over the next 50 years if constructive steps to constrain the rate of growth in expenditures are not taken. In order to avoid repetition of previous mistakes, however, it is vitally important to understand how our current system of care has evolved and to critically examine options for change from multiple policy perspectives.

Five Basic Policy Issues

At present, no coherent long-term care policy exists in the United States. Long-term care under certain pieces of legislation is addressed as a health insurance problem, and under others as a welfare issue. There is a growing awareness that long-term care differs in important ways from the acute medical model of care that has developed and flourished in the United States. The goals of the two models of care differ radically. Increasingly, acute care seeks to sustain life itself, while long-term care seeks to enhance quality of life and to minimize or compensate for functional disability.

Chronically ill individuals require a range of social and medical services if they are to compensate for their functional impairments and maintain their precarious health status and independence in the least restrictive setting possible of their own choice over an extended period of time. The chronically ill are not a homogeneous group but vary tremendously by age, income, degree of help available from families, level of education and income, and source of impairment (i.e., mental versus physical). It is generally agreed that need for long-term care services will increase substantially over the next 50 to 60 years, especially as more Americans survive into their 80s and 90s. Services must be provided for this growing population, but the organization and financing of these services must be undertaken in a way that synergistically addresses and maximizes several important attributes of care.

This is a difficult task since, at first glance, many objectives of an ideal system of care may appear to be mutually incompatible. For example, efforts to lower costs are argued by some to require reductions in quality of care provided. However, it is the contention of this book that five basic policy issues must constitute a framework for analysis of long-term care reform and that while trade-offs may be necessary, the trade-offs concern questions of degree rather than of zero-sum game. The basic issues that must be addressed include: access, equity, affordability, quality, and continuity of long-term care services. We argue that any future long-term care policy that addresses one of the above issues to the exclusion of the others is preordained to fail, since minimal levels of all five attributes must exist, and it may be possible with some creative planning to maximize many of them. Each attribute is briefly defined below and will be referred to repeatedly in chapters to follow.

Access. Access to care means that an individual who needs care is able to obtain it in a timely manner. Until now, access to long-term care service has been limited because of our heavy dependence on institution-based care and our lack of financing mechanisms which enable persons to purchase care. Many individuals who require care may not seek it because the "cost" of leaving home is too high. Access to care may become even more constrained in the future. At present, most nursing homes in the United States average 90 percent occupancy levels. Despite the fact that facilities are virtually full, many states use denial of certificates of need for new nursing home construction as a way of limiting increases in cost of care. This method of cost control may severely reduce access to needed care among future generations of the elderly.

Equity. Equity is the distribution of access to care across different population groups. Inequity in the current system is seen in the fact that instituiton-based services have been funded to the exclusion of in-home services. For example, if two people have the same disabling condition, one can enter a nursing home, spend down to Medicaid eligibility levels, and receive Medicaid-reimbursed long-term care. Another individual living in the community with exactly the same type of disability may be unable to receive publicly subsidized care of any type. This is inequitable.

Affordability. The United States is facing a $200 billion annual budget deficit. Blue-ribbon committees have been formed in the last few years to seriously reevaluate the capacity of the Medicare trust fund to provide substantial entitlements to our growing numbers of elderly citizens. The cost of institutional long-term care has increased from $1 billion to $30 billion over the period 1965–1984. It is clear that any coherent long-term care policy must make affordability a prime concern.

Quality. Long-term care regulators and providers have been concerned with quality of care issues for a long time. Seventy percent of long-term care institutional beds are located in investor-owned for-profit or proprietary homes. Proprietary agencies also constitute one of the fastest-growing segments of the home care industry today. Profit making per se is not inconsistent with the provision of quality services. However, it is important that long-term care reimbursement and delivery policies encourage quality care for individuals who might be unable to speak for themselves, through the structuring of quality incentives of some type into the system.

Continuity. While some might argue that continuity of care is one aspect of access or quality, we argue here that continuity of care for the chronically ill is so important that it justifies highlighting as a separate issue. At present, lack of knowledge on the part of consumers and their physicians regarding benefits and services, fragmented reimbursement policies, and parallel health and social service delivery systems that do not intersect conspire to hinder the easy transition from one locus of care to another as an individual's health status changes. Clearly, if disease prevention and maintenance of function are desired and the least restrictive and expensive levels and loci of care sought, continuity of care options will become increasingly important.

This brief overview of these important issues by no means completes a discussion of their attributes. Rather, the importance of these attributes will be highlighted repeatedly in chapters to follow as we attempt to demonstrate that they must all be considered simultaneously as part of a critical framework that can be used to reshape our current system of care.

NOTES

1. Katharine R. Levit, Helen Lazenby, Daniel R. Waldo, and Lawrence M. Davidoff, "National Health Expenditures, 1984," *Health Care Financing Review,* Fall 1985, p. 13.

2. Charles Helbing, "Medicare: Participating Providers and Suppliers of Health Care Services," *Health Care Financing Notes,* 1981, p. 2.

3. William G. Weissert, "Size and Characteristics of the Noninstitutionalized Long-Term Care Population," *Urban Institute Working Paper 1466–20,* September 1982, p. 10.

Esther Hing, "Characteristics of Nursing Home Residents, Health Status, and Care Received: National Nursing Home Survey, United States, May–December 1977," *Vital and Health Statistics,* Series 13, no. 51 (April 1981), p. 2.

4. Marc L. Berk, Gail Lee Cafferata, and Michael Hagan, "Persons with Limitations of Activity: Insurance, Expenditures and Use of Services," *NCHES Data Preview, 19* (PHS) 84–3363.

5. Dorothy P. Rice and Jacob J. Feldman, "Living Longer in the United States: Demographic Changes and Health Needs of the Elderly," *Milbank Memorial Fund Quarterly: Health and Society,* Summer 1983, p. 384.

CHAPTER TWO

Development of Long-Term Care in the United States

- The majority of long-term care services in the United States are provided by unpaid families and friends (informal caregivers).
- The public financing of formal (paid) long-term care services has encouraged the haphazard growth of institutional care and has inadvertently fostered the development of a largely proprietary (70 percent of beds) institutional provider capacity that must be taken into account when assessing the feasibility of alternative policy options.
- Compared to institutional care, community-based care is a relative newcomer that has demonstrated impressive growth in recent years.
- As a result of different funding sources, community services are provided by two parallel social and medical service systems which rarely intersect. More interaction among all three systems is necessary in order to realize the full potential of available care options.

Long-term care in the United States is currently provided by three sources: informal caregivers (the relatives and friends of impaired individuals) and the formally organized, parallel health and social service systems. The bulk of long-term care is provided by informal caregivers. However, over the last 50 years, formally organized services have grown considerably, often as the unexpected by-product of government legislation that was originally intended to achieve very different objectives. Most formal long-term care services are provided in institutional settings, but noninstitutional or community-based services also form an important part of the long-term care picture and have been growing more rapidly. The historical development of care in both settings is intertwined; however, for the sake of simplicity, their development will be treated separately in this review.

INSTITUTIONAL LONG-TERM CARE

The United States has never had an explicit, coherent policy toward the organization and financing of long-term care. Rather, our policy for care of the chronically ill has evolved incrementally and disjointedly, often as an afterthought or add-on to other pieces of health and social legislation. Although not part of a larger design, certain key pieces of legislation passed during the last 50 years have significantly impacted the provision of long-term care. As Figure 2–1 demonstrates, the legislation can be roughly categorized into two types: laws that expanded the demand for long-term care services by increasing the pool of eligible recipients and laws that increased the supply of providers by initiating direct subsidies of some type.

In the early part of the century, formal long-term care services were mainly provided by poorhouses, state mental hospitals, and voluntary homes for the aged that were established by different ethnic and religious groups. According to Vladeck and Waldman, the Social Security Act of 1935 played an important role in expanding the demand for proprietary and voluntary nursing home care by providing aged individuals who qualified under a means test with income (Old Age Assistance or OAA) that could be used to purchase personal and nursing care.[1] Framers of the Social Security Act believed that the elderly used almshouses because they lacked income

FIGURE 2–1 Development of Institutional Long-Term Care

Decade	Demand Stimulus	Supply Stimulus
1930s	Old Age Assistance under the Social Security Act allows aged individuals to purchase personal and nursing care.	
1950s	Disability Assistance under the Social Security Act extends coverage to the disabled. Social Security Amendments allow direct payments to vendors of health services for disabled medically indigent and federal matching of medical vendor payments under Old Age Assistance program.	Hill-Burton Act extends federal funding for grants, loans, and loan guarantees to nonprofit and government nursing homes. Small Business Administration loans and loan guarantees to proprietary homes. Federal Housing Authority mortgages (loan guarantees) for proprietary homes.
1960s	Kerr-Mills Act, Medical Assistance to the Aged, provides means-tested benefit for medically indigent elderly. Medicare, Title XVIII of the Social Security Act, adds universal health care for the aged. Medicaid, Title XIX of the Social Security Act, expands the Kerr-Mills Act to welfare recipients and the medically indigent of all ages. Miller Amendments allow vendor payments to newly created intermediate care facilities and extend coverage to the mentally retarded.	
1970s	PL 92–603, Social Security Amendment extends Medicare coverage to kidney transplants, renal dialysis, or long-term disability.	
1980s	Tax Equity and Fiscal Responsibility Act mandates prospective payment for Medicare hospital care (limits hospital services and/or length of stay).	

to support themselves in the community. They therefore reasoned that provision of income would eventually obviate the need for almshouse use. On the basis of this logic, they included a provision that prohibited payment of OAA benefits to people already residing in public institutions. However, Vladeck states that this provision was generally unsuccessful in emptying almshouses because many elderly residents were incapable of caring for themselves independently in the community. Instead of achieving its intended goal, the provision ultimately enabled other elderly people not already residing in almshouses to purchase care on their own, thus marking the supplanting of public facilities by proprietary "Mom and Pop" homes for the elderly.[2]

This shift to proprietary sources of care accelerated 15 years later, in 1950, when income assistance under social security was expanded to the disabled (Disability Assistance or DA), again on a means-tested basis. Even more significantly, the 1950 Social Security Amendments also authorized welfare agencies for the first time to make direct payments to providers (vendors) of health services, including providers of nursing home services. The states were allowed two options to determine level-of-income eligibility for OAA and DA. Under the "in or out" option, eligibility was based solely on whether an applicant could meet an income-based means test at the time of application. Under the "spend-down" option, applicants with higher incomes could become eligible if medical expenditures reduced their income to means-tested levels. Since nursing home care was relatively costly, many people in "spend-down" states who were not eligible for income assistance per se became eligible for publicly financed nursing home care. This extension of coverage to both the disabled poor and to the aged and disabled medically indigent significantly increased the pool of publicly financed long-term care recipients.

While the pool of eligibles was expanding, certain other government policies directly influenced nursing home supply. First, in 1954 in response to increased demand for care, federal funding for grants, loans, and loan guarantees was extended under the Hill-Burton Act of 1946 to nonprofit and government nursing homes capable of providing "high level, skilled nursing care."[3] The expansion of Hill-Burton coverage to nursing homes marked the beginning of federal involvement in setting standards in the nursing home industry and significantly influenced the medicalization or the transformation of small voluntary homes into miniature hospitals.

The next infusion of public funding into the industry occurred in 1956. At that time, in response to charges from proprietary homes that they were unfairly excluded from participation in the Hill-Burton program, Small Business Administration loans and loan guarantees were made available. However, proprietary homes charged that the loans were too few and covered too short a time period. In 1959, they succeeded in influencing the passage of legislation that made FHA mortgages available to proprietary homes. The legislation initially guaranteed 75 percent of a loan over a 20-year period but was subsequently expanded to guarantee 90 percent of a loan over a 40-year period. According to Vladeck, availability of FHA mortgage guarantees eventually succeeded in generating close to $1 billion in mortgage loans to the proprietary sector of the nursing home industry.[4]

Medicare and Medicaid

By the late 50s, many groups had been expressing alarm concerning increasing costs of health care. Strategists who had lobbied unsuccessfully in the late 1940s for national health insurance with universal coverage began to realize that health insurance for the elderly might be an achievable first step. In an effort to stem the liberal tide of feeling on this issue, Wilbur Mills successfully engineered the passage of the Kerr-Mills Act (Medical Assistance for the Aged or MAA) of 1960. MAA differed from OAA in two ways. First, states were allowed to define medical indigency separately from cash-income eligibility. Second, there was no ceiling on federal matching of state payments, although the federal share was specified to range from 50 to 80 percent in inverse ratio to the per capita income of a given state. Participation in MAA was voluntary on the part of the states; consequently, the program was implemented quite variably. For example, five of the states with 31 percent of the nation's elderly accounted for 62 percent of federal MAA funds, and nine states never participated at all. In the states which participated, vendor payments for nursing home services increased tenfold within a five-year period.

Speculating on the cause for this rapid growth, Vladeck attributes it to a combination of three factors: the attractiveness of even very low reimbursement rates to proprietary homes, the convenience that the nursing home provided social workers as a "safe" discharge option for marginally functioning elderly, and the spend-down feature which expanded the potential pool of welfare program recipients.[5] However, it is also true that the size of the elderly population was increasing during the 1960s, reflecting the high birthrate and immigration rates of the late 19th century, and mortality rates were also beginning to decline. The combined influence of increases in supply and demand for long-term care service was beginning to be felt.

Under the great wave of social legislation marking Lyndon Johnson's early presidency, Medicare (Title XVIII of the Social Security Act) was finally signed into law in 1965, providing universal health insurance for the aged. The main purpose of Medicare was to protect elderly individuals from the risk of total payment for acute hospital care. Therefore, the long-term care benefit in the bill was very modest, consisting of 100 reimbursed "extended-care facility" or nursing home days following a hospital stay. This benefit was intended to shorten hospital stays by providing a less expensive level of care where the elderly could convalesce following an acute illness. Nursing home benefits under Medicare were also originally intended to apply only to those nursing homes owned or operated by hospitals. However, recognizing that most recipients would be effectively denied the service benefit by this restriction, Congress later allowed payments to homes having transfer agreements with specific hospitals.

Meanwhile, during the controversy which accompanied the passage of Medicare, Medicaid (Title XIX of the Social Security Act), the most significant legislation to affect long-term care, was signed into law almost as an afterthought. In order to accommodate liberal supporters of Medicare, conservative supporters of the Kerr-Mills approach, and American

Medical Association pleas for voluntary physician coverage, Wilbur Mills put together a "wedding cake" health insurance package. Medicaid was the bottom, Medicare Part A the middle, and Medicare Part B the top layer.[6] Medicaid expanded the coverage of the Kerr-Mills Act to all individuals, regardless of age, who were either welfare recipients or medically indigent. In order to participate in the Medicaid program, states had to provide five "basic" services of which skilled nursing home care was one. Continued federal matching funds of 50 to 83 percent were made available, again, without a ceiling on total level of federal expenditures. Although Medicare payments for nursing home care were specified to be cost related, no similar provision was made for Medicaid nursing home reimbursement rates, which were left to the states to determine.

The different administrative homes of the two new social security titles reflected their different sponsorship, intent, and relative importance. Medicare was housed in the Social Security Administration since it was an entitlement and was to be administered as an insurance program. Medicaid, in contrast, was housed in the Medical Services Administration Office of the Social and Rehabilitation Service (formerly the Welfare Administration) since it was a social welfare benefit and not an insurance entitlement. The federal administration of the Medicaid program was to prove woefully inadequate to the program's needs. For example, Stevens and Stevens described the 1968 Medicaid task force of the New York City Health Department to be better staffed than the national Medicaid program.[7] It was not until 1977 that a single new agency, the Health Care Financing Administration, was created by an act of Congress to oversee the joint management of both programs.

Retrenchment

Although the original Medicare long-term care provisions were never overly generous, regulations subsequently developed to guide their implementation made them increasingly restrictive. Two events caused this retrenchment. The first concerned nursing home conditions of participation in the

Medicare program, and the second, rapid increases in overall Medicare program expenditures in its early years. Originally, framers of the Medicare legislation intended to upgrade the quality of nursing home care by insisting on transfer agreements with specific hospitals. However, a mere 6 percent of the 13,000 nursing homes existing in 1966 could fully comply with the conditions of participation.[8] To prevent denial of care to most elderly beneficiaries, regulators developed a new category of Medicare participation called "substantial compliance," thereby enabling another 3,200 homes to participate.

Second, all Medicare expenditures, including those for long-term care, increased rapidly during the first few years following the implementation of the legislation. The actual first-year cost of Medicare extended-care benefits alone was five times greater than originally estimated. The expansion of coverage to facilities in "substantial compliance" and the reliance on cost-based reimbursement are both advanced by Vladeck as causes of this surge in costs. Furthermore, extended-care benefits were originally assumed to be a substitute for higher-cost hospital inpatient days. It appeared, instead, that the services were used as an add-on to acute care benefits.[9]

Faced with increasing health care costs on every front, the new Nixon administration attempted to retrench where it could through the development of more restrictive regulations. In April of 1969, Medicare benefits for both nursing home and home health care were severely curtailed by the introduction of the "skilled nursing care" regulation. For the first time, intermediaries were provided with an itemized list of services that had to be provided by a vendor in order to qualify for Medicare reimbursement. These services were limited to conditions requiring skilled nursing care such as intravenous feedings, sterile dressing changes, and frequent intramuscular injections. Intermediaries were also advised that erring on the side of increased denials of reimbursement claims was preferred to erroneous approvals. Retrospective denials of claims began immediately, and mass confusion reigned for an ensuing three-year period. Retrospective denials increased from 1.5 percent of nursing home claims during the first six months of 1969 to 8.2 percent during early 1970.[10] The number of extended-care days reimbursed by Medicare dropped from a high of 17.6 million in 1969 to 6.6 million in 1972.[11] In three years, the contribution of Medicare to long-term care costs was halved, and over the decade 1969–1979, the proportion of institutional long-term care expenditures reimbursed by Medicare fell from 5.3 percent to 1.1 percent.

During the same decade, the industry also faced increased demands regarding structural and staffing standards of care. Once the government increased its share of service costs, legislators (specifically the subcommittee on long-term care of the Senate Special Committee on Aging, chaired by Senator Frank Moss) began to voice concerns about improving nursing home standards. The "Moss" Social Security Act Amendments were passed in 1967, signed into law in early 1968, and implemented in June of 1969. These amendments mandated the disclosure of financial interests in nursing homes; the establishment of standards for record keeping, dietary services, drug dispensing, medical services, and environment and sanitation; the development of transfer agreements with hospitals for acute care needs of patients; and a program of peer review of professional services and utilization review to be administered by the states.

Regulations subsequently developed to implement the Moss Amendment also specified that in states lacking more stringent fire codes, the Life Safety Code of the National Fire Protection Association become the standard for enforcement. Finally, the regulations also required the employment of at least one full-time RN during the day shift, with nonwaivered LPN charge nurses during afternoon and evening shifts, after July 1, 1970. According to Scanlon and Feder, the combination of uncertainty regarding Medicare reimbursement for skilled care conditions and the more stringent Medicare quality-assurance regulations resulted in the closing by 1976 of more than 6,000 (28 percent) of the homes operating in 1971.[12] Somewhat paradoxically, during the same five-year period, 4,800 new homes opened. The new homes differed significantly, however, from their predecessors. On average, they were twice as large, causing the average size of a nursing home to increase from 54.5 to 68.9 beds. Comparatively speaking, they were better equipped administratively to handle the increased complexity of nursing home management.

In response to the increased technical emphasis of the skilled nursing reimbursement regulations and the Moss Amendments, the nursing home industry fought back, proposing the establishment of a different category of care, the intermediate care facility (ICF). Nursing home providers argued that a substantial number of residents did not require 24-hour skilled nursing care and could be cared for less expensively if grouped together. Emanating from the Senate Finance Committee, the Miller Amendment of 1967 authorized vendor payments for this new level of care under the cash assistance titles (OAA, DA) of the Social Security Act but not through Medicaid. The intent was to provide a middle level of care which would prevent both excessively medicalized care and the reimbursement of custodial care only. The Miller Amendment also again significantly expanded the pool of publicly supported long-term care recipients by including residents of nonskilled care nursing homes, residents of homes for the aged, and the mentally retarded as eligible recipients.

During the next two years, confusion reigned as nursing homes reclassified residents and states reclassified providers. In 1971, in an effort to clarify the situation, legislation was enacted that transferred the ICF benefit back to the Medicaid program with the option once again of eligibility based on medical indigency if states so chose. Reimbursement was limited to 90 percent of the statewide rate for skilled nursing facilities (SNFs) and federal standards for staffing and safety (somewhat lower than SNF levels) were formulated. During 1971, the Nixon administration also created an Office of Nursing Home Affairs within the Department of Health, Education, and Welfare (HEW) and announced its support of expanded federal funding for enforcement of regulations.

Finally, in 1972, under the PL 92–603 Social Security Amendments, a number of steps were taken to clarify and stabilize the confused long-term care picture and, once again, to expand the potential pool of recipients. The 1972 Social Security Amendments were originally intended by the reelected Nixon administration to form the basis of a complete overhaul of the U.S. public welfare system. However, consensus on a national welfare policy for the majority of recipients, families with dependent children, could not be reached. It was possible, however, to reach agreement regarding the then less controversial issue of care for the aged, blind, and disabled. As a result of this legislation, Medicare extended-care facilities (ECFs) and Medicaid SNFs were redefined as falling within the same SNF level category of care, and HEW was instructed to develop a single set of SNF standards. A new category of "presumptive eligibility" for patients with certain diagnoses was established as a means of ending the retrospective denials problem for Medicare SNF admissions. Newly created professional standard review organizations (PSROs) were also charged to review SNFs and ICFs regarding appropriateness of level of care provided. Full federal funding of the states' long-term care enforcement activities was also authorized. Importantly, these 1972 amendments also expanded Medicare coverage to a new pool of recipients: patients of all ages undergoing kidney transplants and patients requiring dialysis for kidney failure.

Finally, and perhaps most importantly, Section 249 of the 1972 amendments for the first time also required Medicaid reimbursement for SNF and ICF care to be cost related in an effort to counteract the popular argument of providers that quality of care was impossible to achieve because of low reimbursement rates. This section also encouraged the states to experiment with ways to determine "reasonable cost," thus accounting for the present variety in state rate setting for Medicaid long-term care.

The 1972 amendments at first appeared to signal that substantial progress was occurring in long-term care. However, by the time the amendments were passed into law, the Nixon administration was totally preoccupied with Watergate, and the Medicaid cost-related reimbursement regulations for nursing homes were not implemented until January 1, 1978, a delay of six years.[13]

Recent Developments

By the late 70s, price controls on health care had been lifted, and the cost of nursing home care was increasing rapidly. The states were becoming alarmed at the increasing size of their Medicaid expenditures and increasingly concerned about the portion of Medicaid budgets designated for reimbursement of nursing home care. This was the climate in which two other recent pieces of legislation that have had profound impact on the provision of institutional long-term care in the 80s were passed. The new Reagan administration, committed to reductions in federal spending as a means of controlling inflation, successfully engineered the passage of the 1981 Omnibus Budget Reconciliation Act (OBRA). This legislation reduced the level of the federal share of Medicaid by 3 percent in fiscal year 1982, 4 percent in fiscal year 1983, and 4.5 percent in fiscal year 1984. These reductions in federal Medicaid matching funds occurred at precisely the same time as one of our worst economic recessions. Thus, at a time when unemployment and welfare expenditures were at their highest levels and income tax revenues were declining, states had to come up with larger outlays for Medicaid expenditures. As several other chapters of this book will demonstrate, the OBRA Medicaid reductions caused several states to take the draconian measures of declaring moratoria on certificate of need approvals for any new nursing home construction, reasoning that a nonexisting bed could not be filled by a Medicaid eligible patient.

The second important piece of legislation which will reverberate through the subsequent chapters of this book is the Tax Equity and Fiscal Responsibility Act of 1982 (TEFRA). This revolutionary legislation required the Department of Health and Human Services to develop a Medicare prospective payment system (PPS) for hospitals and skilled nursing facilities. As a result, a prospective payment system based on 470 diagnosis-related groups (DRGs) was implemented in 1983 to become universally applied (with the exception of four waivered states) to all hospitals in the United States by the fall of 1985. By paying a fixed amount prospectively based on a patient's specific DRG category at discharge, regulators hoped to provide hospitals with incentives to limit costs. Costs could be controlled by limiting the types of services provided and/or limiting a patient's length of stay. The theory underlying PPS was that efficient hospitals would do well because they could pocket the dollars saved, whereas inefficiently managed hospitals would suffer. Although prospective payment for nursing homes has not yet been implemented, this injection of a competitive twist to hospital financing has had profound implications for long-term care because many acute hospital users are the chronically ill. With hospitals limiting their involvement with these patients and rushing to discharge them, the need for long-term institutional and community-based care has increased tremendously. Thus recent developments on the institutional side of the long-term care picture have simultaneously capped our long-term care bed supply and stimulated the demand for long-term care services.

By the late 70s and early 80s, the public was becoming increasingly aware of fraud and quality-assurance problems in the long-term care industry as a result of exposes like Mendelson's *Tender Loving Greed* and Moss' *Too Old, Too Sick, Too Bad.* Demographers were beginning to write about decreased mortality rates among the very old who are heavy long-term care users, and the trust funds for both social security and Medicare were projected to expire in the near future. The stage was thus set in the 80s for a critical reexamination of long-term care services and searches for alternatives to our reliance on expensive institutional care. One of the alternatives which has been most intensively researched is community-based care, heretofore the orphan of the long-term care system. We turn now to an examination of this parallel system of care, one that did not grow as fast as institution-based care but grew equally haphazardly.

Community-Based Long-Term Care

Community-based long-term care in the United States has evolved in a way that results in a very fragmented picture today (see Figure 2–2 on page 24). Community-based services span a continuum of intensity, varying from skilled nursing care in the home (as an alternative to hospital or SNF care) to adult day care services, congregate meals, and sheltered housing. Analysis of the current structure and historical development of community-based care reveals that, in the United States, this care has developed according to two distinct and parallel service models: the medical model and the social

FIGURE 2–2   Development of Community-Based Long-Term Care

Decade	Demand Stimulus	Supply Stimulus
1950s	Social Security vendor payments for incapacitated welfare recipients allowed for homemakers/home health aids.	
1960s	Medicare, Title XVIII of the Social Security Act, includes skilled home health care benefits for the aged. Medicaid, Title XIX of the Social Security Act, includes home health care benefits for welfare recipients and the medically indigent.	
1970s	PL 92–603, Social Security Amendments extend home health care benefits to persons with long-term disability or end-stage renal disease. Title XX of the Social Security Act provides federal-state funds for services allowing the chronically impaired and elderly to remain independent in the community. Title III of the Older Americans Act establishes offices to disseminate information and provide referral to services for the elderly. Title VII of the Older Americans Act provides funding for home-delivered nutrition services.	Health Revenue Sharing and Health Services Act, P.L. 94–63, provides grants and loans to demonstrate the development and expansion of home health care. Section 222 Day Care/Home Care waivers fund "expanded" home care demonstrations.
1980s	Omnibus Reconciliation Act, P.L. 96–499, eliminates Medicare limits on the number of home health care visits and 3-day prior hospitalization requirement.	1981 Omnibus Budget Reconciliation Act allows proprietary home care agencies to become Medicare certified.

FIGURE 2–2 *(concluded)*

Decade	Demand Stimulus	Supply Stimulus
1980s	Tax Equity and Fiscal Responsibility Act, mandates prospective payment system for hospital reimbursement and hospital length of stay shortens; establishes new Medicare Hospice benefit.	
	Omnibus Budget Reconciliation Act (P.L. 96–499), Section 2176 waiver for community-based care under Medicaid.	

---

services model. These models originated in the public health nursing programs and the voluntary social welfare organizations of the early 1900s.

The Medical Model

Medically oriented home care services originated in the public health/visiting nurse programs of the progressive era when nurses began making home visits to educate and treat mothers of newborn children and sufferers of contagious diseases.[14] The purpose of the service was to reduce the unnecessary morbidity and mortality of children arising from poor child care practices and/or unsanitary living conditions and to reduce the threat of contagious disease to the community at large. From 1920 until the present, many public health department and visiting nurse programs sprang up across the United States to provide these services. During the 1940s, hospitals began to develop home care programs, most notably at Montefiore Hospital in New York City. The purpose of this new type of home care was to shorten expensive hospital stays by providing appropriate convalescent-level nursing and personal care services to patients in their homes.[15]

Despite a plethora of descriptive articles advocating the expansion of hospital-based home care, less than 100 such programs were established by the late 1960s.[16] This zero growth occurred despite widespread agreement on the soundness of the concept and official endorsement of home health services by such prestigious and disparate groups as the American Medical Association and the American Public Health Association. Essentially, the industry failed to grow because most health insurance plans did not provide home care benefits during this time.

Proponents of home health care did succeed, however, in engineering the inclusion of home health care benefits into Medicare and Medicaid legislation in 1966. Home care was viewed at that time not as a long-term care service option but rather as a way to encourage early discharge from expensive acute care hospitals, and subsequent Medicare home care regulations reflected this viewpoint. Like Medicare coverage of nursing home care, home health agencies reimbursed by Medicare were required to meet specific conditions of participation in the program. Under Part A of Medicare, patients were required to undergo hospitalization or SNF admissions for at least three days during the two weeks prior to admission to home care and were limited to 100 home care visits for that benefit period. Under Part B, patients were limited to 100 visits per calendar year and were required to pay a deductible before receiving service if the deductible had not yet been reached for other Part B services during that year. Under both Parts A and B, patients were required to have prior certification from a physician that they were homebound and required intermittent, as opposed to continuous, skilled nursing care or physical or speech therapy. The regulations also required that the services provided be necessary for further treatment of the condition for which the patient received care in the hospital or SNF and that reimbursement cease when a patient reached maximum rehabilitation potential.

Under Medicaid, states were also allowed to include a home care benefit. However, home care was not one of the five basic services required of the states, and the benefit was implemented quite variably. In contrast to the Medicare home care regulations, states were allowed discretion under Medicaid in defining the type of home care service reimbursed. For example, some states opted to provide expanded personal care services for Medicaid home care recipients. However, in most states, the Medicare skilled care model was also adopted for Medicaid.

Retrenchment

Despite the limitations of both Medicare and Medicaid home care benefits, home care proponents believed that public funding signaled the dawn of a new era. However, increased public support was short lived. Just as rapid increases in the costs of inpatient acute medical care caused restriction in coverage for institutional long-term care benefits, Medicare home health care benefits quickly became subject to complex regulations designed to prevent overutilization.

Simultaneous with the nursing home experience previously described, in 1969, home care fiscal intermediaries were instructed to interpret the Medicare skilled nursing requirements quite stringently. These reviews resulted in industry-wide chaos for an ensuing three-year period. The 1969 skilled care regulations had two important effects, one temporary and one more long lived. First, just as in the nursing home case, Medicare reimbursements for home health services decreased sharply from 1969 to 1971, and a number of agencies went out of business. The number of home health care visits used by Medicare recipients decreased from 8.5 thousand in 1969 to 4.8 thousand in 1971, and total reimbursement declined 27 percent, from 78.1 million to 56.8 million, over the same two-year period.[17]

Second, the emphasis on skilled care further intensified the medical focus of home health agencies participating in the Medicare program. In many cases, home care agencies had no prior assurance that their services would be reimbursed by Medicare. As a result, they accepted for care only those patients with fairly sophisticated nursing needs. Ricker-Smith and Trager, in describing the California home care experience from 1966 to 1974, have documented a substantial reduction in the number of elderly people cared for, particularly those 75 years of age and older, as a result of this shift in focus to acute care needs.[18] This shift in target population is important because chronic impairment and the subsequent need for long-term care is often a function of advanced age. The skilled care emphasis of the Medicare home care benefit has thus substantially limited its potential relevance to long-term care.

Just as in the nursing home case, the Social Security Amendments of 1972 also played an important role in stabilizing the turbulent home care field. These amendments eliminated the 20 percent coinsurance fee for home care services under Part B of Medicare (effective January 1, 1973) and, more importantly, authorized the secretary of HEW to establish by diagnosis the periods of coverage under Part A for individuals with specific conditions. In other words, a DRG-like prospective reimbursement system was implemented in 1972 in the home care industry. The amendment also sought to protect both agencies and beneficiaries from the vagaries of fiscal intermediaries who reviewed claims for payment. This was done by allowing payments for services that neither home health agencies nor beneficiaries could reasonably be expected to anticipate were not covered by Medicare. These amendments also extended Medicare home health care benefits to a new class of beneficiary: persons receiving social security on the basis of long-term disability or end-stage renal disease (effective July 1, 1973). Finally, and perhaps most importantly, Section 222(b) of these amendments authorized the use of waivers by the Human Resources Administration of HEW to finance experiments to test the cost effectiveness of community-based alternatives to institutional care. Under these Section 222 waivers, a decade of experimentation ensued. Although the results of these experiments have been somewhat inconclusive, it is probably fair to say that they have generated a community-based constituency or lobby that is responsible for both the present community care experiments and the several bills that propose expansion of Medicare home care benefits pending in Congress.[19]

The 1972 amendments were critically important in stabilizing the nascent home care industry and promoting its growth through expanding demand for care. In 1975, the Health Revenue Sharing and Health Services Act (P.L. 94–63) further stimulated growth in supply through the appropriation of $3 million annually for grants and loans to demonstrate the development and expansion of home health ser-

FIGURE 2–3   Growth in Medicare-Reimbursed
Home Health Visits, 1969–1983

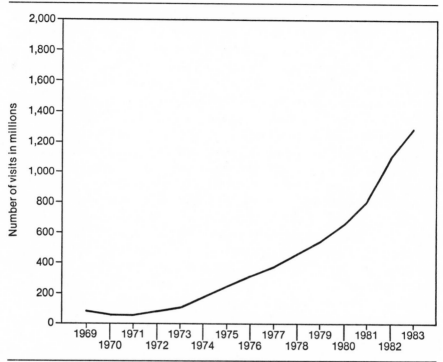

vices. This act still provides development grants to public and nonprofit home health agencies and loans to proprietary agencies. Figure 2–3 demonstrates the impact which these various pieces of legislation had in totally reversing the downward trend in Medicare reimbursement for home health services that occurred nationally before 1972. Medicare home care funding literally took off in 1973 and has been growing rapidly ever since.

As mentioned earlier, home health care services were also available on either a means-tested or spend-down basis to individuals eligible for Medicaid during this same time period. However, several factors combined to restrict the growth of home care services under Medicaid. First, the population covered was limited either to people categorically eligible because of low income or people with documented medical expenditures reaching the spend-down level. Medical expenditures to the spend-down level were difficult for persons receiving ambulatory services to accumulate. Therefore, only a relatively few community-dwelling Supplementary Security Income (SSI) eligible individuals received home care under this payment category.

Home care was not a required service option under Medicaid during the first four years of its existence. However, in 1970, as a result of growing concern at the federal level regarding increased expenditures for institution-based long-term care, states were mandated to include home health and personal care services in their Medicaid programs. Although this mandate allowed states to expand their support for home care services, 23 of the 49 participating states chose the more restrictive Medicare reimbursement guidelines.[20] These states not only retained the Medicare homebound and skilled nursing care regulations but also required prior Medicaid authorization for initiation of service. Participating home care agencies were also required to qualify for participation in Medicare, thus continuing the Medicare emphasis on skilled care during acute illness provided by agencies with medical or clinical credentials. Under these provisions, Medicaid reimbursement of home care services was implemented quite variably across the states and generally accounted for a negligible portion of state Medicaid expenditures. A notable exception to the rule, however, was New York State which passed legislation named Nursing Home Without Walls in 1977. Under this legislation, certain agencies received contracts allowing them to provide Medicaid-reimbursed home care services to individuals certified by an assessment team to require ICF-level or SNF-level institutional care, providing the cost of the home services did not exceed 75 percent of the institutional cost. In 1976, in San Francisco, Medicaid waivers were also used to provide adult day care services for the chronically ill elderly. Both the New York and San Francisco experiences were to prove significant harbingers of developments to come.

Expansion

Two final pieces of legislation that accelerated growth in both Medicare and Medicaid home care services were passed in 1980 and 1981. These laws were a direct response to criticisms that the skilled care regulations seriously diminished the relevance of Medicare home care services to the chronically ill. A number of federally funded demonstrations of expanded home care programs had been undertaken with mixed results regarding cost savings. Although Congress was unwilling to increase Medicare expenditures, many members wished to appear to accommodate supporters of the popular community-based care movement. As a result, several pieces of legislation affecting home care were incorporated into the 1980 Omnibus Reconciliation Act (P.L. 96–499). This act removed Medicare limits on the number of home health agency visits, eliminated the three-day prior hospitalization requirement for services under Part A and added occupational therapy as a qualifying service need for home care benefits. These provisions became effective July 1, 1981. The new regulations appeared to be significantly more generous, and the industry responded to these provisions with a spurt of new agencies in 1982. However, the 1980 Omnibus Reconciliation Act is probably more noteworthy because it failed to remove the skilled care regulation. The retention of the skilled care restriction still prevents Medicare-reimbursed home care services today from providing meaningful care to the chronically ill over extended periods of time.

Rather than expanding entitlement for chronic home care services under the federally funded Medicare program, states were encouraged a year later to apply for Medicaid waivers for community-based care for those at risk of requiring institutional care through Section 2176 of the Omnibus Budget Reconciliation Act of 1981. The response generated by this legislation provides a good index of the states' desperation regarding the increased cost of Medicaid institutional long-term care (described in greater detail in Chapter 2). Originally, about 50 percent of the states were expected to apply for the waiver, whereas, to date, close to 100 percent have applied and have been approved for the Section 2176 waivers. We have thus embarked in the 80s on an era of rapid growth in community-based long-term care services, fueled by regulators' and legislators' concerns about the rising costs of institution-based care as typified by both the hospital and the nursing home.

The prospective payment system for hospital reimbursement that became effective October 1, 1983, only served to accelerate this already existing trend. However, home care services organized according to the medical model represent only one side of the community-based services picture. Although not as significant in terms of volume of services or costs, other services organized according to a social services model of care also deserve mention.

The Social Services Model

In contrast to the acute care orientation of the medical model of community-based care described above, the social services model of home care services developed in voluntary social welfare agencies during the early part of this century. Originally, these services were provided to families with young children whose mother was incapacitated by illness. Their purpose was to reduce the negative impact of illness on the family and minimize disruption in family functioning. To accomplish this goal, voluntary agencies provided social work counseling and homemaker services to families on a sliding-scale fee based on ability to pay, sometimes over extended periods. In 1956, these services became reimbursable through Social Security vendor payments for incapacitated individuals and families who were income eligible for other public welfare benefits.

Agencies that are organized according to the social services model provide household support services geared to nurture and maintain an individual in the home without the requirement of prior hospitalization. The agencies are community based and provide homemaker/home health aides whose practical functions include activities such as cleaning, laundry, shopping, meal preparation, escort services, and financial management (bill paying, check cashing, etc.). The

services are available on a short-term or long-term basis de
pending on need. In sharp contrast to medically organized
home care agencies, these agencies provide few if any medical
services and do not maintain any transfer agreements with
Medicare home care agencies, physicians, or hospitals. This
lack of medical involvement can create serious problems with
respect to the coordination and continuity of health care services for clients of these agencies, just as the lack of social
services provided by Medicare and Medicaid home care services can impede optimal rehabilitation or maintenance in the
community of the chronically ill.

Title XX

Until recently, these personal social services have been provided to families with young children. However, there is a
growing awareness of the needs of chronically impaired adults
and elderly for services of this type on a part-time but consistent and long-term basis.[21] Limited funding for these services
has been provided by Titles III and IV of the Older Americans
Act and Title XX of the Social Security Act. Title XX was
implemented in 1974 to assist individuals of all ages to remain independent in the community and thus minimize the
use of more costly institutional care. Unlike its predecessors,
however, Title XX was "capped" soon after its passage, and
funding for it has leveled off to the point where the program
does not exceed $2.5 billion annually. Services were originally
financed by a combination of federal (75 percent) and state (25
percent) matching funds; however, in 1982, the state matching
requirement was eliminated, and the program became a federal block grant to the states.

An attractive feature of the Title XX program is the flexibility that the states enjoy in assembling service packages for
different target populations. As a result of this flexibility,
services provided under Title XX can vary widely from state
to state and can include adult day care, homemaker and chore
services, home-delivered meals, senior centers, and companion programs. In 1978, according to Blum and Minkler, states
spent approximately 13 percent of their Title XX budgets on
home-based care.[22] In administering Title XX services, states

can provide direct service or contract with either a formal or informal provider. Until 1981, Title XX services were available only to those individuals whose income was less than 110 percent–120 percent of the poverty level. The removal of this income restriction may increase the availability of Title XX as a service option to the public at large. However, the ceiling on Title XX funds and its mandate to serve many diverse populations limit its contribution to long-term care expenditures.

Older Americans Act

The other source of funding for community-based care of the social services type are Titles III and VII of the Older Americans Act. Title III was intended to facilitate coordination of services for the aging through the establishment of a network of local and state offices whose function is to disseminate information about available services and expedite referrals to service for elderly citizens. Title VII, in contrast, provides funding for home-delivered meals and nutrition services.

Both Title XX and the Older Americans Act provide valuable services to older adults. However, as Table 2-1 demonstrates, neither program interacts in any way with Titles XVIII and XIX.

In many states, Section 2176 Medicaid community-care waivers can be used to purchase personal service for individuals at risk of long-term care institutionalization, thus augmenting Title XX funds. However, expenditures for this type of care vary widely by state and are still quite small compared to outlays for institutional care. The end result is that only a small portion of potential demand for care is being met nationally by existing community-based programs.

Summary

We thus have developed independent, institution-based and community-based, parallel social and medical systems of care which by definition do not intersect. This lack of interaction and separate but equal status severely limits the degree to which available programs can complement one another, since providers in one system frequently have little formal contact

TABLE 2–1 Comparison of Essential Characteristics of Four Public Programs Funding In-Home Services

Characteristics	Programs			
	Social Security Act			Older Americans Act
	Title XVIII	Title XIX	Title XX	Title III
1. Services authorized				
Nursing	X	X		X
Therapy	X	X		X
Home health aide	X	X	X	X
Homemaker/chore			X	X
Medical supplies and appliances	X	X		
2. Program eligibility requirements				
Age	X			X
Income		X	X	
Skilled nursing care	X	Varies		
Homebound	X			
Physician prescribed	X	X		
Included in state plan	n.a.	X	X	X
3. Administration	Federal	State	State	State
4. Funding	Open-ended	Open-ended	Capped	Capped

n.a. = not applicable.

SOURCE: U.S. General Accounting Office, *Improved Knowledge Base Would Be Helpful in Reaching Policy Decisions on Providing Long-Term, In-Home Services for the Elderly,* Washington, D.C., October 1981, p. 26.

with their counterparts in the other. Responsibility for the coordination of service has thus, by default, resided with the chronically ill person or with an involved family member or friend. Critics have charged that the resulting confusing array of services, eligibility requirements, and reimbursement sources frequently creates barriers to care, especially for the frail elderly who may have the most difficulty negotiating complex service systems. A large part of this confusion stems from our fragmented method of financing care, which we turn to next.

NOTES

1. Bruce C. Vladeck, *Unloving Care: The Nursing Home Tragedy* (New York: Basic Books, 1980), p. 36.

Saul Waldman, "A Legislative History of Nursing Home Care," in *Long-Term Care: Perspectives From Research and Demonstrations,* ed. Ronald J. Vogel and Hans C. Palmer (Washington, D.C.: U.S. Department of Health and Human Services, Health Care Financing Administration, 1983), p. 509.

2. Vladeck, *Unloving Care,* p. 37.

3. Waldman, "A Legislative History of Nursing Home Care," p. 510.

4. Vladeck, *Unloving Care,* p. 44.

5. Ibid., p. 47.

6. Richard Harris, *A Sacred Trust* (New York: The New American Library, 1966), p. 187.

7. Robert Stevens and Rosemary Stevens, *Welfare Medicine in America; A Case Study of Medicaid* (New York: The Free Press, 1974), pp. 137, 172.

8. Vladeck, *Unloving Care,* p. 57.

9. Ibid., p. 56.

Michael J. Connor and Sandra B. Greene, "Should Extended Care Following Hospitalization Be Encouraged?" *Inquiry,* Fall 1983, p. 262.

10. Vladeck, *Unloving Care,* p. 57.

11. Judith Lave, "Medicare: Use of Skilled Nursing Facilities, 1980," *Health Care Financing Notes,* September 1983, p. 5.

12. William J. Scanlon and Judith Feder, "The Long-Term Care Marketplace: An Overview," *Health Care Financial Management,* January 1984, p. 6.

13. Vladeck, *Unloving Care,* p. 69.

14. R. H. Bremner, *From the Depths* (New York: New York University Press, 1956).

R. E. A. Winslow, *The Evolution and Significance of the Modern Public Health Campaign* (New Haven: Yale University Press, 1923).

15. M. Field and B. Schless, "Extension of Medical Social Services Into the Home," *Social Casework,* March 1948, pp. 22–25.

I. Rossman, S. D. Eager, and M. Cherkasky, "The Treatment of Cardiac Patients on a Home Care Program," *Modern Concepts of Cardiovascular Disease,* 14, no. 7 (1950).

16. Ibid.

17. Donald N. Muse and Darwin Sawyer, "The Medicaid and Medicare Data Book, 1981," *Health Care Financing Program Statistics,* April 1982, p. 31.

18. Katherine Ricker-Smith and Brahna Trager, "In-Home Health Services in California: Some Lessons for National Health Insurance," *Medical Care,* March 1978, p. 179.

19. Susan Hughes, "Apples and Oranges? A Review of Community-Based Long-Term Care Demonstrations," *Health Services Research,* 20, no. 4 (October 1985), p. 481.

20. Scanlon, "Long-Term Care Marketplace," p. 2.

21. Anne Somers and Florence M. Moore, "Homemaker Services: Essential Options for the Elderly," *Public Health Reports,* 91, no. 4, p. 355.

22. Stephen R. Blum and Meredith Minkler, "Toward a Continuum of Caring Alternatives: Community-Based Care for the Elderly," *Journal of Social Issues,* 36, no. 2 (1980), p. 146.

CHAPTER THREE

Paying for Long-Term Care: The Record to Date

- Long-term care costs have been increasing more rapidly than acute hospital costs in the United States, largely reflecting the increase in the population over age 65.
- At present, available public financing favors institutional versus community-based care by a ratio of 3:1.
- In order to receive help with the costs of institutional care, long-stay residents must divest themselves of resources to become Medicaid eligible.
- Institutional long-term care now constitutes the largest expenditure in state Medicaid budgets.
- Fifty percent of institutional long-term care costs are paid for directly out of pocket with very little private insurance for long-term care currently available. Long-term care thus represents a catastrophic burden that is currently financed very inadequately in the United States and is a prime candidate for reform.

Long-term care is moving to the center of the health care stage primarily because of policymakers' concerns over increased costs. Since the passage of Medicare and Medicaid, expenditures for all types of health care in the United States have increased rapidly. The consumer price index (CPI) for all goods and services produced in the United States more than tripled between 1950 and 1980, reflecting across-the-board inflation in our economy. During the same time period, however, the medical care component of the CPI has quintupled.[1] Hospital and physician charges account for the largest share of medical care expenditures, but long-term care, narrowly defined to include institution-based care only, ranks third. Increased availability of public financing has resulted in both increased demand for nursing home care and higher nursing home prices. As costs of nursing home care have risen, increased numbers of people have resorted to Medicaid as the payor of last resort for extended nursing home stays. Medicaid outlays for nursing home care have consequently grown at an average rate of 14.5 percent from 1976 to 1980, faster than the rate of growth in all other Medicaid expenditures. Nursing home outlays now constitute one third of all Medicaid expenditures nationally.[2] The portion of this expenditure borne by the states varies from 22 to 50 percent depending on per capita income. Despite the federal share, however, the states' expenditures have risen substantially.

As a result of this relentless upward spiral, as Table 3–1 demonstrates, 21 of the states spent more than 40 percent of their total Medicaid budgets on nursing home care in 1980. Although state and federal policymakers are concerned about past increases in long-term care expenditures, they are even more concerned about projected increases in future costs. In this chapter, we describe the components of these cost increases, the respective roles of public and private funding sources in paying the long-term care bill, and projections regarding future cost increases.

COST INCREASES AND THEIR COMPONENTS

Concern over increased costs of acute hospital care in the United States is commonplace and has resulted in major changes in our acute care reimbursement system. Prospective

TABLE 3-1 State Medicaid Expenditures for Nursing Home SNF and ICF Care, Fiscal Year 1980

Percent of Total Medicaid Budget	Number of States	Percent of States
0–9%	1*	2%
10–19	0	0
20–29	10	20
30–39	18	36
40–49	16	32
50–59	4	8
60–69	1	2

*Washington, D.C.

SOURCE: U.S. GAO, "Medicaid and Nursing Home Care: Cost Increases and the Need for Services Are Creating Problems for the States and the Elderly," 1983, p. 42.

payments, preferred provider organizations, and community coalitions to reduce runaway health care expenditures have become the norm. This activity basically reflects concern about the size of our largest category of health expenditures, the hospital bill. However, although acute hospital care consumes the largest dollar share of expenditures, its rate of growth pales by comparison with growth in expenditures for long-term care.

As Table 3–2 demonstrates, the total health systems cost per capita (all costs related to direct patient care, including services and supplies) in the United States increased from $69 in 1950 to $1,288 in 1983 and is projected to rise to $2,274 by 1990. Acute hospital care accounted for 35.4 percent of this expense in 1950, 47 percent in 1983, and is projected to increase to 47.1 percent by 1990, growing at an average annual rate of 9.9 percent. In contrast, the share of total health systems cost attributable to nursing home care over the same 40-year period has almost quintupled, increasing from 1.7 percent of all health care costs to a projected 9.4 percent share, an average annual growth rate of 13.9 percent.[3]

TABLE 3–2   Percentage of Total Health Systems Cost Attributable to Hospital versus Nursing Home Services, Selected Years, 1950–1990

Year	Total Systems Cost per Capita Current Dollars	Percent for Hospital Care	Percent for Nursing Home Care
1950	69	35.4%	1.7%
1960	125	38.4	2.2
1965	177	39.0	5.8
1970	305	42.8	7.2
1971	333	43.0	7.8
1975	521	44.8	8.6
1979	811	45.9	9.2
1980	926	46.2	9.3
1981	1,062	46.3	9.4
1982	1,181	47.4	9.3
1983	1,288	47.0	9.2
Projections			
1985	1,504	45.8	9.3
1988	1,938	47.1	9.4
1990	2,274	47.1	9.4

SOURCE: Mark S. Freeland and Carol Ellen Schendler, *Health Care Financing Review,* 6:3 (Spring 1985), p. 20.

Table 3–3 shows these same increases over the same time periods in dollar amounts. The increase in the portion of all health care costs attributable to nursing home care is even more remarkable because these figures reflect institution-based care only, thus omitting parallel increases in costs of Medicare and Medicaid home care, as well as Title XX and Older Americans Act (OAA) community-based care expenditures, private expenditures for community care, and public welfare expenditures for sheltered, domiciliary and foster care of the chronically ill. Since nursing home care is still the major publicly funded service option for long-term care, a closer examination of the components of cost increases for this type of care is warranted.

To understand why costs increase over time, it is necessary to quantify the relative role of at least four cost components: (1) inflation, (2) increase in number and/or type of patients

TABLE 3–3   Rate of Increase in National Hospital
and Nursing Home Expenditures at
Five-Year Intervals, 1960–1990
(amount in billions)

Year	Hospital Care		Nursing Home Care	
	Amount	(Percent Increase)	Amount	(Percent Increase)
1960	9.1	—	0.5	—
1965	13.9	53	2.1	320
1970	28.0	101	4.7	128
1975	52.4	87	10.1	115
1980	101.3	93	20.4	102
Projected				
1985	170.6	68	34.6	70
1990	277.4	63	55.1	59

SOURCE: Mark S. Freeland and Carol Ellen Schendler, *Health Care Financing Review*, 6:3 (Spring 1985), p. 20

cared for, (3) increase in number of services provided or their technologic intensity, and (4) profits. As we have already demonstrated, the annual rate of increase in the medical care component of the consumer price index has consistently (with the exception of 1979) outstripped the rate of increase for all goods and services combined. This suggests that factors other than inflation per se are responsible for the steady surge in costs of long-term care.

In their most recent analysis of nursing home cost increases from 1971–1981, Freeland and Schendler have attributed the lion's share of increased costs of nursing homes (excluding ICFs for the mentally retarded) to inflation. Growth in number of days per capita ranked second. Growth in real (inflation-adjusted) expenses per day, or intensity, ranked third, and growth in total population (all ages) and nursing home input prices in excess of inflation tied for fourth place, accounting for approximately 7 percent each. The proportion of cost increases attributable to general inflation and to population growth is about equal across different segments of the health care industry and also applies to other nonhealth sectors of the economy. However, the portion of cost increases attributable to the remaining three factors, that is, increased

---

FIGURE 3–1   Health Sector Specific
Factors Accounting for
Growth in Expenditures for
Hospital and Nursing
Home Care, 1971–1981

Hospital	Nursing home *
100%	100%
28.5%	17.0%
61.3%	33.1%
10.2%	49.9%

☐ Input prices in excess of inflation

▨ Intensity per patient day

▤ Patient days per capita

---

*Excluding ICF-MRs.

SOURCE: Mark S. Freeland and Carol Ellen Schendler, *Health Care Financing Review,* 1983, pp. 30 and 9.

days per capita, increased intensity, and input prices in excess of inflation, according to Freeland and Schendler is caused by factors specific to the health care industry. Figure 3–1 treats the sum of these factors as accounting for 100 percent of health care-sector specific cost increases and compares the pattern of cost increases for the hospital and nursing home industries.

As can be readily seen, the distribution of factors differs substantially, with growth in per capita patient days accounting for 50 percent of the increases in nursing home costs versus 10.2 percent for hospitals. Freeland and Schendler attribute this growth in patient days to the increasing number of elderly 75 years of age and older in our population. They demonstrate that aggregate nursing home days (excluding ICFs for the mentally retarded) increased at an average annual rate of 3 percent from 1978 to 1981, the same rate of increase as that of people aged 75 and over.

Other factors which play a role in increasing the aggregate number of nursing home days may be the increasing wealth of successive cohorts of the elderly and the increased availability of public funding for nursing home care. However, the specific role of these forces is currently unknown and is difficult to ascertain.

Interestingly, growth in real expenses per day, or intensity, accounted for only 33 percent of the growth in nursing home costs, as opposed to 61 percent of the growth in hospital costs over the same time period. These figures suggest that technologic intensity does not play as prominent a role in the nursing home industry but still accounts for a sizable portion of growth in costs. This figure is also consistent with survey data reported by the General Accounting Office (GAO) showing increased functional impairment in nursing home residents over time and increased nursing home responsibility for heavy-care patients in recent years.[4]

The third factor specific to the health sector, input prices in excess of inflation, reflects increases in items such as medical supplies and equipment or safety requirements. These costs account for a somewhat smaller proportion of nursing home (17 percent) versus hospital (28.5 percent) cost increases.

Freeland and Schendler's analysis of increased costs does not address our fourth cost component, profits, for a good reason. Data on nursing home profits are not readily available. A research team at the University of Washington headed by Kenneth McCaffree examined profits, growth and reimbursement systems in the nursing home industry over the years 1969 to 1973.[5] Using growth in beds as a proxy for profitability, the study found that nursing homes were rewarded for inefficient borrowing at high interest rates because of pass-through reimbursements for interest on debts.

They also found that beds per 1,000 elderly grew more rapidly in states that reimbursed according to level of care required, since this reimbursement scheme allows homes to reclassify patients upward. Finally, they observed that growth in beds was unassociated with either vertical or horizontal integration among multifacility nursing home chains. It is important to note that findings from this study are limited in their generalizability because the study data were restricted to the years 1969–1973, which was a time of great upheaval for the industry. However, a more recent analysis of this issue described below has also pointed to the method of reimbursing capital costs of nursing homes as a major culprit in increasing nursing home supply and costs.

In the late 60s and early 70s, policymakers were mainly concerned that patients achieve access to needed long-term care and that the care be of good quality. As a result, the use of cost-based reimbursement for nursing home care was expanded to apply to both Medicare and Medicaid in 1972. Cost-based reimbursement was viewed as a means of attracting providers to participate in Medicare and Medicaid while simultaneously encouraging good quality care by paying a reasonable fee for service. The pros and cons of specific types of reimbursement for nursing home care are discussed in more detail in Chapter 8. However, the relationship between cost-based reimbursement and nursing home profits merits some discussion here.

Cost-related reimbursement includes payments for both direct hands-on patient care and for return on capital investment. Until fairly recently, many state Medicaid programs reimbursed nursing home capital costs by including a pass-through for interest on debts or mortgages and a depreciation allowance. According to Baldwin and Bishop in a recent analysis of this issue, sophisticated investors were quick to take advantage of this double windfall, and numerous instances of abuse occurred during the 70s. For example, in multicorporate situations, nursing home owners borrowed from their own related enterprises to purchase a facility at both excessive and fully reimbursed rates of interest. Similarly, interrelated owners sold facilities at inflated prices, thus increasing the basis for depreciation allowances with each sale.

In both cases, owners benefited twice: first, from higher Medicaid payments, and second, from federal tax deductions for the same expenditures. As Baldwin and Bishop point out, this type of investment is most attractive to investors in higher tax brackets who seek tax shelters. They conclude that it is no surprise that new investors attracted to the industry during the 70s were not small owner operators but "for profit corporations that could benefit from the cash flow, tax savings, and capital gains or real estate transactions" that this method of reimbursement made possible.[6] As a result, the nursing home industry is now heavily proprietary with 80 percent of the homes and 70 percent of the beds operated for profit, as opposed to 12.5 percent of hospitals and 8.8 percent of the hospital beds.[7]

In recent years, many of the loopholes in Medicaid reimbursements have been tightened. As a result, many long-term care analysts have expressed concern over the declining rate of growth in the nursing home bed supply. This decline in bed supply is attributable to states' increasingly restrictive stances regarding approval of certificate of need applications in an effort to contain Medicaid expenditures. While this cost containment strategy undoubtedly may prove effective in the short run, many argue that state Medicaid programs are only deferring the crisis until a later date, when problems of access to long-term care will be magnified by the growth in our "old-old" population. Before discussing projected future costs, however, an examination of the current payors of long-term care is appropriate.

Purchasers of Long-Term Care

Two other unique attributes of the long-term care industry that distinguish it from the acute care health sector are its heavy reliance on public versus private payments for care and the virtually total absence of any meaningful degree of private insurance for care. Turning first to the financing of institutional care, Table 3–4 demonstrates that public payments have accounted for half of all nursing home expenditures during the last decade. As mentioned previously, the proportion of public expenditures reimbursed by Medicare

TABLE 3–4 Estimates of Expenditures for Nursing Home Care as a Percentage of Total Payments, 1973–1983

	1973*	1979*	1980†	1981†	1982‡	1983‡
Total	100%	100%	100%	100%	100%	100%
(Dollar Amount in Billions)	($7.2)	($17.8)	($20.6)	($24.2)	($26.5)	($28.8)
Public Payments	50.3	56.7	55.8	54.5	50.6	48.6
Medicaid	42.9	49.3	49.5	47.9	44.2	43.1
Medicare	2.6	2.1	1.9	1.7	1.9	1.7
Veterans Administration	1.6	1.7	1.9	1.7	1.9	1.7
Other public funds	3.2	3.4	3.4	2.9	2.6	1.7
Private Payments	49.6	43.2	44.2	45.5	49.4	51.7
Direct payments§	48.6	42.0	42.7	44.2	47.9	50.0
Insurance benefits	.23	.65	.97	.83	.75	1.04
Other private funds	.72	.60	.48	.41	.75	.69

*SOURCE: Health Care Financing Administration, Office of Research, Demonstrations and Statistics, Division of National Cost Estimates.

†SOURCE: Robert Gibson, et al., "National Health Expenditures, 1982," *Health Care Financing Review,* 5, no. 1 (Fall 1983), pp. 12, 13.

‡SOURCE: Robert Gibson, et al., "National Health Expenditures, 1983," *Health Care Financing Review,* 6, no. 2 (Winter 1984), pp. 20, 21.

§Compares to 20 percent direct out-of-pocket payments for acute hospital care.

funds is continuing to decline, reflecting the essentially acute care orientation of the Medicare program. In contrast, Medicaid expenditures now account for 89 percent of all public expenditures for institutional long-term care.

Frequently, Medicaid pays for the care of individuals who are not Medicaid eligible upon admission to the nursing home but become eligible as a result of either spending down their assets to the point where they meet the Medicaid eligibility criterion of $1,500 in reserves. Although the public share of long-term care expenditures is large (54.9 percent in 1982), this figure substantially underestimates total public funding because it does not reflect the social security income which Medicaid nursing home residents in the spend down category also pay for their care. Specifically, nursing home residents whose care is reimbursed by Medicaid are required to contribute all but a $25 allowance from their monthly social security payments to their cost of care, with Medicaid picking up the remainder.

In contrast, public funding for noninstitutional care may

appear to be more generous. Table 3–5 demonstrates substantial growth in Medicare home care reimbursements from 1980–1985, from $647 million to $1,273.7 million, an increase of 97 percent. This increase reflects the expansion of the home care benefit to include two new population groups, the permanently disabled and end-stage renal patients in 1972, and the elimination of certain conditions, that is, the removal of the three-day prior hospitalization requirement and the Part B deductible in 1981. Medicare pays 100 percent of home care costs for patients who have met their Medicare deductible under Part A. However, all Medicare patients must require skilled nursing care, which means that intermediate care patients (those needing personal care and chore services with medical monitoring) frequently are not eligible. Reimbursement for care is also terminated once a patient has reached his or her maximum rehabilitation potential, which means that many patients with chronic conditions are left without care once their acute condition has stabilized. Thus, although the benefit on paper appears generous, the program only serves a small percent of total Medicare beneficiaries in any given year.

Medicaid expenditures for home care services have also been growing rapidly, especially since the granting of Section 2176 community care waivers to most states in 1982 and 1983. As Table 3–5 demonstrates, total Medicaid home care reimbursements are substantially lower than Medicare but have climbed steeply from $332 million in 1980 to $597 million in 1983, an increase of 80 percent. However, access to Medicaid-reimbursed care is severely restricted by the fact that most states still require the presence of a skilled care condition for nonwaivered Medicaid home health services in addition to means-tested income eligibility. Services provided under the community care waivers also vary considerably across the states. Some services are restricted to the care of individuals in certain diagnostic categories, such as the mentally ill or mentally retarded, while others that are targeted to the physically infirm elderly frequently cover chore and housekeeping services only, thus lacking a sorely needed medical component.

In contrast to the increased expenditures under Titles

TABLE 3-5 Federal Expenditures for Community-Care Services by Program Source, 1980–1985 (in millions)

	1980	1981	1982	1983	1984	1985
1. Social Security						
Medicare*	646.6	802.6	1,086.5	1,273.7	—	—
Medicaid†	332.0	428.0	496.0	597.0	—	—
Title XX‡	2,681.9	2,878.3	2,400.0	2,675.0	2,675.0	2,725.0
Subtotal	3,660.5	4,198.9	3,982.5	4,545.7		
2. Older Americans Act						
Social services and senior centers§	247.0	249.5	238.5	240.5	240.9	265.0
Home-delivered meals§	50.0	54.5	56.8	57.4	62.0	67.9
Subtotal	297.0	304.0	295.3	297.9		
Total	3,957.5	4,412.9	4,277.8	4,843.6		

*SOURCE: Bureau of Data Management and Strategy, Health Care Financing Administration, Department of Health and Human Services. Medicare Data, Table no. AA11. (This table contains data based on bills approved by fiscal intermediaries and recorded in central office files as of December 30, 1983. Data are summarized by the period in which claims were approved and should be considered preliminary for all periods after 1982 due to processing lags.)

†SOURCE: Chris Howe, Division of Medicaid Cost Estimates, Bureau of Data Management and Strategy, Health Care Financing Administration.

‡SOURCE: Division of Grants and Contracts Management, Department of Health and Human Services. (Figures cited for 1980 and 1981 are actual expenditures; figures for 1982–1984 are appropriated funds.)

§SOURCE: Region V, Administration on Aging, Office of Human Development Services, Department of Health and Human Services. (The exact expenditures of Title III funds for supportive (social) services and centers and for home-delivered meals are not readily available. This is because in any given year expenditures are made from several different annual allotments due to varying fiscal years among the states and their grantees. States are also permitted to transfer funds between allotments. Thus, the figures cited are the annual allotments or operating levels, which are relatively close to the expenditure level for any given year.)

TABLE 3–6 Comparison by Program Source of Federal Expenditures for Institutional versus In-Home Services, Fiscal Year 1983 (in millions)

	Locus of Service	
	Institutional Services	In-Home Services‡
1. Social Security		
Title XVIII (Medicare)	394.6*	1,273.7
Title XIX (Medicaid)	13,867.0†	597.0
Title XX (Social services)	—	2,675.0
2. Older Americans Act		
Title III		
A. Social services and senior centers	—	240.5
B. Home-delivered meals	—	57.4
Total	14,261.6	4,843.6

*SOURCE: Bureau of Data Management and Strategy, Health Care Financing Administration, Department of Health and Human Services. Medicare Data, Table no. AA7. (This table contains data based on bills approved by fiscal intermediaries and recorded in central office files as of December 30, 1983. Data are summarized by the period in which claims were approved and should be considered preliminary for all periods after 1982 due to processing lags.)

†SOURCE: John Smyth, Office of Research and Demonstrations, Health Care Financing Administration.

‡For source information, see Figure 3–5.

XVIII and XIX, Table 3–6 demonstrates that public outlays for community-based long-term care services under Title XX and the Older Americans Act remained fairly stable. Since Title XX has always been "capped," overall program expenditures have not risen substantially. In fact, they have declined as a result of Reagan administration cutbacks. Similarly, OAA expenditures for in-home services show a relatively flat trend over time, consistent with the general decline in popularity of social services in general during the Reagan administration.

Taken as a whole, the increases in public outlays for community-based care represent a small but significant change in our public long-term care policy. As Table 3–6 illustrates, public outlays for institutional care still outweigh those for community-based care by approximately 3:1. The figures cited under institutional care expenditures also substantially underestimate the total level of public funding since they do not include federal subsidies for nursing home care included in Hill-Burton funds, FHA mortgages, and tax deductible bonds. However, despite the massive investment of the past in institutional care, the major growth in recent years has clearly taken place in community care. Research recently undertaken at Northwestern University's Center for Health Services and Policy Research clearly indicates a preference among the elderly for this locus of care. A remarkable 80 percent of elderly surveyed in Chicago stated they would prefer to receive long-term care services at home.[8] The preferences of this group should be an important indicator of future changes since, as our next section demonstrates, the elderly are the second largest payors of long-term care services.

The Private Payors

As Table 3–5 demonstrated, the long-term care industry is probably most remarkable because of its heavy reliance on out-of-pocket payments and the almost total absence of private insurance. Private insurance payments accounted for a mere 1 percent of long-term care financing in 1983. One reason insurers cite for the lack of development in this area is a lack of demand. However, statistics on growth of nursing home use tend to refute this allegation. In 1973, approximately 1 million individuals resided in a nursing home on any given day. In contrast, by 1977, this number had increased by 21 percent to 1,303,000. It is clear from these figures that use of long-term care services is increasing substantially.

The lack of both private insurance for long-term care and a comprehensive long-term care benefit under Medicare, forces individuals to rely on their own resources to purchase extended care. Typically, nursing home residents pay for the first few months of care until they have spent down their resources and become eligible for Medicaid. From that point forward, long-stay residents contribute all but $25 of their social security to the nursing home and Medicaid picks up the rest.

This current method of paying for nursing home care has several obvious drawbacks. First, many individuals, most of whom are elderly, are forced to become paupers because they have survived spouses, siblings, or offspring who are no longer available to care for them in the community. Second, once residents have spent down their resources, it is almost impossible for them to return to the community if their conditions stabilize or improve because they usually do not have the financial or family resources to arrange suitable housing. Finally, this all or nothing method of public financing encourages the planned transfer of assets from the elderly to family members. Since prospective residents know they have to spend their accumulated assets, why not transfer them to a family member instead?

Unfortunately, catastrophic out-of-pocket expenditures for long-term care are not limited to institutional care. A recent analysis by Soldo and Manton of the 1982 National Long-Term Care Survey data indicates that about 1.1 million or 25 percent of all functionally restricted community-residing elderly receive some level of formal services at home at a cost of approximately $99 million per month.[9] Over 75 percent of this group receiving community care financed all service costs out-of-pocket with expenditures peaking for the oldest (age 85 and over) and most disabled group at $466 per month. Previous research by Soldo has also indicated that the availability of help from family members is a major inhibitor of use of formal community-based care by the elderly. Specifically, disabled elderly who lived with a spouse or adult child were unlikely to use formal community care services until they experienced substantial and severe impairments—incontinence or need for 24-hour supervision.[10]

In view of these findings the recent attitude of the Reagan administration toward family responsibility is somewhat ironic. Recently, the Reagan administration has focused some attention on the issue of relatives' responsibility for financing care, and states have been authorized to assess relatives' ability to help support their institutionalized family members. However, this approach is very unpopular politically and has been implemented in only a few states with very little success to date. In addition to its political unpopularity, the concept of relative responsibility assumes that relatives with disposable income are available but have not been contributing because they have not been requested to do so. In fact, however, most surveys of long-term care populations have shown that long-term care users differ significantly from non-users of the same age, sex, and health characteristics by virtue of having substantially fewer social supports. Most users of institutional long-term care services are females who were never married or were widowed and have no or only one surviving child.[11]

The question of relative responsibility in our opinion is better addressed by turning the situation around and recognizing the substantial contribution which many families make to the care of the chronically ill in their homes. For example, while 1.3 million individuals currently receive care in institutional settings, it is estimated that another 6 million are similarly impaired but are residing in the community where they are being cared for by family and friends.[12] The public does not directly pay for the care of these individuals but subsidizes their care through a federal income tax credit for the care of elderly relatives. At present, we have very little idea of the true costs of informal care, but care requires time, and time devoted to care must be taken away from other activities, some of which might otherwise be productive. In recent research on this issue, Paringer has attempted to define the upper and lower bounds of the range of costs of informal care for the chronically ill, using unadjusted and adjusted foregone earning-opportunity costs. The unadjusted method calculates the earnings potentially available to caregivers of particular age, race, sex, and education categories and assumes that all caregivers were equally likely to be labor force participants during the year in question. The second method uses the same approach but adjusts the earnings by actual labor force participation rates.

The first method overestimates the total cost by including individuals who might not necessarily have worked, and the second underestimates costs by failing to place any value on homemaking activities. Based on estimates of caregiver time from the Canadian Manitoba longitudinal study, Paringer applied this method of calculating costs to the estimated number of people who were reported by the National Health Interview Survey to require care in the community and shared a household with a potential caregiver. Using this method, she found that the value of intrahousehold informal care currently provided in the United States ranges from $7.2 to $16.1 billion, with about 45 percent of total care costs directed to individuals who require help with eating and/or transferring from bed to chair.[13]

Using an alternative replacement cost method to compute costs yielded similar estimates. Replacement costs assume that, in the absence of the informal caregiver, formal paid services of an agency would be required. According to this method, providing all chronically impaired people with paid aide service in lieu of informal care would cost approximately $9.6 billion. However, this figure is probably an underestimate because it is based on the average rate that nursing home aides were paid in 1978, $3.23 per hour.[14] Public policy that seeks to increase the financing role of families seems to ignore this substantial contribution which relatives and friends already make to the care of the chronically ill, and thus, seems preordained to fail.

In addition to citing a lack of demand for insurance policies, private insurers have also expressed concerns about adverse selection, i.e., fear that only those who need care (the chronically ill) will buy the policies. The risk pool would then be small relative to the number of beneficiaries, and the industry would lose money. In most existing nursing home and home care insurance policies, benefits are closely modeled after Medicare benefits and reimburse for skilled nursing care for a limited time following an acute illness. Few policies offer an intermediate care benefit, and virtually none offer a custodial care or an expanded long-term home care benefit.

Insurers are also reluctant to expand benefit packages because they fear that moral hazard will result. Moral hazard is a term used by economists to describe a tendency to increase the use of a service when one does not pay for using extra units of that service. For example, if totally insured for home-aide visits, an individual will not have to pay for these visits and will consequently not consider costs in deciding the amount of aide services to use. Those insurance companies that provide an institutional long-term care benefit rely on the inherent unpopularity of nursing home care among consumers to reduce moral hazard. Consequently, they fear that expanding the benefit package to include more popular types of care, such as home care, would result in excessive and uncontrolled utilization.

We will deal at greater length with these issues in the final chapters of this book. However, it is worth pointing out here, that as a result of the limited insurance coverage currently available and the institutional bias of current public reimbursement policies, we are experiencing what Paringer terms "market-basket moral hazard." Referring to the multiple services provided in the nursing home as a market basket, she writes that the nursing home user is compelled under current reimbursement conditions to purchase either the entire market basket of services or no services at all. She argues rather convincingly that a more comprehensive array of service and reimbursement options would be much more efficient.[15]

Interestingly, on the community-care side of the long-term care picture, there has been a significant increase over the past 10 years in the number of insurance policies that offer home health care benefits. However, this benefit is usually strictly modeled after the Medicare home care benefit, has a strong skilled care orientation, and is primarily intended to reduce acute hospital and short-stay SNF days. Thus, it would appear that there is substantial potential to expand the provision of private insurance for both institution-based and community-based long-term care. Furthermore, the advantage to government of stimulating growth in private long-term care insurance is even more compelling in view of projected cost increases for long-term care.

Projections Regarding Future Costs

The preceding sections of this chapter demonstrated that costs of long-term care have risen rapidly over the last 15 to 20 years. The infusion of uncapped funds, a reliance on cost-based reimbursement, and expensive loopholes in our Medicaid reimbursement system have been identified as major causes of this cost explosion. In Chapter 4, we will discuss the fourth major factor, which is demand for care. The primary users of long-term care are individuals over 65 years of age. Their numbers are expected to increase dramatically over the next 50 years, and it is their spectre which confronts policymakers today, especially at the state level. As mentioned earlier, in 21 states, long-term care now consumes more than 40 percent of all Medicaid expenditures. Nursing home care alone cost $20.4 billion nationally in 1980. By 1990, it is projected to cost $55.1 billion.

Outlays for nursing home care and home care constitute the fastest growing expenditures nationally for Medicare and Medicaid. If we assume that there will be no major breakthroughs in the reduction of mortality rates from the treatment of chronic disease, it is estimated that the number of people requiring institutional long-term care will increase from 1.5 million in 1980 to 5.2 million in 2040.[16] Although costs of long-term care have been described as catastrophic, no major piece of national health insurance legislation has ever included a provision for long-term care. The Federal government is attempting to reduce a $200 billion annual deficit, and the solvency of the Medicare trust fund is in question. Clearly, the needs of individuals for long-term care over the next 50 years will not go away but will instead increase as the at-risk population grows. Just as clearly, there are limits to the role of public funds in underwriting the costs of long-term care. The question then to be addressed in subsequent chapters is not "Will our system of financing long-term care change?" but "How and in what directions?" Before looking at changes in the system, however, an understanding of the consumers and providers of long-term care is necessary.

NOTES

1. Barbara G. Weichert, "Health Care Expenditures," *Health: United States, 1981* (Hyattsville, Md.: U.S. Department of Health and Human Services, Office of Health Research Statistics and Technology, 1981), p. 83.

2. U.S. GAO, "Medicaid and Nursing Home Care: Cost Increases and the Need for Services are Creating Problems for the States and the Elderly," DHHS Pub. no. (IPE–84–1), January 1984, p. i.

3. Mark S. Freeland and Carol Ellen Schendler, "National Health Expenditure Growth in the 1980s: An Aging Population, New Technologies, and Increasing Competition," *Health Care Financing Review,* 6:3 (1985), p. 29.

4. U.S. GAO, p. 26.

5. Kenneth McCaffree et al., "Profits, Growth and Reimbursement Systems in the Nursing Home Industry," *Health Care Financing Grants and Contracts Report,* April 1981.

6. Carliss Y. Baldwin and Christine E. Bishop, "Return to Nursing Home Investment: Issues for Public Policy," *University Health Policy Consortium Working Paper DP-50,* January 1983, p. 24.

7. American Hospital Association, Hospital Statistics, 1982, p. 6.

8. Aravindan Rangaswamy and Susan Hughes, "Marketing Long-Term Home Care Services to the Elderly: A Survey," Working Paper 88 (Evanston, Ill.: Northwestern University, Center for Health Services and Policy Research, 1982), p. 4.

9. Beth J. Soldo and Kenneth G. Manton, "Health Service Needs of the Oldest Old," *Health and Society,* 63:2, 1985, p. 304.

10. Beth J. Soldo, "In-Home Services for the Dependent Elderly: Determinants of Current Use and Implications for Future Demand," *Research on Aging,* 7:2, (June 1985), p. 281–304.

11. Peter Townsend, "The Effects of Family Structure on the Likelihood of Admission to an Institution in Old Age: The Application of a General Theory," in *Social Structure and the Family,* ed. E. Shanas and G. F. Streib (Englewood Cliffs, N.J.: Prentice-Hall, 1965), p. 175.

12. William G. Weissert, "Size and Characteristics of the Noninstitutionalized Long-Term Care Population," *Urban Institute Working Paper 1466-20,* September 1982, p. 10.

13. Lynn Paringer, "The Forgotten Costs of Informal Long-Term Care," *Urban Institute Working Paper 1455–28,* June 1983, p. 35.

14. Ibid., p. 39.

15. Lynn Paringer, "Economic Incentives in the Provision of Long-Term Care," in *Market Reforms in Health Care,* ed. Jack Meyer (Washington, D.C.: American Enterprise Institute, January 1983).

16. Dorothy P. Rice and Jacob J. Feldman, "Living Longer in the United States: Demographic Changes and Health Needs of the Elderly," *Health and Society,* 61:3, 1983, p. 385.

PART TWO

Long-Term Care Populations, Providers, and Delivery Systems

CHAPTER FOUR

The Consumers:
Demand for Long-Term Care

- Contrary to popular stereotypes, consumers of long-term care are diverse, including as many individuals under age 65 as above, with needs that span social, psychiatric, educational, rehabilitative, and medical care.

- The greatest increase in demand for care is projected to occur among the "old-old" elderly (those age 80 and above), especially with respect to long-stay users of institutional care.

- Linear projections of demand based on past and current use are fraught with risk. Specifically, changes in mortality and morbidity, advances in the treatment of conditions like Alzheimer's disease and osteoporosis, changes in the composition of family supports, and increased financing options can substantially affect the need and demand for specific types of long-term care services and will need to be monitored carefully and used in interactive planning models in the future.

Demand for long-term care is expected to increase substantially over the next 50 to 60 years because of three long-term trends: (1) increased survival of the elderly; (2) continued advances in medical technology that will enable the chronically ill to survive and to be cared for in a greater variety of settings; and (3) continued search for less expensive care settings than the acute care hospital. Because long-term care has been touted by many as a major growth area, many new providers (hospitals and hospital chains, in particular) are entering this arena. It is very important that new entrants to this market understand that, despite popular stereotypes, users of long-term care services are not a homogeneous group. At least four subgroups of community and institutional long-term care users can be broadly described. These are the young chronically ill, the mentally ill and mentally retarded, those over 65 suffering from a time-limited condition requiring skilled care, and those over 65 who require long-term maintenance, intermediate, or skilled level care. Although these groups overlap, for the sake of simplicity they are described here as distinct subgroups. In this chapter, we address all four, with emphasis on the last because of its predominance in terms of both current and predicted volume.

The Young

We use a very broad definition of young to encompass those individuals under 65 years of age who do not have a primary diagnosis of mental illness or disability. This group includes such diverse subgroups as congenitally handicapped children; adolescent, young adult, and adult trauma victims; and victims of iatrogenic medicine who require supportive services.

The number of children receiving long-term care is difficult to determine with exactness but appears to be growing. Local newspaper headlines recently publicized the successful hospital discharge of an infant who weighed less than one pound at birth. This child now weighs five pounds at age six months and apparently has no neurological or other long-term side effects of prematurity. Other children are not as fortunate and may require substantial amounts of medical and social services over their lifetimes.

According to a recent study by Newacheck et al., data from the most recent National Health Interview Survey reveal that the number of children suffering limitation of their activities because of health or disability has doubled from 1 to 2 million over the last 20 years.[1] In another study dealing with this issue, Smyth et al. reported that the estimated average expenditure for health services by a group of chronically ill children (most of whom suffered from cystic fibrosis, cerebral palsy, and myelodysplasia) was 10 times that of a comparison sample of "average" children.[2] These reports indicate that the prevalence of chronic illness in children may be increasing, with important implications for health care costs.

Part of this increase may result from advances in medical technology that have allowed many congenitally handicapped children who might not have survived 20 years ago not only to survive but to receive care in their own homes. President Reagan made news a few years ago when he publicized Katie Beckett's situation. Katie is a child who had been in a hospital for several years because she was dependent on a ventilator, and her care at home was not reimbursable under her state's Medicaid program. Since the publicity attending her case, the Katie Beckett waiver (Section 132 of the Tax Equity and Fiscal Responsibility Act [TEFRA]) has been passed and made effective in October 1982. Under this waiver, states have been given the option to approve Supplemental Security Income (SSI) payments to disabled children under 18 years of age who are being cared for at home. Under Medicaid deeming rules announced in June 1982, states may now apply to the Health Care Financing Administration (HCFA) on a case-by-case basis to waive family members' income and resources which otherwise would have been deemed attributable to the care of a disabled child. This waiver enables children qualifying for SSI under the Katie Beckett provision to receive Medicaid coverage for home care. As a result of this waiver, more children who previously were confined to hospital intensive care units at a cost of $1,800 a day for years (so-called "million dollar babies") are now receiving long-term care at home. Specifically, ventilator-dependent children in three cities across the country are now being cared for at home. Children being served in Chicago programs include those suffering from high spinal cord injuries, respiratory distress syndrome, bronchopulmonary dysplasia, and hyaline membrane disease.

The estimated monthly cost savings associated with home care services are $23,000 per child treated.[3]

As a result of President Reagan's personal interest in this issue, the Office of the Surgeon General has actively supported national conferences on the delivery and financing of care for technology-dependent and other chronically ill children.[4] These conferences have stimulated many previously isolated public and private agencies dealing with this issue to exchange information and to reach a consensus regarding future policy research needed in this area. As a result, both community-care alternatives and more innovative private financing mechanisms are being reviewed.

According to a recent article in the *New England Journal of Medicine,* nursing homes in certain states are also beginning to care for sufficient numbers of multiply handicapped children to warrant the establishment of special pediatric units.[5] The presence of multiple state payment, rehabilitation, and education oversight agencies has been described as a serious barrier to the provision and coordination of high quality care to these children. As a result, several states are beginning to share experiences on this issue in an effort to develop more streamlined methods of financing and monitoring the care of the severely, multiply handicapped child. Numerically, the population of children who use long-term care services is still small. However, if technology continues to enable more of these children to survive, this group can be predicted to constitute a small but costly group of users in the future.

Technology is also responsible for both good and bad news regarding the number of young to middle-aged adults surviving traumatic accidents or coping with chronic illnesses. According to the National Center for Health Statistics, the number of Americans with physical disabilities increased by more than 49 percent between 1970 and 1981.[6] On the positive side, advances in rehabilitation research have made it possible for many of the young disabled to live in the community, either totally independently or with others. Many individuals with spinal cord injuries, for example, who 10 years ago would have been unable to manage without a 24-hour attendant, are now driving specially equipped vans. Substantial numbers of young adults suffering from cystic fibrosis and cerebral palsy are now surviving into their 20s, creating new demands on primary care providers who are unused to caring for these former pediatric-specialty patients.[7]

The National Institute of Handicapped Research was established in 1978 to promote the development of special services and technical aids for the disabled. An increase in the number of independent living centers from none to 100 nationwide is also providing a new source of community support for these individuals. Technological advances in intravenous feeding and kidney dialysis have also made it possible for many working-age persons with serious chronic illnesses to remain at home engaged in their own self-care and gainfully employed. "Hi-tech" home care services and medical supplies for this group have been touted in the press recently as major growth areas in the health care industry. At the other end of the spectrum, however, are the totally dependent individuals who remain in nursing homes over extended periods in essentially comatose conditions, requiring total 24-hour care.

According to the most recent National Nursing Home Survey, 14 percent (about 183,000) residents during 1977 were under age 65.[8] Diagnostic data from the survey indicate that residents under age 65 generally have very different medical conditions than older residents, who constitute the majority. Mental illness, mental retardation, and paralysis unrelated to stroke were most prevalent among residents under age 65, as opposed to arteriosclerosis, heart trouble, and senility among those 65 and above. In the future, continuing advances in medical technology will probably enable increased numbers of younger individuals with chronic handicapping conditions to live independently or in congregate living arrangements in the community. On the other hand, medical technology will also enable severely impaired younger adults to be maintained over extended periods of time as heavy-care patients of long-term care institutions.

The Mentally Ill and Developmentally Disabled

Another group of long-term care users are the mentally ill and developmentally disabled individuals under age 65. One unintended result of public financing for long-term care can be seen in the transfer of individuals with these diagnoses from treatment facilities for the mentally ill to nursing homes during the 70s. Services tend to follow reimbursement dollars. Thus, it is not surprising that the federal share of Medicaid long-term care expenditures, coupled with the trend over the past 20 years to deinstitutionalize the mentally ill and developmentally disabled, has resulted in the transfer of many mentally ill individuals from state hospitals to nursing homes. It has also led to the development of a new type of nursing home, the intermediate care facility for the mentally retarded (ICF-MP).

The community mental health movement began in the mid-sixties when the availability of psychoactive drugs held the promise of treating formerly unmanageable psychotic patients in the community. Within 15 years, the population of state mental hospitals was reduced by two thirds. Although it was estimated that 1,500 community mental health centers would be required nationally to replace institutional care, only 600 were funded. Mentally ill patients between age 21 and 65 are generally not eligible for Medicaid benefits if they are hospitalized in facilities that care exclusively for mental disorders. However, Medicaid benefits for this same group are available for maintenance care in nursing homes. As a result of this policy, as Figure 4–1 demonstrates, many patients were shifted from mental health facilities to nursing homes.[9] In 1974, the National Nursing Home Survey reported that 22 percent of the residents under age 65 were diagnosed as mentally ill or retarded. By 1977, this proportion increased to 32.3 percent, with psychosis (15.1 percent) and mental retardation (17.9 percent) responsible for the majority of cases.[10] It is not clear whether this transfer of patients in the 70s caused a one-time bulge in these statistics or whether this is the beginning of a long-range trend. However, in the absence of future new public funding for the treatment of the mentally ill or disabled, it seems reasonable to expect that nursing homes will continue to care for a sizable portion of these individuals. Whether they are well equipped to do the job adequately is another matter which is addressed in chapters to follow.

FIGURE 4–1 Population of Nursing Homes and of State and Private Mental Hospitals, 1963 and 1969

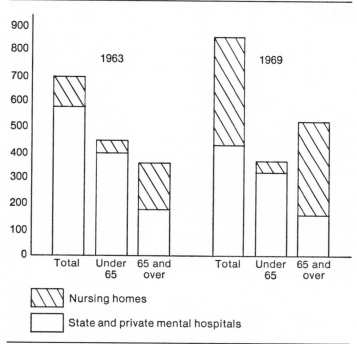

The 65+ Short Stayers

Just as services follow dollars, service use is heavily in- fluenced by funding sources. Although Medicare pays for a steadily shrinking portion of all nursing home care, the avail- ability of Medicare and private insurance coverage for short- stay, skilled nursing home care has produced a distinct sub- group of short-stay nursing home users. The characteristics of short-stay users are not exactly understood because our knowledge of users is limited by the cross-sectional or snapshot approach used to date in studying them.

Most data on service users are derived from the National Nursing Home Surveys (NNHS) which use cross-sectional versus longitudinal survey methods. The NNHS obtains information on two representative samples of nursing home users: (1) a cross section of nursing home residents in a given year and (2) a sample of residents discharged during the previous year. As Liu and Palesch have pointed out, both samples bias our understanding of typical nursing home users.[11] Specifically, residents included in cross-sectional samples are more likely to represent long stayers, while short-stay patients are overrepresented in the sample of discharges. To surmount this problem, without going to the expense of conducting a national longitudinal survey, health services researchers have recently developed a rather ingenious method of creating, from the available 1976 data, a hypothetical "all user" population for that year as well as a hypothetical "cohort of admission" in that year.[12] Reports from these analyses have finally given us reasonable approximations of those characteristics of nursing home users that are associated with short versus long length of stay.

First, and most importantly, these studies revealed that twice as many elderly individuals as previously believed used nursing homes in 1976. For example, reports for the last 10 years, which were based on cross-sectional data, estimated that a stable 4.7 percent of persons over age 65 use nursing homes in any given year. This new method increases that estimate to 8.9 percent. A major reason for the difference in the two estimates is the presence of a higher volume of short-stay patients than was previously understood. In analyzing a hypothetical cohort of new admissions, for example, Liu and Manton reported that 40 percent of all residents of nursing homes in 1976 were new admissions and that a substantial number of these new admissions (60 percent) were discharged within two months.

These short stayers have been undercounted in previous surveys of residents because they were not present in the facility at the time of the survey. As expected, the short-term users differed substantially from their long-stay counterparts. Specifically, 98.3 percent of the residents whose primary payment source was Medicare were discharged within two months of admission. Further analysis of residents by status at discharge revealed that 59 percent of the people admitted in a given year were also discharged during that year, 73 percent alive and 27 percent dead. Of those discharged alive, more were married (54 percent), suffering from hip fractures (67 percent) and/or cancer (40 percent), and least disabled at admission. Alternatively, people who suffered from cancer and were also bedridden at admission were most likely to be discharged within one year of admission because of death. Finally, although new admissions accounted for 40 percent of the total number of nursing home patients in 1976, their share of total nursing home days was only 22 percent, with the subset of admissions who were also discharged accounting for only 7 percent of nursing home days. This difference reflects the fairly rapid turnover of these patients.

As a body, these statistics are important because they demonstrate that a significant proportion of nursing home patients receive recuperative care over a relatively short period. The presence of this subset of skilled care, short-term users is important to recognize in projecting future demand for nursing home use and in developing specific interventions to reduce institutional use. For example, as Liu and Palesch have pointed out,

> it is important to recognize which type of nursing home user is likely to be affected by specific policies. Failure to recognize the effects of specific policies on subsets of the nursing home population will result in erroneous projections of policy impact. On the other hand, the financial burden of specific policies may not be as formidable as expected, if improved estimates become available on the policies' prospective target population.[13]

This subset of skilled care users can only be expected to grow in the future as a result of two long-term trends: the overall increase in the number of elderly and the new prospective payment system for hospital Medicare patients. As a result of both trends, it will be in the future interest of hospitals to provide an aftercare option to this skilled care group. Through either direct provision of aftercare services or through shared or joint-ventured services or transfer agreements, hospitals will be able to expedite the timely discharge of this group of patients, while simultaneously assuring their continuity of care and likely future use of the hospital.

Statistics previously cited suggest that nursing homes already play a substantial role in the provision of skilled aftercare services. The other option for this group requiring recuperative care is Medicare-reimbursed home care. Although statistics similar to the nursing home survey data on characteristics of Medicare home care users are not available, we know that most clients who use Medicare home care services are over age 65 and that they must suffer from similar skilled care conditions for their care to be reimbursed by Medicare. The potential growth in this elderly skilled care group makes involvement in one or both of these types of aftercare services a very attractive proposition for hospitals today. However, while this group of elderly short-term users is expected to grow, it is important to keep in mind that its growth pales in comparison to our next group of users, the long-term users.

The 65+ Long-Term Users

The short-stay users of long-term care services have been described as younger, married elderly who suffer from acute illness, who constitute 40 percent of nursing home admissions in a given year, and represent an unspecified but probable substantial majority of Medicare home care clients. In contrast, recent analyses of long-term users suggest that this population is quite different. Specifically, more long-term users tend to be single or widowed and female.[14] In addition, more long-term users suffer from chronic brain syndrome and are incontinent of both bowel and bladder.[15] While there is clearly a relationship between advanced age and likelihood of nursing home use, recent analyses of this issue suggest that age per se does not predict long-term versus short-term use. Risk of nursing home admission doubles from roughly 9 percent probability at age 65 and over to 20 percent at age 80 and over. On the basis of this relationship and the fact that 70 percent of nursing home residents are over age 75, a number of rather grim projections have been made regarding future demand for long-term care. Since a great deal rests on the relative accuracy of these projections, we address them in some detail in this chapter.

Future Growth in the Elderly Long-Term Care Population

A great deal of attention has focused recently on the burgeoning numbers of elderly survivors in the United States. It is now a cliché to speak of the "graying" of America. In fact, so much has been made of the survival of the elderly, that federal policymakers have been willing to undertake few, if any, meaningful initiatives in long-term care in the recent past, perhaps correctly reasoning that when one doesn't know what to do, the best thing to do may be nothing.

There is no question that the number of elderly in the United States has been increasing rapidly and is expected to continue to do so. Persons over age 65 constituted 4.1 percent of our population at the beginning of this century.[16] They now constitute 11.1 percent. As in Figure 4–2 on page 72, the proportion of elderly in the United States has grown particularly rapidly since 1960. Specifically, during 1960–1980, the total elderly population in the United States increased twice as fast as the nonelderly population. More importantly, however, within the elderly population, the subset of very old elderly grew even more rapidly, with those over age 85 increasing by a startling 174 percent over the same time period.

This increase in the number of very old, coupled with projections regarding their future growth, is the cause of much concern. Because the very old are particularly high-volume users of long-term care, projected increases in their number have been cited as a source of considerable alarm. Any conclusion regarding whether or not this degree of alarm is actually warranted requires closer scrutiny of the assumptions underlying these projections. It is particularly important, for example, that the multiple factors that influence use of long-term care services be examined. Thus, projections regarding future demand for long-term care services should address not only demographic shifts in the age of our population but also trends in mortality, stability of social supports, and purchasing power of successive elderly cohorts over time. In addition,

---

FIGURE 4–2   Change in Age Distribution in United States
Population, 1960–1980

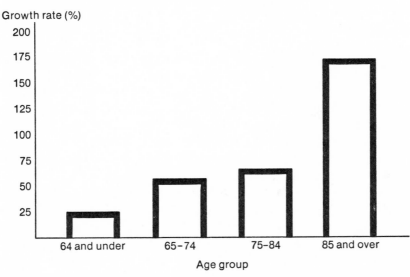

several unknown factors, such as changes in morbidity and technological advances in the treatment of chronic disease, should be factored in as well.

The single most important piece of information which predicts the size of future cohorts of the elderly is the fertility rate. This rate, together with information on net immigration rates and assumptions about mortality, forms the basis for projections regarding future numbers of elderly in our society. Given the fact that life expectancy was 73 years in the United States in 1980 and the fact that all members of these birth cohorts have already been born, we can make reasonably sound projections now about the numbers of elderly who will survive through the middle of the next century.

The Census Bureau has been developing these projections, using three different sets of statistics or series: lowest, middle, and highest estimates regarding fertility, life expectancy, and immigration.[17] Most reports use the middle-series statistics, with the lowest and highest-series estimates forming the lower and upper bounds of the estimates' error. Recently, Rice and Feldman combined the census middle-series data with Social Security Administration actuarial data on mortality to project the demographic and health needs of the elderly through the year 2040.[18] They report that major declines in mortality due to vascular disease are expected to continue well into the 21st century. As a result, the proportion of elderly in the population will increase from 11 percent to 20 percent by 2040. Forty-five percent of the elderly in 2040 will be age 65-74; however, the majority (55 percent) will be 75 and older. In other words, because of declining mortality rates, average life expectancy will increase from age 70.7 for males in 1981 to 73.3 in 2050 and from 78.3 for females to 83.6 by 2050.[19]

It is important to note, however, that most analysts believe that the life span of the human species is not increasing. The life span of humans is believed to be relatively fixed at a little over 110 years of age. However, more and more people are surviving to the upper limits of the life span, mainly as a result of lower infant mortality rates, better immunization rates, the use of antibiotics, and, most recently, declining death rates from cardiovascular disease. This increase in number of very old citizens is important and is anticipated to profoundly affect our society. For example, a recent census report has projected that the rate of centenarians (people surviving to age 100) in our population will increase from the current rate of 1 in 6,500 people to 1 in 2,500 by the year 2000, 1 in 300 by 2050, and 1 in 165 by 2080.[20] These projections have particularly profound implications for strategic planners of health services.

Morbidity

The increased survival of the very old is anticipated to tax our health and social services because increased age, unfortunately, is often accompanied by increased prevalence of chronic impairment. Reports from the National Health Interview Survey, for example, indicate that the proportion of individuals suffering from limitation of activity increases with age, rising from 7.3 percent of the population age 45 and under to 24.1 percent of those 45–64 and 46 percent of those 65 and over.

As Table 4–1 demonstrates, within that large population of individuals over age 65, the need for help with activities of daily living increases substantially with age, especially for those over 85. Thus, it appears there is a close linear relationship between advanced age and decline in functional capacity. However, Weissert's research on this issue indicates that, despite this relationship, care of the elderly may still be manageable in the future. His analysis of data from the National Nursing Home and National Health Interview Surveys suggests that only 15 percent of the elderly are dependent in both personal care and mobility, the two characteristics which most strongly predict need for nursing home care.[21]

Additionally, many have argued that a direct linear projection of past morbidity levels to the future is inappropriate and potentially seriously misleading. Fries, for example, has argued that the combination of improved lifestyle and technological advances in the treatment of chronic disease may substantially postpone the onset of chronic diseases and limit the degree of morbidity or functional impairment customarily associated with them.[22] In this case, society would experience not only a rectangularization of the mortality curve, with more persons surviving to advanced age, but a rectangularization of morbidity as well. In the latter case, older people in the future would be relatively free from disease until the last years of life when they would succumb to senescence or to multiple simultaneous organ failures as a result of decline in lifetime organ reserves. Other researchers have argued that the exact opposite may occur; i.e., more and more individuals will reach advanced old age but only at the cost of a pandemic of chronic disease, resulting in extraordinary and unprecedented use and cost of health and social services.

Until recently, we have had scant knowledge regarding the prevalence of chronic disease and even less ability to forecast trends in this area. However, recent advances in statistical techniques have profound implications for our ability to make more accurate predictions. The actuarial analysis of life tables is a well recognized analytic technique that has enabled life insurance companies to grow and prosper financially during

TABLE 4-1 Rate per 1,000 Adults Who Need Assistance at Home by Type of Need, Age, and Sex, United States, 1979

Type of Need	All Adults	55–64 Years M	55–64 Years F	65–74 Years M	65–74 Years F	75–84 Years M	75–84 Years F	85 Years and Older M	85 Years and Older F
					Age and Sex				
Needs help in one or more basic physical activities	22.5	28.0	29.3	49.4	29.3	101.7	121.4	301.7	372.0
Walking	16.1	20.5	17.6	37.7	17.6	73.5	89.7	204.8	289.7
Going outside	13.7	12.2	15.9	28.0	15.9	52.6	86.2	225.3	292.7
Bathing	9.1	10.5	11.6	22.8	11.6	45.6	53.7	149.0	185.5
Dressing	7.1	8.7	9.0	14.3	9.0	31.3	34.1	111.7	118.1
Using the toilet	5.5	6.0	6.0	12.0	6.0	22.0	32.0	72.6	122.0
Getting in or out of bed	4.9	6.1	5.9	8.0	5.9	20.1	29.2	63.3	78.4
Eating	2.0	4.0	1.6	5.2	1.6	7.3	9.1	33.5	39.7
Adults who usually stay in bed	5.5	9.0	7.0	11.9	10.9	29.4	27.6	61.5	45.6
Has device or other trouble controlling bowels or bladder	10.1	8.7	16.3	14.6	28.8	49.1	49.0	117.3	108.1
Needs help of another person in one or more of the above activities	31.7	34.3	45.3	55.3	81.1	127.6	180.8	353.8	479.2
				Both Sexes					
Needs help in one or more home management activities	26.5	31.9		57.3		141.8		399.0	
Shopping only	4.0	4.1		11.1		25.6		71.2	
Chores only	3.8	7.1		9.0		12.1		26.6	
Meals only	0.5	.9		1.3		2.3		5.8	
Shopping and chores	3.4	4.1		7.6		23.6		43.4	
Meals, shopping, chores	4.1	6.6		10.4		18.3		60.9	
No help reported needed	973.5	968.1		942.7		858.2		601.0	

SOURCE: National Center for Health Statistics, "Americans Needing Help to Function at Home," *Advance Data*, no. 92, September 1983.

the 20th century. At the beginning of this century, average life expectancy was 47 years, and there was a clear need for dependent families to be protected from potential loss of income due to the premature death of the family breadwinner. With advances in average life expectancy and increased prevalence of chronic disease, disability insurance has become more important or as important as life insurance. Recent advances in combining epidemiologic data on disease prevalence, incidence, and functional status are making it possible to project years of functional health, a breakthrough comparable to the years of survival measure with which we have been familiar in the past.

Several researchers have been working on the development of bioacturial methods to forecast functional health of the elderly. From available data, Katz et al. have constructed Activity of Daily Living (ADL) Scales for a statewide probability sample of the noninstitutionalized elderly in Massachusetts in 1974 and 1976.[23] Using life-table methods, the study team then calculated active life expectancy or remaining years of independent ADL functioning for this sample. Findings included an observed decrease in active life expectancy with age, ranging from 10 years of remaining active life expectancy for people aged 65 to 69, to 2.9 remaining active years for those 85 and older. Interestingly, in each age group studied, active life expectancy was longer for the nonpoor than the poor (those known to receive Supplemental Security Income, Old Age Assistance, or Medicaid). Nonpoor elderly aged 65 to 69 enjoyed 2.4 additional years of active life; this declined to less than one additional year at age 75 or older. Women experienced longer periods of dependent years of life, consistent with their longer life expectancy. Finally, Katz's group observed that although ADL dependency fluctuated for 20 percent of the study sample (i.e., some persons experienced decline followed by improvement in functional status), it remained stable or declined over time for most (80 percent) of the sample studied.

Using similar bioactuarial methods but concentrating on a specific disease and emphasizing the importance of understanding the latent period of chronic disease, Manton and Liu demonstrated the application of these research techniques to the study of chronic lung disease.[24] At present, because of annual household surveys conducted by the National Center for Health Statistics, we have reasonable information regarding the prevalence (number of individuals suffering from) and incidence (number of new cases in a given time period) of several chronic diseases. What is not clearly understood, however, is the nature of the delay from exposure to risk of contracting the disease to actual onset of clinical symptoms. This information is important for two reasons. First, if we know when people are at risk of exposure to a disease, we will also know when to target interventions to vulnerable populations. This improvement in targeting would greatly improve both the efficiency and effectiveness of primary prevention efforts and considerably aid the decline in morbidity that Fries has predicted. Second, knowledge about the time lag between exposure and manifestation of clinical symptoms can help planners to predict more accurately the future health services utilization and manpower resources required for those exposed to the disease.

While these bioactuarial models are in their infancy, their potential is revolutionary in scope because they will permit, for the first time, sophisticated analysis of the multiple types of indicators that influence long-term care use. As a result, government analysts and private insurers will have new tools with which to forecast future demand and expenditures for long-term care.

For example, in addition to mortality and morbidity, these analytic methods can be also used to assess three other important factors which may either reduce, exacerbate, or facilitate the use of long-term care services in the future. These are technological advances in the treatment of chronic disease, changes in our social support systems, and increased wealth of future cohorts of the elderly.

Technological Breakthroughs

Straight linear projections of ADL dependency by age from current data to the future may also substantially overestimate demand for long-term care because of the unknown contribution of technological breakthroughs in the treatment of chronic diseases. Twenty years ago, for example, very few individuals survived cardiac bypass surgery. Today, the mortality rate associated with this procedure is almost nil. Similarly, artificial joint implants to enable sufferers of arthritis to regain mobility and lens implants for sufferers of cataracts were unknown. At present, two of the major conditions associated with need for institutional long-term care are Alzheimer's disease and urinary incontinence; both are currently the subject of concentrated research efforts funded by the National Institute on Aging.

However, just as improvements in the treatment of disease can reduce demand for care, they can also result in the sustaining of life for severely dependent individuals. The use of life-sustaining treatment is an issue that will require continued legal and ethical discussion. As a result, use of "living wills" may increase. Just as more people have arranged to allow use of their organs after death, so too, as people begin to understand their potential risk of extended, unconscious life, they may make their wishes regarding continued treatment or nontreatment under these conditions more explicit.

Informal Supports

Earlier we described the informal support system, the relatives and friends of the functionally impaired, as the major long-term care system in the United States today. While this statement accurately describes the past and present, its application to the future is somewhat tenuous for several reasons. First, the traditional informal caretaker to date has often been described as "the woman in the middle," usually a middle-aged woman who has just finished raising her own children and is then called upon to care for an incapacitated parent or in-law. With the entry of women into the work force continuing to increase, this source of help may not be available in the future.

Second, we have moved from an agrarian to an industrial society, and this transition has had a profound effect on the traditional family network. We do not rely on the extended family for support. Rather, the nuclear family is now the norm. Technological advances, including the automobile, air transport, and rapid transit, have made us a mobile society. This increase in mobility may seriously diminish the availability of assistance to elderly family members.

Third, we have been experiencing a trend toward smaller families. Our future fertility rate is projected to be just a little over two, which is a replacement rate, not a growth rate. Where multiple offspring exist, chances are greater that someone in the family will be available to provide help. The recent trend toward childless marriages among professional couples raises potential problems in this regard.

Finally, until recently, the divorce rate in this country has increased substantially. This factor raises several interesting questions from a legal standpoint. For example, with respect to relative responsibility for financing long-term care services, who is responsible for whom? Is a daughter responsible for her biological mother's care or for her stepmother's care? Furthermore, are out-of-state children as responsible as children residing in the state where the individual is receiving care?

As these trends indicate, the availability of informal assistance in long-term care may substantially diminish in the future. However, this decline in availability of informal supports may be offset somewhat by the final important trend, the increasing wealth of future elderly cohorts.

Disposable Wealth of the Elderly

A considerable amount of evidence suggests that future cohorts of the elderly will differ substantially from those receiving long-term care today. Most elderly people receiving long-term care in institutions today are over age 80. They were born at the turn of this century, many of them as first-generation Americans, if not immigrants, to this country. Consequently, educational opportunities for this cohort differed substantially from those available to younger people who will become our future elderly. For example, 57 percent of people over age 75 in 1977 had only eight years of school or less. In contrast, 67 percent of the people who will be age 65 and older in 1990 will have had some high school education, and 17 percent will have had some college education. By 2020, 30 percent of those age 80 to 84 will have had at least one year of college, and 88 percent will have had at least one year of high school.[25] These figures indicate that a substantial number of future elderly will be well-educated individuals.

Whether this advantage in education will directly translate to an advantage in income is another matter. Recent reports seem to indicate that this is the case. In a recent article, Harold Ting, vice president for marketing of National Medical Enterprises, cited the higher incidence and size of private pension benefits, growth of Individual Retirement Accounts (IRAs), and increases in social security and other retirement benefits associated with increased numbers of two-worker families as factors causing increased private-pay demand for long-term care.[26] As a result of these changes, a recent report indicates that the proportion of elderly families with cash incomes of $25,000 and over (in constant 1980 dollars) will increase from 8 percent in 1985 to 34 percent in 2015.

This shift in the education and income of the elderly has many important implications for planners and long-term care services. It suggests that although the elderly are growing absolutely and proportionately, substantial numbers of them may be able to pay for care and will probably wish to exercise considerable discretion about the type and locus of long-term care services available to them. For example, we recently surveyed a sample of community-dwelling elderly in the Chicago area regarding their preferences for long-term care services. Preliminary data indicate that upper-income elderly (incomes over $15,000) differed from lower-income respondents in wishing to exercise more control over the type and volume of services provided and were quite definite about preferring to retain a relationship with their own physicians.[27] As future cohorts of elderly become increasingly well educated, we can expect that these characteristics will become more dominant.

What Do We Know?

In summary, it seems reasonable to conclude that the number of individuals requiring long-term care will grow in the future. Although long-term care users will continue to be heterogeneous, the largest volume of users will be elderly. Elderly users will be of both the short-term and long-term type. In the absence of specific government policies, such as state or federal income tax credits for the care of elderly family members, it appears that informal supports for the care of the elderly may dwindle over time because of changes in labor-force participation, mobility, and stability of the American family.

However, future cohorts of the elderly will be better educated, have more disposable income, and want to have a substantial voice in deciding what type of services they want or need and where they want to receive them. We will also have much better methods available with which to forecast their health and functional status. On the basis of this larger picture, what emerges is not so much a cause for gloom as a cause for excitement regarding new service markets and substantial opportunities for growth.

NOTES

1. Paul Newacheck, Peter Budetti, and Peggy McManus, "Trends in Childhood Disability," *American Journal of Public Health,* 74:3 (March 1984), p. 32.

2. Kathryn Smyth-Staruch, Naomi Breslau, Michael Weitzman, and Steven Gortmaker, "Use of Health Services by Chronically Ill and Disabled Children," *Medical Care,* 22:4 (April 1984), p. 310.

3. "Kids Who Live in ICUs: HHS Will Send Some Home," *Medical World News,* October 10, 1983.

4. U.S. DHHS, *Report on Activities Following the Surgeon General's Workshop on Children with Handicaps and Their Families* (Bureau of Health Care Delivery and Assistance, Division of Maternal and Child Health, Public Health Service, April 1984).

5. Phyllis Glick et al., "Pediatric Nursing Homes," *New England Journal of Medicine,* 309:11 (September 15, 1983), p. 645.

6. Lawrence Cherry and Rona Cherry, "New Hope for the Disabled," *New York Times Magazine,* February 5, 1984, pp. 52–55, 59, and 60.

7. "Special Adults: New Challenge to Primary Care MDs," *Medical World News,* February 24, 1986, pp. 68–81.

8. Esther Hing, "Characteristics of Nursing Home Residents, Health Status, and Care Received: National Nursing Home Survey, United States, May–December, 1977," *Vital and Health Statistics,* Series 13, no. 51 (April 1981), p. 2.

9. Ellen Bassuk and Samuel Gerson, "Deinstitutionalization and Mental Health Services," *Scientific American,* 238:2 (February 1978), pp. 46–53.

10. Hing, "Characteristics of Nursing Home Residents," p. 15.

11. Korbin Liu and Yuko Palesch, "The Nursing Home Population: Different Perspectives and Implications for Policy," *Health Care Financing Review,* 3:2 (December 1981), p. 15.

12. Korbin Liu and Kenneth G. Manton, "The Characteristics and Utilization Pattern of an Admission Cohort of Nursing Home Patients," *The Gerontologist,* 23:1 (1983), pp. 92–98.

13. Liu and Palesch, "The Nursing Home Population," p. 22.

14. Hing, "Characteristics of Nursing Home Residents," p. 345.

15. Liu and Manton, "The Characteristics and Utilization of an Admission Cohort of Nursing Homes," p. 94.

16. Mary Beard Deming and Neal E. Cutler, "Demography of the Aged," in *Aging: Scientific Perspective and Social Issues,* ed. Diana S. Woodruff and James E. Birrin (Monterey, Calif.: Brooks/Cole Publishing, 1983).

17. Bureau of the Census, *Projections of the Population of the United States: 1982–2050,* (Advance Report). Current Population Reports, Population: Estimates and Projections, Series P-25, no. 922 (Washington, D.C.: U.S. Department of Commerce, 1982).

18. Dorothy P. Rice and Jacob J. Feldman, "Living Longer in the United States: Demographic Changes and Health Needs of the Elderly," *Milbank Memorial Fund Quarterly/Health and Society,* 61:3 (Summer 1983), pp. 362–396.

19. Bureau of the Census, *Projections of the Population of the United States: 1982–2050,* 1982.

20. William Hines, "Many Newborns Expected to Live to 100," *Chicago Sun-Times,* June 21, 1984.

21. William F. Weissert, "Estimating the Long-Term Care Population: Prevalence Rates and Selected Characteristics," *Health Care Financing Review,* 6:4 (Summer 1985), p. 90.

22. James Fries, "The Compression of Morbidity," *Milbank Memorial Fund Quarterly/Health and Society,* 61:3 (Summer 1983), p. 406.

23. Sidney Katz et al., "Active Life Expectancy," *The New England Journal of Medicine,* 309:20 (November 19, 1983), pp. 1218–1224.

24. Kenneth G. Manton and Korbin Liu, "Projecting Chronic Disease Prevalence," *Medical Care,* 22:6 (June 1984), pp. 511–526.

25. Mary Beard Deming and Neal Cutler, "Demography of the Aged," p. 44.

26. Harold Ting, "New Directions in Nursing Home and Home Healthcare Marketing," *Healthcare Financial Management,* May 1984, p. 64.

27. D. Maheshwaran, Susan Hughes, and Ruth Singer, "Marketing Survey of Upper Income Elderly," *Working Paper* (Evanston, Ill.: Northwestern University, Center for Health Services and Policy Research, December 2, 1983).

Providers and Services: Increased Diversity in a Growth Market

- Long-term care providers can be classified according to two dimensions: their level of service intensity and institutional versus community-based location.
- Because of certificate of need, little growth has occurred recently among institutional providers with the exception of increased interest among hospitals in the provision of long-term care services and a substantial increase in the number of continuing-care retirement communities which are privately financed and, in many cases, exempt from state planning requirements.
- In contrast, community care has expanded substantially despite the fact that sources of payment are more uncertain.
- Both types of care will clearly be needed in the future, and easy access between the two systems of care should be fostered.

Both the number and types of long-term care services and providers in this country have grown dramatically over the last 20 years. Just as consumers of long-term care services are increasingly heterogeneous in nature, there is substantial heterogeneity among long-term care providers. Much has been written in the past decade about the need to develop a continuum of service options for the long-term care client. As this chapter demonstrates, we are making remarkable strides toward that goal. As Figure 5–1 indicates, long-term care providers can be roughly classified as falling into one of eight categories depending upon (1) the level of care provided and (2) their institutional versus community-based location.

During 1966–1981, increased survival of the chronically impaired, coupled with increased availability of uncapped cost-based public funding for their care, resulted in major growth of institution-based long-term care services for the chronically ill (cell A2 of Figure 5–1). Recently, however, growth has shifted to other segments of the long-term care market. Specifically, concern over increased costs of care for long-stay institutional users has led to a search for community-based alternative systems (cell B2) of care, especially for those whose care is supported by public funding. The increased education and wealth of future elderly cohorts suggest that growth in community-based long-term care will continue because of the expansion of this private-pay group of consumers who appear to prefer it.

In a similar vein, concern over increased costs of acute care has led to the development of new financing and delivery mechanisms designed to reduce these runaway expenditures. Medicare prospective payment for acute hospital care, health maintenance organizations, and the Medicare hospice benefit represent attempts to reduce outlays for acute hospital care by encouraging the substitution of less expensive care in either an institutional extended-care or home care setting (cells A1 and B1). As a result, many new types of services and service delivery systems have evolved that are already substantially altering the provision of long-term care. They will continue to do so in the future. This chapter describes this array of providers, beginning with those in the institutional column and then moving to the community side.

FIGURE 5–1 Classification of Long-Term Care Providers

Skill Level

Locus of Care

High	
Skilled (acute)	A. Institution
	1. Skilled nursing facilities
Intermediate (chronic)	2. Intermediate care facilities
Sheltered (frail)	3. Homes for the aged, foster care
Congregate	4. Retirement communities, congregate housing
Low	

B. Community	
1. Skilled home care, hospice, high-tech home care	
2. Long-term home care, adult day services, home-delivered meals, lifeline	
3. Homemaker and chore services	
4. Transportation, social and recreational activities	

FIGURE 5-2 Institutional Providers in the Long-Term
Care Market

---

*Service
Intensity*   *Provider Type*

High

        1. Hospital swing-bed and step-down units
        2. Skilled nursing facilities
        3. Intermediate care and sheltered care facilities
        4. Homes for the aged
        5. Continuing-care retirement communities
        6. Foster or domiciliary care
        7. Congregate housing

Low

INSTITUTIONAL PROVIDERS

Institutional care is defined broadly to encompass the wide variety of providers who have recently entered the long-term care marketplace. Figure 5–2 lists at least seven types of institutional providers arrayed according to a continuum of service intensity. Although there is considerable blurring among providers in the middle ranges, these providers have been classified together because they share a common factor. In all cases, consumers using these service options have made a decision that they require the security these facilities offer. In other words, either the user or someone acting on the user's behalf has decided that one of these seven options is preferable to continued independent living in an apartment or home in the community.

Nursing Homes

Tables 5–1 and 5–2 display the growth in the nursing home industry during 1967–1983. As Table 5–1 indicates, the absolute number of nursing homes peaked in 1971 at a high of 22,004 homes and then declined to a low of 18,722 homes by 1978. The 23,065 homes listed for 1980 would appear to signal a resurgence of growth in the industry. However, this figure is quite misleading since it actually reflects a change in classifi-

TABLE 5–1 Growth in Nursing Home Beds and Bed Capacity, Selected Years, 1967–1983

Year	Homes	Beds	Average Bed Capacity
1967	19,141	836,554	44
1969	18,910	943,876	50
1971	22,004	1,201,598	55
1973	21,834	1,327,704	61
1976	20,468	1,414,865	69
1978	18,722	1,348,794	72
1980	23,065	1,537,338	67
1983	21,261	1,851,968	87

SOURCES: Years 1967–1980: National Center for Health Statistics, Data from the National Medical Facilities Inventory, Series 14, no. 4, 16, 23, and 29.

1983: Health Care Financing Administration, Bureau of Data Management and Strategy, "Medicare and/or Medicaid Participating Long-Term Care Facilities and Beds," July 1983.

TABLE 5–2 Characteristics of Nursing Homes, Selected Years, 1967–1980

Year	Bed Size Percent Homes with Less than 100 Beds	Care Provided Percent Nursing Care Homes	Ownership Percent Proprietary
1967	90.7%	55.6%	77.4%
1973	81.2	68.1	76.5
1976	76.1	65.6	75.0
1978	74.3	56.3	74.9
1980	74.2	—	80.9

SOURCE: National Center for Health Statistics, Data from the National Medical Facilities Inventory, Series 14, no. 4, 16, 23, and 29.

cation. In 1980, for the first time, 2,500 adult foster care homes in Michigan and 1,000 residential community care facilities in California were identified as meeting the definitional requirements for inclusion in the National Master Facility Inventory, the most reliable source of information on the number of facilities.[1] As Table 5–1 demonstrates, however, the real story on nursing home growth is not seen in the number of facilities, which fluctuate over time for reasons described in Chapter 2, but rather in the number of beds; here, the growth is impressive. The number of beds increased from 836,554 in 1967 to 1,851,968 in 1983, an increase of 117 percent over a 16-year period. This represents an average annual rate increase of 7.3 percent. Thus, during the same period, the average bed capacity of any given nursing home doubled, from 44 to 87 beds. These figures demonstrate that the industry has changed substantially from the Mom and Pop operators of the 60s to the more sophisticated managers of the 80s.

Table 5–2 also demonstrates this trend. For example, fewer than 10 percent of homes had more than 100 beds in 1967. In contrast, more than 25 percent of homes fit this category today. On the other hand, it is useful to remember that the model nursing home has less than 100 beds. The ownership of nursing homes is also increasingly proprietary; however, the trend in this direction has increased only slightly over time.

Geographically, as Table 5–3 demonstrates, there is marked variety in the distribution of nursing home beds in the United States. The cold weather states in the Midwest (North Central) have the highest ratio of beds per 1,000 elderly. The sunbelt states, characterized by milder climates and younger citizenry, have the lowest despite the fact that significant numbers of elderly relocate in these states during their retirement years. An explanation for this discrepancy can be seen in data from the 1980 census that indicate that the elderly may only relocate temporarily in sunbelt states and move back to stay nearer kin as they become more frail.[2]

Managerially, two other aspects of the industry deserve note. First, as mentioned in Chapter 2, the number of freestanding facilities has declined, replaced by a rapid increase in the number of nursing home chains during the 70s. It is estimated that 10 percent of all nursing home beds are cur-

TABLE 5–3 Average Bed Size of Nursing Homes by Type of Ownership and Geographic Region, United States, 1978

Type of Ownership and Geographic Region	Average Bed Size
All homes	72.0
Type of ownership	
Government	132.6
Proprietary	63.1
Nonprofit	86.9
Geographic region	
Northeast	80.6
North Central	82.4
South	78.6
West	47.8

SOURCE: Genevieve W. Strahan, "Inpatient Health Facilities Statistics, U.S. 1978," *Vital and Health Statistics,* Series 14, no. 24, p. 4.

rently operated by four major nursing home chains, with Beverly Enterprises leading the field. Beverly alone represents 92,777 beds in 822 facilities and 5 percent of the national bed supply.[3]

Second, until recently, there has been some diminution of the skilled care focus of the industry. In 1973, as Table 5–2 indicates, 68 percent of all nursing homes nationally provided skilled nursing care. In 1978, the last year for which these figures are available, only 56 percent of homes provided skilled care. According to many nursing home administrators, this change was due to the significant investment required to qualify for Medicare/Medicaid skilled care licensure and certification. Many administrators felt that this investment was not economically viable and purposely limited their involvement in the skilled care business, preferring instead to emphasize their intermediate care capability. However, with the implementation of Medicare prospective payment for acute hospital care, nursing homes will probably expand their skilled nursing capacity in order to meet the increased demand of hospitals for safe discharge options of elderly in need of subacute care. On the other hand, nursing homes may find some stiff competition in this area from a new source, the hospital itself.

Hospital Geriatric and Extended-Care Services

Many hospitals have been facing shortened length of stay and declining occupancy rates for several years. The implementation of prospective payment has only accelerated that already existing trend. However, coupled as it has been, with insurors' interests in shorter length of stay and increased use of ambulatory care, prospective payment has stimulated a new interest in long-term care among acute care hospitals.

Historically, hospitals have been identified with the rapid acquisition of the newest medical technology and have considered medical school affiliations and number of teaching staff as badges of superiority in a field where knowledge changed rapidly and the acquisition of knowledge was a plus. Rather remarkably, however, the very technology which propelled hospitals to deinvest in more humble community services is now forcing them to take a second look at this decision, since a great deal of medical care now can be provided safely outside of the hospital and third-party payors increasingly recognize this fact. The resulting emergence of birthing centers, high-tech home care, and ambulatory surgery, coupled with increased emphasis on shorter lengths of hospital stay, has hit hospitals squarely in the pocketbook. Hospitals are having difficulty accessing capital for the first time in recent memory and, as a result, are seriously considering entering or have already entered the long-term care arena in one capacity or another.

As representatives of the American Hospital Association have pointed out, it makes a lot of sense for hospitals to cultivate the long-term care market. Hospitals treat a large number of elderly people, with 38 percent of inpatient days in 1980 being used by people age 65 or older.[4] The hospital admission rate of the elderly in 1980 was almost three times higher than that of the nonelderly (400 per 1,000 admissions versus 136 per 1,000). Of elderly persons admitted, 25 percent were readmitted.[5] In other words, the elderly constitute a large share of the average hospital's business. The onset of prospective payment has undoubtedly impacted these statistics somewhat, since it is directly aimed at curtailing the use of hospital care among the elderly. However, given projected increases in the number of elderly in the near future, they will probably continue to constitute a major share of the hospital's clientele.

Hospitals have a competitive advantage in terms of their access to elderly users and in terms of their resources with respect to the skilled care segment of the long-term care industry. As Table 5–4 demonstrates, many hospitals are aware of both factors and have taken steps to capitalize on these advantages by offering a variety of services to their elderly clients. In 1980, 1,056 hospitals operated their own hospital-based nursing home and extended-care facilities. These accounted for an aditional 76,024 beds, or 4.9 percent of the total supply of long-term care beds.[6]

Some long-term care analysts have argued that hospitals should increase their share of long-term care activity by designating certain beds as "swing beds."[7] In response to prevailing sentiments that many areas of the country were oversupplied with acute hospital beds and undersupplied with long-term care beds, the Health Care Financing Administration (HCFA) initiated a swing-bed program. The original HCFA swing-bed regulations allowed hospitals licensed and/or certified for less than 50 beds in rural areas to "swing" beds from acute care to long-term care use. This flexible use of fixed capital resources has been argued by many to be a reasonable way of alleviating the bottleneck of patients waiting in acute care beds for discharge to nursing home care. In 1983 in Massachusetts alone, 300,000 patient days were labelled administratively necessary and reimbursed at less than an acute care per diem rate.[8] This use of acute hospital beds for long-stay Medicaid patients is a source of concern to hospitals, primarily those in the Northeast where the problem appears to be most acute. However, the HCFA restriction of the swing-bed approach to rural areas and to facilities with fewer than 50 beds limits its usefulness in this same area.

Critics of the swing-bed approach have argued that hospital-based long-term care may be twice as expensive as nursing

TABLE 5–4 Types of Special Services for Older Adults Offered by 417 Surveyed Hospitals, 1981

Type of Service	Percentage of Hospitals Reporting
Discharge planning	76.0%
Information and referral	48.0
Patient/family education	43.4
Skilled nursing facility	38.6
Psychosocial counseling	30.7
Intermediate care facility	25.4
Home-delivered meals	24.2
Mental health services	23.3
Inpatient unit (medical-surgical)	22.5
Home health care	22.5
Senior volunteers	22.5
Inpatient unit (psychiatric)	22.1
Screening	21.8
Medical consultation	21.6
Alcohol/drug abuse program	21.1
Case management	19.2
Social/recreational groups	18.5
Outreach	18.0
Follow-up in nursing homes	18.0
Outpatient clinic	17.7
Inpatient unit (rehabilitation)	16.3
Transportation	13.9
Hospice	13.4
Telephone contact/lifeline	13.4
Adult day care	11.8
Physical fitness/wellness	11.3
Satellite clinics	10.1
Congregate meals	9.1
Comprehensive assessment unit	8.9
Outpatient rehabilitation	8.6
Day hospital	7.9
Homemakers/personal care help	7.0
Senior residences/apartments	6.2
Home visitors	5.0
Swing beds	4.3
Health maintenance organization	2.4
Multipurpose senior center	2.2
Life-care community	0.5

SOURCE: Connie Evashwick, "Long-Term Care Becomes Major New Role for Hospitals," reprinted by permission from *Hospitals*, 56, no. 13, July 1, 1982. Copyright 1982, American Hospital Publishing, Inc.

home care because of hospitals' higher fixed overhead and costs. However, recent research by Steven Finkler of New York University indicates that the average swing bed costs less ($26.73 per day, including food, laundry, housekeeping, operations and maintenance, extra labor, and medical products) than nursing home care ($49.05 per day).[9] These savings apply only under certain conditions. Specifically, swing-bed costs are lower only for small numbers of patients (2–8) with temporary needs for subacute care versus larger numbers of patients (40, 60, or 80) who are more economically cared for in nursing homes.

Because of these pressures to retain control over patients in a competitive environment and to shift patients efficiently to less expensive levels and loci of care, many hospitals have been purchasing nursing homes or entering into joint ventures with nursing homes and other long-term care providers. The variety of arrangements used to organize these services will be described in greater detail in Chapter 6. It will suffice to conclude here that the hospital is a new and vigorous entrant in the long-term care market and will be a dominant force in years to come.

Another type of service that hospitals are uniquely capable of providing is geriatric assessment on either an inpatient or outpatient basis for older patients who are beginning to experience functional difficulties and/or whose multiple medical diagnoses cause difficulties in appropriate medical and pharmaceutical management. Since hospitals already have interdisciplinary teams, specialists, and diagnostic testing available, they are uniquely suited to perform these assessments and can reap both community goodwill and access to a new pool of patients by offering the service. Although Medicare reimbursement is not currently available for geriatric assessments per se, many services which comprise the assessment can be billed under Medicare Part B. As a result of recent research that has demonstrated the effectiveness of this approach in producing better patient outcomes and reducing cost of care, reimbursement for this service may be more readily available in the future.[10]

Finally, although there are many potential advantages accruing to both hospitals and patients from hospital involvement in long-term care, there are potential drawbacks as well. Hospitals have long been identified with the provision of high-tech, high-price care. Their entry into the long-term care market place may therefore signal a new medicalization of care that traditionally has encompassed both medical and social components. In the past, hospitals have reorganized into ambulatory and home care divisions in part to offset fixed capital or overhead costs. Regulators have been concerned about these cost shifts for some time and will be looking for evidence of this behavior by hospitals in their long-term care ventures. To the extent that hospitals can provide long-term care adequately and cheaply, they will be hard to beat. To the extent that they manipulate the market to cost shift and to recycle patients through acute care beds, their involvement may ultimately be short-lived.

Continuing-Care Retirement Communities

The lines between institutional providers listed in Figure 5–2 have become increasingly blurred during the last 30 years. As Vladeck has pointed out, long-term care was originally provided by homes for the aged which included a few infirmary-type beds for the care of ill residents. Many of these voluntary homes converted beds to intermediate and skilled care use to qualify for Medicare and Medicaid reimbursement. However, as a result of tougher certificate of need approvals for expansion of nursing home beds and burgeoning numbers of elderly, a number of nursing homes and hospitals are rediscovering the home for the aged but renaming it the continuing-care retirement community (CCRC) and building in new amenities for a more sophisticated clientele. CCRCs vary widely, but most provide independent living units as well as social, recreational, and health care services on a fee basis to residents. Until recently CCRCs have differed distinctly from other providers in requiring a life-care contract. Under the terms of this contract, which can cover as little as a year or as long as a remaining lifetime, the CCRC agreed to provide housing, health care, and other services, and the resident agreed to pay specified fees in advance to defray the cost of the services. Although earlier CCRC's required residents to turn over all their assets in return for lifetime shelter and care, most communities today require a substantial entrance fee accompanied by a monthly service charge. In return, the resident receives shelter and services but no title or ownership rights. According to a recent study of CCRCs by Winklevoss and Powell, the average entrance fee in 1981 was $35,000 and the monthly fee $550, depending on the type of housing selected within the community and the number of occupants of the unit.[11] The CCRC essentially acts like an insurance mechanism and pools revenues received from residents as well as Medicare, Medicaid, and private insurance payments when applicable. To limit their risk of exposure to heavy care, most CCRCs screen applicants carefully and generally select candidates who are healthier and wealthier than the elderly population as a whole.

There has been a surge in the number of CCRCs constructed during the last 20 years. Estimates of the current number of CCRCs vary from 300 to 600 nationally, depending upon the specificity of criteria used in defining them. Most are located in states with large elderly populations, such as California, Florida, Pennsylvania, Ohio, and Illinois. The majority continue to be owned by voluntary, often church-related groups with only 5 percent to 10 percent operated for profit. However, as many as one third are being managed by outside proprietary companies. In the early 80s, growth in CCRCs was slowed by high interest rates and a soft resale housing market; however, with the new stability in the economy, CCRCs are predicted to double if not triple in number by 1990.

The CCRC provides the ultimate in continuity of care to the discerning elderly consumer, and most enjoy reputations of providing high quality care. Until recently, however, the range of fees has not been within the grasp of most elderly people. Some CCRCs have also been plagued with significant financial risks and have gone out of business. When this happens, not only does the business suffer but the elderly resident is left homeless and penniless.

As the Winklevoss study points out, a sound actuarial base for a CCRC includes accurate calculation of residents' fees, based on estimates of plant operating costs, renovation and replacement costs, number of deaths, nursing facility transfers, and new admissions anticipated in given years. Since CCRC populations tend to be healthier than most, the use of standard morbidity and mortality tables, which fail to adjust for this selection advantage, can cause problems since these tables overestimate the rate of turnover in residents served. CCRCs also have to maintain adequate reserves to protect against uncertain future turnover rates and operating costs and be willing to raise monthly fees as needed. However, their ability to do the latter is hampered by the fact that most residents live on fixed incomes.

Since substantial opportunity exists for fraud and mismanagement in the CCRC business and because the real estate transactions therein are anticipated to offer tax advantages to proprietary chains, states are beginning to regulate these providers more carefully. Currently, all states require registration and certification of new CCRCs prior to operation; however, definition of what constitutes a CCRC varies widely from state to state. States also require public disclosure of financial status and are moving to require entrance-fee escrows and the maintenance of actuarially sound reserve funds. Because of the anticipated growth in income of the elderly over time, this type of long-term care can probably be expected to increase in the future; however, new entrants who are well capitalized up front (as opposed to the independent nursing home proprietors who are highly leveraged) will have a strong competitive advantage.

Congregate Housing

In contrast to the high capital requirements of the CCRC, which is obligated to provide lifetime care, congregate housing may be a somewhat less risky proposition for the provider wishing to expand into long-term care. Through Section 202 of the National Housing Act, low interest federal mortgages used to be available from the Department of Housing and Urban Development for the construction of specially adapted housing for the elderly and handicapped. Through Section 8 of the same act, tenants who met income guidelines could receive federal rent subsidies if their rent in approved low-income housing exceeded 25 percent of their income. Many elderly who are unable to manage totally unassisted in their homes do not require skilled or intermediate nursing care. For this group, the meals, housekeeping assistance, and social activities provided in congregate housing can make a critical difference, enabling them to be sustained in a less restrictive setting than the nursing home for several years. According to a survey conducted by the International Center for Social Gerontology in 1978, however, only 151 congregate housing facilities, representing 22,559 residential units, existed in the United States. In contrast, the existing need is estimated to be between 3.0 and 6.2 million units.[12] Although many analysts have urged the expansion of congregate housing, the Section 202 program has been cut back under the Reagan administration. According to Vladeck, Section 202 provided only $200 million per year at its peak, allowing for the construction of only 5,000 units nationally (the equivalent of less than a week's worth of ICF admissions).[13]

Traditionally, congregate housing has involved the construction of new housing, resulting in fairly prohibitive capital investments and high rents. However, many argue that the recycling of existing buildings could be a more efficient way to go in the future and that the economies of scale derived from bringing in services to concentrated numbers of elderly would offset the rehabilitation costs. An additional problem with the congregate housing option is the increased frailty of residents over time. Congregate housing located in close proximity to a hospital or to other extended-care units, or part of a campus, makes sense since individuals would be able to move around fairly easily as their needs for care change. At the same time, residents would not be bound to a facility by a life-care contract but would be free to relocate if dissatisfied with service. As future cohorts of elderly possess greater purchasing power, the congregate housing option may become, with or without public subsidies, a more popular and commercially viable option.

Share-A-Home

Share-A-Home is another type of care that has developed in recent years as part of the effort to sustain impaired elderly in least restrictive settings at low cost. The Share-A-Home concept is remarkably simple; namely, for every elderly person suffering from a particular handicap, there is another who is capable in that domain but needy in another. Share-A-Home programs essentially arrange matches whereby one elderly person's problem becomes another's solution. Those needing housing are matched with those having housing to spare but needing income or companionship. The visually impaired are matched with the sighted, the mobile with the immobile, and so forth. Share-A-Home programs have grown in recent years, largely in response to the lack of new federal housing initiatives for the elderly. It is estimated that approximately 500 such programs exist nationwide. Usually a nonprofit agency worker acts as a broker in bringing interested parties together. The sharers themselves then work out the details of their particular arrangement. Share-A-Home programs appear to be relatively easy to run with a small staff. Many programs are funded, at least initially, by local foundations and reap a return in public relations that is at least as great if not greater than their cost. While not the answer for everyone, this simple, cheap, and low-tech approach seems to be one that is destined to grow in popularity in the future.

The options described above share one common feature; they all require people to move from a familiar home environment in order to receive care. Some elderly don't mind leaving home. For some, congregate or shared housing represents a new lease on life and for some, life in a retirement community represents a desired level of security and freedom from worry. For others, however, continued living in cherished homes may be paramount and for this group, the number of options are also expanding rapidly.

COMMUNITY-BASED SERVICES

While it is true that individuals without caregivers who need 24-hour care and/or supervision may require institution-based long-term care, the variety of services which can be provided safely and economically to patients remaining in their own homes is growing daily. Three major trends are fueling the expansion of in-home services. First, the number of elderly is growing and most of them prefer to remain in their own homes if possible.

Second, technological advances have made the provision of sophisticated care possible in the home setting. Third, runaway costs of institution-based care have caused a search for less expensive alternatives. As a result of all three factors, home care services have grown rapidly during the last 10 years and now comprise the fastest growing segment of the long-term care marketplace. A recent survey by Frost and Sullivan estimated the total home care market at $5.3 billion in 1981 and projected it to grow to $9.1 billion in 1985 and $16.3 billion in 1990.[14] Like institutional services, home care services also span a continuum of service intensity, and it is important that specific types or models be defined in describing these providers. At least four different types of home care services can be described based on service intensity. These are high-tech, hospice, Medicare skilled, and long-term home care.

High-Tech Home Care

Most recently, major growth has occurred in the high-tech and durable medical-equipment segments of the home care market. Since it is in the interest of hospitals to discharge patients quickly under prospective payment, high-tech home care is an appealing postdischarge alternative. At present, it is possible to provide enteral and parenteral nutrition as well as chemotherapy, antibiotic therapy, and respiratory therapy to seriously ill patients in their homes. As a result, major alliances have developed between drug and medical supply companies, home care agencies, and hospitals. Home care agencies claim that they can care for high-tech patients at one third the cost of a hospital, while simultaneously improving the patient's quality of life. The cost of serving a typical home health care parenteral patient is estimated to be $40,000 to $50,000 a year compared to hospital charges of $200,000. This message has proved particularly attractive to health insurance companies and health maintenance organizations.

The high-tech movement began in 1968 when patients without functioning digestive organs (due to intestinal cancer or some other severe disease) were sustained for the first time through total parenteral nutrition. At first, the therapy involved hooking patients up to intravenous (IV) bottles for 24 hours a day. However, in the early 70s, pumps permitted more rapid infusion of the solutions, ultimately freeing patients from tubes and bottles for up to 16 hours a day. The next step was allowing therapy to take place outside the hospital where it reportedly costs 50 percent to 75 percent less. In 1983, approximately 2,500 patients received parenteral nutrition therapy at home at the cost of $150–$250 a day, or about $200 million a year.[15] According to a 1983 article in *Barron's,* the American Society for Parenteral and Enteral Nutrition estimates that there could be 15,000 to 20,000 home parenteral patients by 1990, entailing expenditures of $1.6 billion per year.

Not much is known about the clientele or agencies that provide high-tech home care. Home Health Care of America, a proprietary chain with 22 branch offices, Baxter Travenol, and Abbott Laboratories are the major providers of high-tech care, with Baxter and Home Health of America reporting revenues of $46 and $43 million, respectively, in 1983.

Although the precise size of the high-tech population is unknown, it is estimated that 150,000 people a year receive parenteral therapy alone. The typical patient receiving high-tech service is generally younger than other home care clients, with the average patient being a 38-year-old adult recovering from major abdominal surgery.

High-tech services can last anywhere from one week to a lifetime and include a heavy educational component. Patients and family members must be instructed in storage and maintenance of IV equipment, nurses periodically visit to draw blood for lab tests, and IV solutions are delivered weekly or monthly according to a prearranged schedule. Patients can administer the therapy when it is convenient for them, with many choosing to do so at night in order to live a normal lifestyle including going to work during the day.

Spurred by news reports of high before-tax profit margins of 25 percent or more, many smaller providers have recently scrambled into the high-tech service area. However, as many of the more established leaders in the field have discovered, quick returns on investment are more elusive than early reports suggested. According to recent reports, two factors have caused some of the "bloom to fade from the high-tech rose."[16] The first is concern about adequate numbers of patients to sustain the growing number of providers. Not all patients with nutrition-absorption or respiratory disorders want to or are capable of engaging in self care at home. To manage successfully on a self-care regimen, patients have to be well motivated to follow fairly rigid sterile procedures, be resourceful in dealing with complications as they arise, and be able to provide a reasonably safe, clean environment and extra refrigeration for storage of IV solutions. In addition, their doctors have to be convinced that the quality of care provided in the home will be adequate. As a result, only a percentage of all clinically eligible individuals are appropriate for and will select the high-tech home care option. Thus, many providers believe that a comprehensive initial patient assessment in the hospital is a critical factor in determining who will or will not do well on these programs.

The second potential drawback to growth is a somewhat uncertain picture regarding third-party reimbursement. According to reports, Home Health Care of America recently reserved 15 percent of its revenue for bad debt in 1984 and posted a fiscal second-quarter net loss of $1.7 million after years of soaring growth, mainly because of difficulties in obtaining Medicare reimbursement for services rendered. At present, Medicare regulations on high-tech reimbursement are fuzzy. For example, the Health Care Financing Administration (HCFA) currently classifies in-home antibiotic therapy as an outpatient drug, rendering it totally unreimbursable, and only approves in-home chemotherapy if an infusion pump is used. The regulations in part reflect concern that nursing homes could abuse IV therapy by using it for patients who could otherwise be spoon-fed. They also reflect concern that payment approvals would create a new class of patients who would be entitled to expensive home care, in much the same way that extension of coverage to end-stage renal patients caused a surge in home care costs during the 70s. Despite these short-term setbacks, however, most providers are optimistic about continued growth in high-tech services, mainly because underlying trends, that is advances in technology and hospital reimbursement, clearly indicate long-term growth in in-home therapies. However, providers with good access to hospital inpatients and good cash flow situations will enjoy a distinct competitive advantage.

Hospice

Although the antithesis of the high-tech approach in terms of its underlying high-touch philosophy, hospice care is also a rapidly growing type of in-home care. Hospice care is usually not long-term but does offer many individuals an attractive alternative to receiving acute hospital or skilled nursing home care during the last six months of a terminal illness. Technically speaking, hospice services can be provided in a variety of institutional settings; however, the recent Medicare hospice regulations clearly favor the provision of hospice services in the home.

The hospice movement began in the United States in 1975 as a voluntary grass roots effort to recognize and meet the special needs of the terminally ill. In particular, hospices advocate the treatment of the terminally ill in homelike settings, the provision of palliative versus heroic treatment measures if patients are clearly terminal, and an emphasis on emotional support of patients and family by trained volunteers. As a result of substantial discontent regarding technically competent but emotionally sterile hospital care of the terminally ill, the number of hospice organizations grew from 1 in 1975 to 200 by 1979 and HCFA was mandated by Congress to conduct a multisite demonstration/evaluation of this new mode of treatment. Preliminary findings from both the HCFA demonstration and from a Blue Cross hospice study indicated major savings in hospital costs for home care hospice programs. The hospice lobby capitalized on these favorable returns and successfully engineered the inclusion of a new hospice Medicare benefit in the 1982 Tax Equity and Fiscal Responsibility Act. The regulations then became the subject of a tug of war between providers, Congress, and HCFA before finally being published in December 1983.

According to the current regulations, Medicare pays for

physical, psychological, social, and spiritual services when an individual who is eligible for Medicare (Part A) is certified by a physician as having a maximum of six months to live, elects hospice care, and waives Medicare benefits for curative or duplicative services.[17] The eligible patient may change hospices once during an election period (every 90, 90, and 30 days) and may revoke hospice care at any time. If care is revoked, the patient loses any benefit remaining during that election period.

Services covered include nursing care, medical social services, physician's services, counseling, short-term inpatient care, medical appliances and supplies, home health-aide services, and physical, occupational, and speech therapies. Agencies must be able to provide service on a 24-hour basis, and annual reimbursement is capped at no more than $6,500 per patient served. This cap does not apply to each individual patient served but reflects an overall average annual cost per patient which Medicare payments will not exceed.

As of this writing, 200 providers have been fully certified to participate in the Medicare hospice benefit. In addition, most Blue Cross and Blue Shield plans as well as other insurance carriers also provide hospice coverage. However, despite the fairly rapid proliferation of this model of care, some serious problems with the Medicare benefit remain. Physicians are concerned that in many cases prediction of a patient's remaining lifespan is total guesswork, for which no valid scientific underpinning currently exists.[18] The substantial degree of variation in individual disease courses can lead to two problems. First, physicians and hospices may be overly conservative and delay accepting the patient until he or she is so close to death that palliative care is unnecessary. Alternatively, a physician may be too liberal in certifying remaining months of life, with the result that the patient will outlive his or her benefit period and require the most intensive care at that point. In this case, the hospice program would be unable to discharge the patient but would remain liable for care. The hospice program would also bear the burden of any successful treatment cases in which palliative care actually resulted in substantially extending a patient's life. For this reason, most hospices are reluctant to admit patients unless it is quite clear that death is imminent. Physicians are concerned that patients or their families might sue them for wrongfully denying a patient care during the earlier months of the terminal illness. Alternatively, physicians fear that if patients outlive their six-month benefit period, hospices may bring suit for wrongful prognosis.

As a result of the cap on total reimbursement, demanding staffing requirements, problems in prognosing remaining months of life, and liability for care after benefits have expired, many home care agencies have adopted a wait and see attitude rather than actively pursuing Medicare certification to provide hospice care. Finally, even more fundamental than the restrictive Medicare regulations is the fact that the number of terminally ill patients is (fortunately) finite and those selecting the hospice benefit even smaller. Thus, growth in the number of hospice programs can probably be expected to stabilize in the near future. Given the uncertainties associated with Medicare hospice reimbursement, many home care providers are choosing instead to provide high-tech home care for the terminally ill patient. However, despite the limitations of the Medicare hospice benefit, it is providing many individuals who wish to elect the hospice care option that important entitlement.

Medicare Home Care

The high-tech and hospice models of home care represent some of the newer wrinkles in the home care industry. However, despite the current fashionableness of these new models, the Medicare skilled care model remains the undisputed "cash cow" from the providers' perspective. Unlike hospice care payments, Medicare skilled home care payments were uncapped until 1985 and theoretically are available until a patient reaches his or her maximum rehabilitation potential following an acute illness for which a physician certifies that intermittent skilled nursing care in the home is necessary. Of 5,000 home care agencies in the United States in 1981, 3,000 (60%) were Medicare certified.

Until 1986, when discipline-specific cost limits were imposed on Medicare home care visits, everything about Medi-

TABLE 5–5   Medicare Home Health Data, 1966–1983

	Number of Home Health Agencies	Number of Visits (millions)	Number of Beneficiaries (thousands)	Medicare Reimbursements (millions)	Average per Visit Charge
1966	1,019	—	98.5	10.4	—
1967	1,151	—	244.0	46.0	—
1968	1,269	—	299.2	67.0	—
1969	1,380	8.5	235.0	78.1	9.18
1970	1,465	6.0	—	61.5	10.25
1971	1,515	4.8	250.0	56.8	11.83
1972	1,585	5.2	—	65.9	12.67
1973	1,683	6.4	315.6	92.9	14.51
1974	1,786	7.9	393.0	144.3	16.44
1975	1,919	10.4	500.0	217.0	19.08
1976	2,057	13.1	588.7	294.6	21.45
1977	2,248	15.3	689.7	366.5	24.26
1978	2,446	17.2	769.7	426.9	26.89
1979	2,662	19.3	836.7	518.2	29.31
1980	2,864	22.3	956.4	662.1	32.17
1981	3,187	24.9	1,068.0	973.2	35.53
1982	3,765	30.9	1,082.0	1,110.0	39.11
1983	4,258	—	—	—	—

SOURCE: Compiled from HCFA data by the National Association for Home Care Research Division, August 1984.

care-reimbursed home care has grown. As Table 5–5 shows, there are now four times as many Medicare-certified home health agencies in the United States as there were in 1966. The number of Medicare home care beneficiaries has increased tenfold, reimbursements 100-fold, and average per visit charges fourfold. Although the total number of Medicare-certified home health agencies has increased considerably in the past 10 years, this growth is not uniform across all types of providers. Table 5–6 illustrates the accompanying changes which have occurred between 1966 and 1983 in Medicare-certified home care providers by type. As this table demonstrates, in 1966, official agencies (public health departments) and visiting nurse associations clearly dominated the field, accounting for 89 percent of all providers. In contrast, these traditional providers accounted for only 42 percent of all providers in 1983, their lead having been overtaken by the growing number of proprietary and private nonprofit agencies. The

TABLE 5-6 Change in Composition of Medicare-Certified Home Care Providers by Type, 1966 versus 1983

Type	Percent of All Agencies			
	1966 (N = 1,019)		1983 (N = 4,245)	
VNA	34.0 ⎱ 89%		12.0 ⎱ 42%	
Official	55.0 ⎰		30.0 ⎰	
Combination	1.9		1.4	
Rehabilitation-based	.3		.4	
Hospital-based	7.2 ⎱		14.0 ⎱	
SNF-based	.1 ⎱ 9%		3.2 ⎱ 57%	
Proprietary	.3 ⎰		24.0 ⎰	
Private nonprofit	1.4 ⎰		16.0 ⎰	
Other	.4		.8	
Total	100%		100%	

SOURCE: Adapted from official HCFA data as of January 18, 1984.

growth in number of proprietaries has been particularly impressive. In 1966, proprietary agencies accounted for only 0.3 percent of all home care providers. By 1983, their share had risen to 24 percent. Similarly, the private nonprofit types, excluding visiting nurse associations, accounted for only 1.4 percent of all agencies in 1966 but increased to 16 percent by 1983. Together, the proprietaries and private nonprofit providers now account for 40 percent of all Medicare-certified home care providers.

Two other trends in type of Medicare home care provider deserve note. These are the increases in the number of hospital-based and SNF-based providers in recent years. As Table 5-6 indicates, these groups were slow to climb on the home care bandwagon but once aboard increased rapidly. Most of their growth occurred after 1981, probably in anticipation of the impact of Medicare hospital prospective payment. Together, these two providers now account for about 17 percent of all Medicare-certified home health agencies. Their share, particularly that of hospital-based agencies, can be expected to grow in the future.

Despite the increased growth in home care providers, we still know relatively little about the Medicare home care consumer. A recent study conducted by Kramer and colleagues at the University of Colorado suggests that Medicare home care patients are quite different from the average patient cared for in a nursing home.[19] Specifically, Kramer et al. studied case mix differences between four groups: (1) a sample representing all home health patients; (2) a sample representing nursing home patients; (3) a sample representing Medicare home health patients only; and (4) a sample representing Medicare nursing home patients only. The study found that Medicare nursing home and home care patients were most similar, but Medicare nursing home patients were much more likely to be dependent in activities of daily living. It was concluded that Medicare home care can substitute for the last days of an acute hospital stay and may substitute for SNF care for less dependent SNF patients but that Medicare SNF care would continue to be needed for individuals requiring both highly skilled care and functional assistance.

As mentioned earlier, Medicare reimburses for home care only when patients require skilled nursing care or speech, physical or occupational therapy and continues to reimburse only until a patient reaches his or her maximum rehabilitation potential. Although the three-day prior hospitalization and 100-visit limitation have been lifted, fiscal intermediaries still review claims for payment in terms of degree of skilled care required and provided. Thus, use of this skilled home care benefit can be expected to reduce acute hospital and skilled nursing facility days. Therefore, it is an attractive option for insurers and employer groups.

Non-Medicare Home Care

Medicare statistics only tell half the story about our home care supply, however. Specifically, an increasing number of non-Medicare certified home health agencies also provide a variety of in-home services. These agencies are largely proprietary, serving private pay patients. Many provide only a single service, such as homemaker or home health-aide services, and can not obtain Medicare certification because they do not provide skilled nursing services. Since these agencies are not licensed, their real numbers are unknown. However, estimates of the number of non-Medicare home health agencies range from 6,000 to 10,000.[20]

Long-Term Home Care

The relevance of Medicare home care to the frail old, suffering from chronic disease and in need of long-term assistance, is rather limited. For this group, a new type of home care is being tested under the title of expanded or "long-term" home care. During the last decade, a substantial amount of attention and research funding have been devoted to the issue of expanded home care. In response to critics' charges that the technical and time-limited attributes of Medicare home care services limit their relevance to the chronically ill, as many as 15 demonstrations and evaluations (D/Es) of expanded home care have been conducted. In general, most D/Es attempted to test whether expanded home care could reduce health care expenditures for the chronically ill or would be used as an add-on to supplement customary acute hospital and nursing home care.

Because of substantial variations in the targeting of these services and problems in their evaluation designs and implementation, there is little consistent evidence in the literature pointing to either a cost savings or to other clinical benefits achieved by these programs. However, many of the demonstrations were flawed insofar as they targeted younger or acutely ill persons for chronic care and/or tested services that differed little or not at all from the Medicare skilled home care model.[21] Our research on a long-term home care program demonstrates several positive benefits of long-term home care provided by the Five Hospital Program in Chicago.[22]

Using a two group pretest-posttest, quasi-experimental design, we evaluated outcomes of long-term home care nine months and 48 months after acceptance to care. The two groups studied were 157 consecutively accepted clients of the Five Hospital Program and 156 consecutively approved clients of a home-delivered meals program operated by the local area office on aging. Subjects in the two groups resided in geographically contiguous areas of the city and were required to be over age 60 and homebound. Outcome measures included comprehensive functional status, mortality, and acute hospital and institutional long-term care use. Findings at nine months included no difference in mortality. There was a decrease in the level of previously unmet service needs, an increased sense of physical well-being, and mixed improvement and decline in ADL functioning in the Five Hospital sample.[23]

Although no differences attributable to the Five Hospital Program were noted in rate of hospital use, a significant and substantially reduced risk of permanent admission for sheltered and intermediate nursing home care over 48 months was observed in the Five Hospital group. We concluded that the services reduced institutional long-term care days and improved patients' quality of life without increasing their use of acute care hospitals or mortality. Per capita costs of all services were 25 percent higher in the Five Hospital group. However, this figure is substantially lower than the add-ons of 35 percent to 60 percent previously reported by other investigators and reflects both the presence of a small group of high service users and the extremely low public aid reimbursement rates for sheltered and ICF care in Illinois.[24]

Even more fundamentally, a comparison of services provided by the Five Hospital Program to the services reimbursed by Medicare home care demonstrated substantial differences between the two models of care. As Figure 5–3 demonstrates, in the Medicare "acute" model, skilled nursing visits predominate, accounting for 59 percent of all service visits. Social work visits account for less than 3 percent of all visits reimbursed, and home health-aide visits for 34 percent. In contrast, in the Five Hospital Program long-term home care model, home health-aide visits predominate, followed by skilled nursing visits, and social work visits are six times higher.

At present, only a handful of long-term home care programs that provide this low-tech constellation of services exist in the United States. Section 2176 Medicaid Community Care waivered services generally fall into this home care category. However, Section 2176 waivers usually reimburse for home-

FIGURE 5–3 Service Composition:
Acute versus Long-Term Home Care

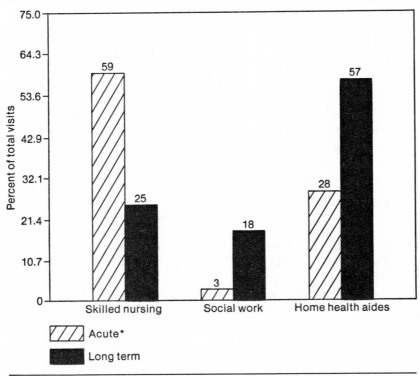

*U.S. Department of Health, Education, and Welfare, "Medicare: Use of Home Health Services, 1976," *Health Care Financing Program Statistics,* HCFA Pub. no. 03050, May 1980.

maker and chore services or respite care only and incorporate neither a combined sociomedical case-managed approach to care nor direct home health care services.

In our study of the Five Hospital Program, we became convinced that the program's comprehensive case-managed approach to care was responsible for improved client outcomes. On the basis of this research, which could benefit from replication and testing elsewhere, we inferred that a combined sociomedical approach is essential in caring for the frail elderly in the community.

Two underlying trends point toward the ultimate expansion of this type of home care service. First, as mentioned earlier, the Medicaid Section 2176 waiver seems to be heading in this direction. For example, in Illinois, the waiver has been administered by the state's department on aging and has reimbursed for homemaker and chore assistance only for individuals who are at risk of nursing home admission. In the winter of 1985, a demonstration began to test the feasibility of combining homemaker and home health-aide service with home health care services. Policymakers are understandably apprehensive about increased costs once a medical service is added to the service package. Thus, it will behoove participating providers to monitor service use carefully. If they succeed, and results from the demonstration are favorable and affordable, elderly citizens of Illinois will enjoy a much broader scope of long-term care options in the future.

The second trend favoring further growth of long-term home care services rests with the private pay market. As mentioned in Chapter 4, we can expect that future elderly will be increasingly empowered to purchase care of their choice because of the increased availability of pensions, IRAs, and other forms of disposable income. Marketing surveys recently completed suggest that upper-income elderly prefer care at home and want a definite say in what and how services are delivered but are not well informed about costs.[25] Careful marketing and promotional activities with this segment of consumers could potentially yield a whole new clientele for existing long-term home care programs. While it is probably fair to say that those long-term home care programs that exist are struggling, many are finding that aggressive pursuit of multiple funding sources like United Way, Title XX, Medicaid Section 2176 waiver funds, patient fees, and foundation grants can yield sufficient income to mount much needed services which reap tremendous public relations payoffs. Given the increase in number of elderly and the increased competitiveness of the home care market, the proffering of long-term home care services can distinguish a home care program or other long-term care provider and ultimately offer a long-term competitive advantage.

Adult Day Services

Despite their current popularity, home care services are not for everyone. Certain elderly with special kinds of problems like Alzheimers disease cannot function safely during the day in the absence of a spouse or an adult child. Certain other elderly with mild to fairly severe chronic conditions may simply not do well at home where they may be isolated for long periods of the day. They may thrive, however, in the company of their peers. For these individuals, adult day care provides an important new option.

There were approximately 12 adult day-care programs in the United States in 1967–1970. Today there are close to 1,400. On average, they serve approximately 20,000 elderly per day. They are located in hospitals, mental health centers, nursing homes, senior centers, senior housing, and churches. They are primarily administered by nurses or social workers, although most also have physician input of some type on a regular basis. Most programs are state licensed and inspected, are open five days a week, and serve 20–25 clients a day. Most clients do not use the services all five days but come in two or three days per week.

Services are funded by Title III of the Older Americans Act and by Title XX or Social Services block grant funds. At present, adult day care is the third most popular service being requested by the states in their Section 2176 Medicaid waiver applications. Of 60 requests from 38 states for waivers, 50 percent requested adult day care.

Less than 12 adult day-care programs are being offered by proprietary providers. In these cases the services are usually provided as a loss leader, particularly in nursing homes. In these cases, the underlying theory is that the provider's community reputation is enhanced by offering the service and that provision of the service may allow early contact with individuals who might later be candidates for admission.

Very few adult day-service programs are free standing. Given the frail condition of clients served, it makes sense for these services to be offered as an option that can be supplemented by homemaker/chore or other community-based care services.

Durable Medical Equipment/Life Line

The survival of increased numbers of chronically ill and their shift in locus of care also have important implications for manufacturers and suppliers of durable medical equipment. The range of equipment required to care for the chronically ill in either an institution or at home can be substantial, ranging from hospital beds, Hoyer lifts, wheelchairs, tub stools, and commodes to infusion pumps, IV tubing and solutions, and products for incontinence. Consequently, Frost and Sullivan have projected growth in the home care market to $9.1 billion in 1985 and $16.3 billion in 1990. Half of this growth is in durable medical equipment necessary to sustain patients at home. The supplies and equipment necessary for high-tech parenteral nutrition have received the most attention recently in the national press. However, growth in the use of products in the home can be expected across the board as the United States population ages and home care services increase. Similarly, growth in emergency alarm systems and other monitoring devices will occur as more individuals with frail conditions attempt to manage on their own at home.

Summary

As the foregoing review of these multiple and diverse service providers demonstrates, the current bywords for long-term care are choice and change. Even as this chapter is being written, the formerly rigid distinctions between providers based on institutional versus community-based locus of care is breaking down. Nursing homes are beginning to reach out to communities and offer adult day services, health promotion clinics, and other services to nonresidents. Hospitals are providing congregate housing, home-delivered meals, and home care in increasing numbers. In a similar vein, home care agencies are setting up day-care programs and developing relationships with hospitals and nursing homes and durable medical equipment suppliers.

The one constant feature of the current picture is that everyone is getting into the act of providing long-term care services. As a consequence, the range of service options for long-term care consumers is expanding rapidly. A few years ago, community and institution-based services were viewed as competing alternatives. Although results from the community-based experiments suggest some degree of overlap in services provided and target groups served, only a modest degree of overlap (30 percent) has been documented to date.[26] The demonstrations have probably been most helpful in documenting the heterogeneity of consumers and services that currently exist in the long-term care marketplace. As a result, the targeting of services is receiving much more attention, with the real question being what is the least restrictive and most cost-effective care option for a given individual with a particular set of strengths, disabilities, and preferences.

Competition in the delivery of long-term care services is beginning to emerge. This can only be a healthy development for consumers and providers because competition can potentially expand the range of services offered, improve their quality, and reduce their price.

NOTES

1. Al Sirocco, "Nursing and Related Care Homes," *Vital and Health Statistics,* Series 14, no. 29 (1983), p. 1.

2. Glen Collins, "Increasing Numbers of Aged Return North from Florida," *New York Times,* March 15, 1984, pp. 1 and 10.

3. Gary Weiss, "Excellent Prognosis: The Outlook for Nursing Home Chains is Growing," *Barron's,* May 18, 1984, pp. 7 and 8.

4. Connie Evashwick, "Long-Term Care Becomes Major New Role for Hospitals," *Hospitals,* July 1, 1982, pp. 50–55.

5. Gerald Bisbee, Jr., and Donna J. Melkonian, "Hospitals: Major Focus of Medical, Social Services," *Generations,* November 1980, pp. 22–34.

6. American Hospital Association, *Hospital Statistics,* 1981 ed.

7. Bruce Vladeck, *Unloving Care, The Nursing Home Tragedy,* (New York: Basic Books, 1980), p. 240.

8. Edward Campion, Axel Bang, and Maurice T. May, "Why Acute Care Hospitals Must Undertake Long-Term Care," *New England Journal of Medicine,* 308:2 (January 13, 1983), pp. 71–75.

9. *Long-Term Care Management,* ed. Michael Dolan (Washington: McGraw-Hill, February 27, 1986), p. 2.

10. Lawrence Rubenstein, K. R. Josephson, G. D. Wieland, P. A. English, J. A. Sayre, and R. L. Kane, "Effectiveness of a Geriatric Evaluation Unit," *New England Journal of Medicine,* 311, pp. 1664–70.

Mark E. Williams, T. Franklin Williams, James G. Zimmer, W. J. Hall, and C. A. Podgorski, "Report of a Randomized Trial Evaluating the Effectiveness of an Ambulatory Geriatric Consultation Service," paper presented at the American Public Health Association Annual Meeting, Washington, D.C., November 1985.

11. Howard E. Winklevoss and Alwyn Powell, *Continuing Care Retirement Communities: An Empirical, Financial and Legal Analysis* (Homewood, Ill.: Richard D. Irwin, 1984).

12. International Center for Social Gerontology, *Report on Congregate Housing,* (Washington, D.C., 1978).

13. Vladeck, *Unloving Care,* p. 231.

14. Frost and Sullivan, *Home Healthcare Producers and Services Markets in the United States* (New York, 1983), Report no. A1120.

15. Thomas G. Donlan, "No Place Like Home: That's Increasingly True These Days for Health Care," *Barron's,* March 21, 1983, pp. 6, 7, and 32.

16. Jennifer Bingham Hill, "High-Tech Home Health Care is Showing Promise, But Some Big Problems Remain," *Wall Street Journal,* April 14, 1984.

17. "Regulatory Round-up: Final Hospice Regulations Published," *Caring,* February 1984, pp. 5–8.

18. Howard Brody and Joanne Lynn, "Sounding Board: The Physician's Responsibility Under the New Medicare Reimbursement for Hospice Care," *New England Journal of Medicine,* April 5, 1984.

19. Andrew Kramer, Peter Shaughnessy, and Mary Pettigrew, "Cost-Effectiveness Implications Based on a Comparison of Nursing Home and Home Health Case Mix," *Health Service Research,* 20:4 (October 1985), pp. 387–406.

20. U.S. DHHS, Health Care Financing Administration, "Evaluation of the Home Health Agency Prospective Payment Demonstration," Request for Proposals, May 1985.

21. Susan L. Hughes, "Apples and Oranges? A Review of Evaluations of Community-Based Long-Term Care," *Health Services Research,* 20:4, 1985.

22. Susan L. Hughes, David Cordray, and V. Alan Spiker, "Evaluation of a Long-Term Home Care Program," *Medical Care,* May 1984, p. 460.

23. Susan Hughes, Kendon Conrad, Larry Manheim, and Perry Edelman, "Impact of Long-Term Home Care on Functional Status and Mortality," *Working Paper* (Evanston, Ill.: Northwestern University, Center for Health Services and Policy Research, March 1986).

24. William G. Weissert, T. H. Wan, and B. Livieratos, "Effects and Costs of Day Care and Homemaker Services for the Chronically Ill: A Randomized Experiment," (Hyattsville, Md.: National Center for Health Services Research, 1979).

F. A. Skellie, G. M. Mobley, and R. E. Coan, "Cost-Effectiveness of Community-Based Long-Term Care," *American Journal of Public Health,* vol. 72 (1982), p. 353.

Susan Hughes, Larry Manheim, Perry Edelman, and Kendon Conrad, "Impact of Long-Term Home Care on Hospital and Nursing Home Use and Cost," *Working Paper* (Evanston, Ill.: Northwestern University, Center for Health Services and Policy Research, March 1986).

25. Aravindan Rangaswamy and Susan Hughes, "Marketing Long-Term Home Care Services to the Elderly: A Survey," *Working Paper 88,* (Evanston, Ill.: Northwestern University, Center for Health Services and Policy Research).

26. William G. Weissert, "Seven Reasons Why It Is So Difficult to Make Community-Based Long-Term Care Cost Effective," *Journal of Health Services Research,* 20:3 (October 1985).

_____

CHAPTER SIX

Consolidating Services in a Competitive Market: $(1 + 1 = 3)$

- Horizontally integrated, multiunit, long-term care systems currently operate under investor-owned, voluntary, and public ownership, although the investor-owned systems predominate. At present, horizontal integration affects only 10 percent of the long-term care bed supply but appears to be growing. The long range consequences of this trend toward consolidation (e.g., economies of scale and consumer name brand recognition) are unknown and merit study.

- The capacity for vertical integration among long-term care providers appears to be growing as an unanticipated byproduct of Medicare prospective payment and an increasingly competitive environment. Increased vertical integration can promote increased control over patient flow for providers and increased levels of care and care options for consumers.

The long-term care industry has grown rapidly during the last 15 years, marked by expanding public reimbursement, increased demand for care, and rapid growth of institutional and community-based providers. For 20 years following the passage of Medicare and Medicaid, the industry mushroomed in an uncoordinated fashion, with market conditions at times resembling the boom towns of the wild West. While the past was marked by rapid growth and expansion, the future appears to be quite different. Concerned over increased costs of care and probable increases in demand linked to demographic changes beyond their control, policymakers at both state and federal levels are trying to control growth in long-term care expenditures. The hospital industry is already coping with Medicare prospective payment, Preferred Provider Organizations (PPOs), Health Maintenance Organizations (HMOs), and business and consumer coalitions concerned with reducing or stabilizing the costs of acute medical care. Congressionally mandated studies of prospective payment and competitive bidding for long-term care providers are already underway. It is only a matter of months until new reimbursement systems will be announced and implemented. At the same time that long-term care has become increasingly regulated, the level of public reimbursement has declined and possibly will be capped.

The market is thus changing drastically from an immature to a maturing one. As a result, competition has increasingly become the name of the game. Under the conditions described above, i.e., increased regulation, increased competition, and lower reimbursement, organizations possessing superior access to services, capital, and manpower have strong competitive advantages. Under these conditions, two types of organizational integration, horizontal and vertical, can make a critical difference. Each is described in this chapter, along with case examples and suggestions regarding the implementation of integrated systems approaches to the provision of care.

HORIZONTAL INTEGRATION

Goldsmith has applied Alfred Chandler's theories on how businesses adapt to changing market conditions to the acute care hospital industry. The same analysis can be performed in long-term care.[1] Chandler identified the four evolutionary phases as: (1) initial expansion and accumulation of resources,

(2) internal rationalization and consolidation, (3) diversification into new products and expansion into new markets, and (4) development of a decentralized multidimensional corporate organization. According to Goldsmith, horizontal and vertical integration are prominent activities undertaken in phase one.

In 1981, over 80 percent of the nation's hospitals participated in some form of shared services and approximately 30 percent were part of formal multiunit systems. By 1984, this figure had increased to 35.5 percent.[2] The proportion of nursing homes belonging to a formally organized multiunit system in 1977 was roughly similar at 28 percent, which indicates that both acute and long-term care providers are participating in this trend. As figures in Chapter 5 demonstrated, the long-term care industry has been expanding for years, with growth occurring among both institutional and community-based providers. The industry is now embarking on a new phase, however, that of consolidation. The trend toward consolidation is noticeable at almost every level, from the trade organizations themselves down to the individual provider level. Growth through consolidation can be achieved in a number of ways, including horizontal and vertical integration. Some of the obvious advantages of horizontal integration include the pooling of and greater access to capital, along with increased bulk purchasing power, alleged economies of scale, and more sophisticated management capacity.

Horizontal Integration in Institutional Settings

One hears a great deal these days about nursing home chains. Generally, the chains are referred to as big proprietary organizations that are rapidly consuming the rest of the market. While it is true that horizontal integration is occurring at a rapid pace, it is not true that the proprietaries are the only players in the game.

Horizontal integration among public, voluntary, and investor-owned institution-based long-term care providers is not new. For example, the Veterans Administration (VA) has been providing nursing home and home health care at numerous sites in the United States during the last 10 to 20 years. As Table 6–1 demonstrates, the VA operated 106 nursing

TABLE 6–1   Nursing Homes Owned, Managed, or Leased by Multifacility Chains, 1984

	Chains	Facilities	Beds
1. Public Veterans Administration	1	106	10,600
2. Nonprofit	92	311	32,489
3. Investor-owned	48	2,435	284,010
Total	141	2,852	327,099

SOURCES: Veterans Administration, *Summary of Medical Programs,* Office of Information Management and Statistics, September 1984; American Association of Homes for the Aging, *Directory of Members,* 1985; William A. Spicer, "Measuring Long-Term Care's Corporate Sector," *Contemporary Administrator for Long-Term Care,* June 1984, pp. 32–35.

homes nationally in 1984, accounting for 10,600 nursing home beds.[3] That same year, the VA also provided more than 10,000 intermediate care beds in its acute care hospitals, caring for more than 17,000 veterans overall. At a total of more than 20,000 beds, the VA ranks as the fourth largest nursing home chain in the United States. However, its actual rank is still higher since these figures do not reflect the amount which the VA spends for contract nursing home care, e.g., care provided in private nursing homes to veterans under contract with the VA. In 1984 for example, the VA paid for the care of another 35,551 veterans in non-VA community nursing homes at an average per diem cost of $58.38.

The bed size of VA nursing homes ranges from 26 to 300, with most newer facilities being built in units of 120 beds. The veteran population is of considerable interest to long-term care policy analysts because it reflects a high preponderance of World War II veterans who are, on average, 10 years older than the general population. In 1980, 10.6 percent of all veterans (3 million) were age 65 and older. By 2000, this age group will constitute 8.9 million or 37 percent of all veterans.[4] This increase is important because veterans over age 65 are not required to have a service-connected disability in order to receive free VA health care. Thus, until this year, the VA has been obligated to serve any veteran over age 65 who applied for care if care was available. In anticipation of the peak in demand resulting from the aging of its population, the VA's nursing home budget has increased substantially from $220 million in 1981 to a requested $398 million in 1985. During this time, the number of nursing home beds increased by 23 percent. Interestingly, the number of hospital ICF beds has declined slightly, but these are expected to pick up substantially in the future as more VA administrators convert acute surgical beds to ICF use. Since existing VA nursing home beds are currently experiencing a 93.4 percent occupancy rate, the VA's investment in long-term care will probably continue in the future. However, the VA has recently initiated an income-based means test to determine eligibility for care among veterans over age 65. At present, the income criterion is set at the relatively high level of $20,000. If this level is substantially reduced in the future, growth in the VA system could substantially moderate.

As Table 6–1 indicates, nonprofit nursing homes also belong to horizontally integrated systems of care. It is difficult to determine exactly which nursing homes in the United States belong to multiunit chains because this piece of information is monitored but data are not broken down by type of ownership in government surveys. For example, according to the 1977 National Nursing Home Survey, 5,300 or 28.1 percent of all nursing homes in the United States belonged to a group of facilities operating under one general authority or owner.[5] However, no other cross-tabulations are reported on multiunit status by type of ownership or bedsize. Therefore, the best approximations available today are derived from an examination of the membership of the nursing home trade organizations or the trade publications. According to the *1985 Directory of Members* of the American Association of Homes for the Aging, 311 nonprofit nursing homes belonged to one of 92 multifacility sponsors. These 311 facilities represent 11 percent of all United States nursing homes which belong to a multifacility system. On average, however, the nonprofit systems are quite a bit smaller than either the VA or the proprietary chains, encompassing only 3.4 facilities apiece and 2 percent of all United States nursing home beds.[6] In contrast to their proprietary counterparts, most voluntary nursing home chains are religiously affiliated and have been in the nursing home business for a long time.

During the 70s, proprietary chains first began entering the long-term care marketplace in a major way. Capitalizing on the Medicaid depreciation policies described in Chapter 2 and approaching the industry more as a real estate than as a health services venture, several national chains sprang up rapidly. Some of the early profit takers have left the field in response to increased regulation and decreasing public reimbursement rates. As a result, the existing chains now participate in a more mature market where competition and regulation are more common and management is considerably more challenging.

Multifacility chains of all types account for approximately 19 percent of all nursing home beds in the United States. It is difficult to estimate the exact number of proprietary chains, but the *Contemporary Administrator* June 1984 survey of the corporate nursing home sector received responses from 48.[7] Although there are fewer proprietary than voluntary chains, the average proprietary chain tends to be considerably larger, with an average of 51 facilities per proprietary chain versus 3.4 for the voluntaries. As Table 6–1 demonstrates, proprietary chains also account for the largest share (87 percent) of chain-operated beds.

According to data in Table 6–2, four proprietary chains occupy the lead, accounting for roughly 12.6 percent of the national nursing home bed supply. Beverly Enterprises, the nursing home giant at 102,000 beds, clearly leads the field. Hillhaven, which ranks second, has also been steadily increasing its holdings and acquired 49 new facilities during 1983 alone. Both Beverly and Hillhaven are linked to multihospital investor-owned chains. Hospital Corporation of America (HCA) until recently owned 20 percent of Beverly stock, and Hillhaven is a wholly owned subsidiary of National Medical Enterprises (NME) to whose total operating profits it contributed 23.6 percent in 1984.

There is no question that the onset of prospective payment for hospital care has fueled the trend toward horizontal integration of proprietary nursing homes. Anticipating a substantial increase in subacute care referrals from hospitals, most chains expanded their operations considerably. Thus, both

TABLE 6-2 Growth in Beds and Revenues of the Top Ten Proprietary Chains, 1982–1983*

Chain	Total Beds			Gross Revenues (millions)		
	1982	1983	Percent Change	1982	1983	Percent Change
1. Beverly Enterprises	72,711	89,441	23%	806	1,100	36%
2. Hillhaven	32,914	37,466	14	283	469	66
3. ARA Living Centers	31,341	30,853	−2	—	—	—
4. Manor Health Care	12,485	15,103	21	164.6	251.2	53
5. Unicare Health Facilities	10,169	13,770	35	38.2	86.3	126
6. Care Enterprises	7,403	8,020	8	55.1	102.3	86
7. Angell Group	6,878	7,879	15	—	—	—
8. National Health Corporation	5,548	5,602	1	61.5	65.4	6
9. Care Corporation	5,238	5,336	2	65.3	81.4	25
10. Health Care and Retirement Corporation of America	3,478	4,735	36	46.5	69.6	50
Total Beds	188,165	218,205	16%	1,520.2	2,225.2	46%

*These companies represent the 10 largest of the 20 multifacility corporations which responded to the *Contemporary Administrator for Long-Term Care* corporate survey in both 1982 and 1983. Figures were reported in the June 1983 and 1984 issues.

1982 and 1983 witnessed substantial growth in the holdings of the investor-owned chains.

In 1983, the number of beds operated by the chains increased by 15.3 percent according to *Modern Health Care*'s 1984 survey and by 16 percent according to the *Contemporary Administrator for Long-Term Care.*[8] Most of the growth occurred in the category of owned or leased beds (up by 17.1 percent) versus those managed, which declined by 4.5 percent. Most of the growth (92.3 percent) also occurred through the acquisition of existing beds rather than through the construction of new facilities. As the bottom line on Table 6–2 demonstrates, the 16 percent overall growth in beds reported by the *Contemporary Administrator* was accompanied by a 46 percent overall increase in gross revenues.

Many have charged that proprietary chains skim, that is, treat less sick, private pay patients, leaving heavier care or public pay patients to the voluntaries. Table 6–3 examines the proportion of all beds classified as private pay in the top 10 chains in 1984 and reveals that this figure varies from a high of 60 percent for Consolidated Resources to a low of 15 percent for Angell Group, with an average of 34 percent private pay beds across all 10 chains. If these figures can be believed, they indicate that at least some proprietary chains provide fairly substantial amounts of publicly reimbursed care. It makes sense for proprietaries to handle public pay business when that business (Medicaid) represents over 45 percent of the market. Although the predominance of Medicaid as a payor makes it very difficult for facilities to totally exclude it as a payment source, all providers may have incentives to select low versus high-care skilled or intermediate care Medicaid patients. Although we mention this issue here, we defer more detailed analysis of it to Chapter 8, which discusses Medicaid reimbursement reforms in greater detail.

Two important factors lie behind the increased numbers of nursing home acquisitions by the chains. First, at least six states (Kentucky, Minnesota, Mississippi, North Carolina, Virginia, and Wisconsin) have imposed moratoria on the construction of nursing home beds in the past few years, reasoning that if the beds do not exist they cannot be filled with Medicaid patients.[9] Those states that have not imposed frank

TABLE 6-3 Growth in Revenues of the Top Ten Proprietary Chains, 1982–1984

Company Name	Total Beds Owned, Managed, and Leased	Percent Private Pay Residents	Gross Revenues (millions)		
			Fiscal Year 1982	Fiscal Year 1983	Fiscal Year 1984
1. Beverly Enterprises Inc.	102,704	33%	806.0	1,100.0	1,400.0
2. Hillhaven Corp.	38,014	33	283.0	469.0	651.9
3. ARA Living Centers	31,610	23	—	—	—
4. Manor Health Care Corp.	19,254	57	164.6	251.2	363.9
5. Care Enterprises	13,183	24	55.1	102.3	151.5
6. Unicare Health Facilities Inc.	12,500	22	38.2	86.3	193.0
7. Angell Group Inc.	9,627	15	—	72.6	98.5
8. Life Care Centers of America Inc.	8,723	46	—	—	—
9. Consolidated Resources Corp. of America	7,064	60	—	—	—
10. Summit Care Corp.	7,130	50	31.0	38.0	60.0

SOURCE: William A. Spicer, "Measuring Long-Term Care's Corporate Sector," *Contemporary Administrator for Long-Term Care*, June 1985.

moratoria are becoming much more restrictive with respect to approval of certificate of need applications. As a result, nursing homes are experiencing an average occupancy rate of 90–95 percent nationally, and construction of new facilities in the industry is at a standstill. This means that organizations seeking to grow can do so only through acquiring existing facilities. With the cost of a new nursing home bed estimated at $30,000, most companies prefer to follow an acquisition strategy and view it as a less expensive alternative than building a new facility.[10]

Another major reason for the growth in the chains has been reduced availability of Industrial Development Bonds (IDBs). IDBs are tax-exempt securities issued under the authority of state agencies. Because they are tax exempt, they have low interest rates. Until the present, nursing homes have used small issue IDBs heavily to finance construction. Legislation passed by Congress early in 1984 imposed ceilings on the amount of bond financing based upon a state's population. This constriction of tax-exempt financing is expected to fall much more heavily on the small owner of one or two long-term care facilities, who will be virtually eliminated from building. However, the impact of tightened access to IDBs in the larger chains with good cash flow is expected to be negligible.

Community-Based Settings

Community-based long-term care providers have also become increasingly aware of the advantages of horizontal integration. In fact, many of the companies which dominate the home care market are multinational firms such as American Hospital Supply, Baxter Travenol, and Abbott. Before its takeover by Baxter Travenol, American Hospital Supply, through its Abbey Medical Division, operated over 100 nationwide home health care retail outlets that provided durable medical equipment and various self-care products. Through its Continu-Care division, American Hospital Supply also provided nursing services, IV therapy products, and blood products. Baxter Travenol, through Travacare, offers parenteral nutrition, blood therapy, renal and urological supplies, and other products and services. Travenol does not provide its own nursing services but instead contracts with Upjohn for this purpose.

Horizontal integration or the development of multifacility chains can also be seen among the direct home care service providers and where it cuts across public, voluntary, or proprietary auspices. To begin with the public sector again, the VA is one of the biggest providers of hospital-based home care, with 43 such programs based at its acute care hospitals across the country in fiscal year 1984.

Through its hospital-based home care programs, the VA treated 9,851 veterans in 1984, providing approximately 200,000 service visits to patients whose average length of stay on active service was 215 days. Although the number of hospital-based home care programs operated by the VA has increased substantially during the last 10 years, future expansion of the program hinges on the ability to withstand moratoria on new programs that have recently been proposed by the Office of Management and Budget. As in the case of institutional long-term care, the VA is also an important purchaser of care from local home care agencies with whom it contracts for service-connected patients on a fee basis.

In contrast to the public and investor-owned segments of the industry, the extent of involvement of voluntary home care agencies in chains appears to be almost nonexistent. The visiting nurse associations (VNAs) represent somewhat of a sleeping giant in this respect. Linked by a similar philosophy of care and similar forms of management, each is a separate corporate entity. It is worth noting that the public health and VNAs have been experiencing either stagnant or negative growth in the recent past, while new hospital-based and proprietary agencies are burgeoning. However, it is important to recognize that VNAs still represent a force, with 520 Medicare-certified agencies in 1983, accounting for $5.7 million in total billings.[11] In view of their considerable size, the VNAs could form a potent market force if they organized. In recognition of this, a new organization was formed in 1982 to link the VNAs. The American Affiliation of Visiting Nurse Agencies and Services, headquartered in St. Louis, now numbers 90 VNAs nationwide among its members. Loosely modeled after the Voluntary Hospitals of America hospital chain, the association hopes to foster communication and cooperation, promote a national image, pool resources for marketing and advertising, and, ultimately create a privately held subsidiary corporation that, among other functions, could market member organizations nationally to large health maintenance organizations. While this organization is still in its infancy, one voluntary Texas-based chain has demonstrated that horizontal integration for the nonprofits is possible.

Home Health-Home Care, Inc. (HHHC) is one of the largest private, nonprofit home care providers in the Southwest. According to a recent report in *Home Health Line,* HHHC is the result of a 1983 merger of three companies (Oklahoma Health Care, Inc., Concepts of Care, and Home Health-Home Care, Inc.) originally run by Louise Maberry. HHHC now encompasses 83 offices serving over 28,000 clients in six Southwest states: Arkansas, Kansas, Louisiana, Missouri, Oklahoma, and Texas.[12]

Maberry originally entered the home care field in 1968, moving from a career in nursing homes, two of which she still owns. Forty-nine of HHHC's 83 offices are Medicare certified and 34 are not. To shield its diversified lines of home care services from Medicare regulation, HHHC has developed a three-divisional structure, which will probably increase to six in the near future and will be more fully described under the vertical integration section.

Although Louise Maberry has demonstrated that private, not-for-profit home care companies can integrate successfully, the most pronounced amount of horizontal integration in home care has occurred among the proprietary companies. It is difficult to obtain good data on the number of proprietary home care chains in the United States at the present time. However, Table 6–4 displays the top 10 proprietary home care chains in the United States as described by the trade journals in 1984. In terms of revenue generated, it appears that Upjohn, Personnel Pool, and Quality Care account for the largest volume of home care services while simultaneously providing the widest geographic coverage. Most proprietary home care chains entered the health care market in the mid-70s as providers of supplemental staffing to hospitals, nursing

TABLE 6–4 Top Ten Proprietary Home Care Chains

		Percent of Business Home Care	Number of Offices*	Revenue (millions)†	Number of States Served*
1.	Upjohn	—	300	131	44
2.	Personnel Pool of America	—	200	162	41
3.	Beverly Enterprises	—	165	—	13
4.	Quality Care, Inc.	90%	163	100	43
5.	Staff Builders Health Care Services	—	100	60	27
6.	Kelly Health Care	—	78	—	25
7.	Kimberly Home Health Care, Inc.	—	72	—	31
8.	Superior Care, Inc.	90%	38	30	17
9.	Hillhaven Home Health Services	—	25	100	5
10.	National Medical Care, Inc.	—	22	—	10

*Esther Fritz Kuntz, "For Profits Adding Home Health Care to Aid Bottom Lines," *Modern Healthcare,* May 15, 1984, p. 168–9.

†Emily Layzer, "New York-Based Proprietary Chains Take Hard Look At Future," *Home Health Line,* vol. IX, April 30, 1984, pp. 101, 106–111.

homes, and home care agencies. However, with fluctuations in demand for hospital staffing, many chains have since begun to develop and emphasize their home care line of business.

Expansion by the proprietary home care chains in the recent past verges on the explosive. A survey of five New York firms in 1984 found a 30 percent to 70 percent compound annual growth rate, most of which resulted from new office openings. One of the major reasons for this growth is proprietaries' greater access to Medicare certification in 1981. Specifically, the Omnibus Reconciliation Act of 1980, implemented in 1981, eliminated a previous Medicare requirement that proprietary home health agencies could participate in Medicare only in those states which permitted licensure of proprietary agencies. This restraint of trade requirement had effectively prevented the proprietaries from competing for the Medicare home care business in 24 states. The combination of the lifting of this requirement in 1981 and the onset of prospective payment in 1983 created a tremendous upsurge in

Medicare home care activity by the proprietary chains. Thus, as Figure 6–1 demonstrates, of 866 agencies certified by Medicare between October 1983 and April 1984, 161 or 19 percent belonged to proprietary chains. Together with new freestanding proprietary and hospital-based, nonprofit agencies, they comprised 75 percent of all newly certified agencies.

Despite their recent interest in Medicare certification, most proprietary agencies continue to consider the private pay market as their primary target and revenue source. At present, there are virtually no statistics available about the size of the private pay market for home care services. In an article on this issue, Harold Ting, vice president of strategic planning for National Medical Enterprises has cited informal communication that 38 percent of all home care in the United States is funded privately.[13] If the growth of the proprietary chains in the past and projections regarding increased disposable income of the aged in the future are considered reliable indicators, this market appears to be substantial in size.

In fact it is this combined ability to offer both private pay and Medicare-certified services that proprietaries view as insuring a competitive advantage. Most home care agencies expect that as a result of prospective payment, eventually every hospital in the United States will either operate its own home care program or contract with or joint venture with an existing home care provider. However, Medicare patients constitute only 29 percent of the average hospital's patient census. Therefore, hospitals will be most attracted to a one-stop home care provider who can provide either Medicare-certified or fee-based care to 100 percent of patients requiring aftercare services.

As a result of this increased demand for full-service providers, most home care agencies have begun diversifying their services. This process of diversification is causing many new structural arrangements to surface in the industry. Thus, it is increasingly common to see relatively small home care agencies form holding companies and pursue corporate restructuring to comply with Medicare certification requirements for their skilled care business and simultaneously protect a for-profit private pay subsidiary from counting as a step-down in its Medicare cost report.

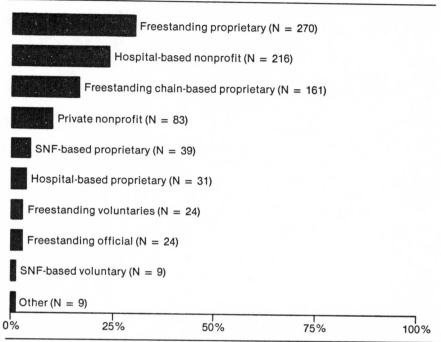

FIGURE 6–1   Percent Home Health Agencies by Provider Type Certified between October 1983 and April 1984 (N = 866)

Freestanding proprietary (N = 270)

Hospital-based nonprofit (N = 216)

Freestanding chain-based proprietary (N = 161)

Private nonprofit (N = 83)

SNF-based proprietary (N = 39)

Hospital-based proprietary (N = 31)

Freestanding voluntaries (N = 24)

Freestanding official (N = 24)

SNF-based voluntary (N = 9)

Other (N = 9)

0%   25%   50%   75%   100%

SOURCE: *Home Health Line,* vol. IV, June 25, 1984, p. 163, and vol. IX, December 17, 1984, p. 303.

Vertical Integration

Although the past decade has witnessed a substantial increase in the number of multifacility chains, the most recent development in the organization and delivery of long-term care services is vertical integration. Vertical integration in industry usually refers to increased backward or forward control of the supplies or resources necessary to run an operation. Thus, it is viewed as a way whereby a firm can increase control over its environment through ownership of vital inputs or distribution processes for its products. Vertical integration, in this classic sense, can be seen in those chains which have relationships with or own durable medical equipment suppliers or construction companies, real estate services, or manpower pools. Recent years, however, have seen a greater appreciation in the health care industry of the importance of control over consumers through greater control over feeder or referral systems. In the health care case, vertical integration thus translates into the provision of multiple levels of care, or the development of a capacity to provide a continuum of care within the parent organization.

A trend toward providing increased levels of care already existed in the long-term care industry at the beginning of the 80s. Many nursing home administrators, for example, were aware of the potential competition of home care agencies for patients. Several of the largest providers anticipated this source of competition by establishing their own home health care business. However, two other regulatory and reimbursement trends, namely certificate of need and prospective payment, account for the major share of this trend's increased momentum.

During the late 70s and early 80s, as mentioned earlier, many states either instituted total moratoria on new nursing home construction or approved very few applications for the same. As the earlier part of this chapter demonstrated, this regulatory stance, together with steep construction costs, fueled the acquisition strategy of the proprietary chains. Nursing home corporations could not grow through construction of new facilities and instead grew through the purchase of existing certified homes. In similar fashion, nursing homes began to integrate vertically by offering other nonnursing-home types of care that either did not require certificate of need approval or could acquire it more easily, i.e., retirement communities and to a lesser extent, home health care services, adult day care, and hospice services. Thus, we have witnessed growth in the number of nursing home affiliates with speculation by some that the nursing home will become the central long-term care provider with a constellation of other services ranging from retirement housing to adult day care, home care, and respite care.

Vertical integration, like horizontal integration, is not new. Both the VA and the voluntary sectors of the nursing home industry have provided vertically integrated care for decades. The VA, for example, not only provides intermediate care beds in hospitals and VA and contract nursing homes, but also domiciliary care, home care, and a variety of other services. Recently, Congress authorized the opening of 30 adult day health care centers in the VA system. However, given the budget trimming that is needed to reduce the federal deficit, it is not clear that the VA will continue to develop and directly provide its own continuum of long-term care services. There are many who advise that it would be more prudent to contract with already existing community services. In response to this sentiment, the VA is beginning to coordinate more closely with area offices on aging to prevent unnecessary duplication of services.

Vertical integration of services can also be found in the voluntary not-for-profit nursing home industry. Information from the American Association of Homes for the Aging Directory indicates that a substantial number (55 percent) of all facilities belonging to multifacility chains offer a variety of outreach services. Retirement living units are provided by 62 percent of facilities belonging to multifacility chains, home-delivered meals by 11 percent, senior centers by 6 percent, adult day care by 5 percent, and home health care by 4 percent (Table 6–5). Although the latter percentages are small, they indicate a growing trend of reaching out to the consumer in the community both before and after a nursing home stay.

A similar trend can also be observed among the proprietaries, who are finding that diversification in today's uncertain economic and regulatory environment can be an asset. As Figure 6–2 demonstrates, a substantial number of proprietary chains are vertically integrating a variety of other services or business capacities. For example, 46 percent of chains with skilled nursing beds offer separate rehabilitation services, and 42 percent have a turnkey development division. A similarly large percentage provided retirement living units in 1983, with Manor Care leading the field with 1,310 owned and 2,439 leased retirement living units. Forum Group was next with 740 owned and 667 managed. Since many states allow exceptions from certificate of need requirements for nursing home beds in life-care centers, continued expansion in this area can probably be expected. Finally, a growing percentage

---

TABLE 6–5 Outreach Services Offered by
Nonprofit Multifacility Chains

Type of Service	Number of Facilities Offering	Percent
1. Retirement living	332	62
2. Information and referral	97	18
3. Religious services	88	16
4. Recreational activities	82	15
5. Other services	71	13
6. Meals on wheels	60	11
7. Counseling	50	9
8. Physical therapy	48	9
9. Congregate meals	36	7
10. Transportation/escort	36	7
11. Senior center	34	6
12. Friendly visiting	31	6
13. Day care	29	5
14. Respite care	27	5
15. Telephone checking (daily)	24	5
16. Occupational therapy	23	4
17. Home health	21	4
18. Homemaker	15	3
19. Speech or hearing therapy	15	3
20. Child day care	4	1
21. Psychiatric care	3	1
22. Hospice	2	0.4

SOURCE: American Association of Homes for the Aging, *Directory of Members*, 1984.

offer adult day care (27 percent), home care (23 percent), and hospice (15 percent).

A Case Example (Large Scale). National Medical Enterprises (NME), one of the nation's leading health management companies, provides one of the best examples of vertical integration on a large scale. In 1984, NME owned or operated 98 acute care hospitals and psychiatric facilities. Through its Hillhaven division, it also owned or operated 291 long-term care facilities in 38 states, 3 retirement communities, and 21 home care agencies (predominantly in California and Washington), as well as durable medical equipment retailers and suppliers through its Home Care Group. This constellation in itself is not that unusual. The distinguishing feature of NME's

FIGURE 6–2   Other Services Offered by Proprietary
Nursing Home Chains

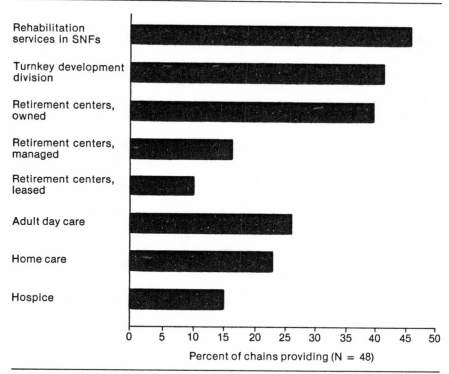

SOURCE: William A. Spicer, "Measuring Long-Term Care's Corporate Sector,"
Contemporary Administrator for Long-Term Care, June 1984.

approach to care lies in its recent inclusion of a financing
mechanism in its portfolio of services. NME has operated
Health PACE as a fully insured health plan in California since
1984. Also, in 1984, NME increased its holdings in this area
by acquiring Av-Med, Inc., a Florida-based operator of federally qualified prepaid and preferred provider health plans.
Both Health PACE and Av-Med will be administered by a
newly established division, Health Care Systems and Services
Group. This group will also manage NME's Instant Care
Centers of America, Inc., and Ambulatory Health Services,
Inc., its ambulatory and occupational health care operations.

At first glance, the interests of an insurance company in controlling hospital costs may seem incompatible with those of an investor-owned hospital chain in increasing hospital revenues. However, in the current climate, volume is more important than per diem rates. Thus, if increased numbers of hospital users can be identified through reduced rates, companies still expect to more than break even at the margin.[14] Through horizontal integration, NME achieved a sufficient volume of holdings to render it one of the major service providers in the United States. It also achieved geographic dispersion that allows it a degree of protection from variable regulatory reimbursement and economic conditions across states. Through its emphasis on diverse holdings in the health care industry, or its vertical integration along the continuum of levels of care, it has also acquired a reputation for having one of the best protected stock offerings among health management companies. While many of these companies have been hurt by uncertainties associated with Medicare prospective payment, NME is regarded as safe for investors because it is not overly reliant on income or earnings from a single source. NME's ultimate goal, according to chairman and chief executive officer Richard Eamer, is to develop complete health care campuses which span the entire continuum of health care services. To that end, Daniel Baty, president of NME's Long Term Care Group, recently described the corporation's strategy as "acquiring or constructing convalescent hospitals in all common locations in order to support the acute care operation," stating that the "real payoff will come when we can offer competitive prices and one-stop shopping to large buyers of health care."[15]

NME is not alone among the major proprietary management companies in pursuing a strategy of vertical integration. Hospital Corporation of America (HCA), the largest investor-owned hospital chain, which owns or manages more than 400 acute care hospitals nationwide, until recently owned 20 percent of the stock of Beverly Enterprises, the nation's largest proprietary nursing home chain and a significant owner of home care agencies. HCA has also begun its own home health care line, TransMed, which is small but operational in three states at this time. Through its Vintage Group division, HCA is now assessing the development of a major long-term care financing initiative possibly modeled after the social/health maintenance organization. Although all of HCA's systems are not yet interfacing in practice, they hold substantial potential for HCA to position itself as an integrated, full-service provider of care in the future.

A Case Example (Small Scale). A different example of a small but vital and diversified nonprofit system is the Bensenville Home Society in Bensenville, Illinois. Established in 1895 by the United Church of Christ, the Bensenville Home provides care to individuals at both ends of the dependency spectrum, children and the elderly. The society currently provides 265 skilled nursing care beds and 22 other services ranging from senior citizen apartments to maternity, adoption, and marital and family counseling. The society reached full circle recently when it cared for a former orphan in its nursing home during this elderly man's last months of life. The Bensenville Home Society currently cares for 450 on-site residents and provides services to an additional 2,500 residents in the community. It has a staff of 350 persons, more than 20 percent of whom have worked for the organization for more than five years. Running a human services organization that spans long-term nursing home care and social services to families and children is a challenge. According to the society president, J. Rex Pippin, the number of elderly residents with limited financial resources is 50 percent higher than it was four years ago, requiring a charity offset in 1985 of $1 million and the establishment of a Life Care Fund.[16] However, both the board and staff enthusiastically endorse the continuum approach to care as providing many opportunities for synergistic programming which can span intergenerational concerns.

Suggestions for the Stand-Alone Provider. Not everyone is a NME, and the number of providers who can develop their own insurance products and in-house real estate capacity is limited. But the principles of networking that the multis illustrate can be adopted by smaller providers as well. In a recent article dealing with this issue, Roger Nauert put forth several constructive suggestions for the smaller provider.[17] Through referral arrangements that range from informal to formal in nature, stand-alone providers can become part of a network that can greatly enhance their revenue streams, service capacity, community image, and marketability, while simultaneously decreasing dependence on a single-market niche. Service capacity can be increased by networking with existing community service programs so that an increased array of benefits is available to residents or clients. Sharing professional services with another provider is an additional way of expanding a service offering and increasing marketability without incurring full overhead costs. Armed with data from a good marketing survey, providers can identify those additional services that consumers want and are willing to pay for. Networking with hospitals and HMOs can also lead to better treatment of residents or clients and possibly allow the exercising of some financial leverage with respect to discounted rates or possibly shared laundry, lab, or nutrition services. Close relationships with physicians or physician groups can also be mutually beneficial as can be arrangements with retirement centers and home care agencies.

Vertical Integration: Community-Based Care

Many proprietary home care chains have been in both the private-pay home care and hospital and nursing home staffing businesses for quite some time. As mentioned earlier, the new feature of the proprietary home care chains is their recent pursuit of Medicare home care certification. There are two reasons for this trend. First, the Omnibus Budget Reconciliation Act of 1981 made it possible for proprietary agencies to apply for Medicare certification. Prior to this time, proprietors had actually been restrained from participating in the Medicare home care business. However, most administrators of proprietary home care chains admit they are not pursuing Medicare certification for the dollars that are involved. Rather, they want to be able to provide Medicare home care services for acute care hospitals. The chains believe that Medicare certification will help them forestall the wholesale movement of hospitals into this area and allow them to contract with hospitals.

Starting a home care operation is not too complicated for hospitals. They are already in the health care business and may, under prospective payment, have a surplus of nurses. However, setting up a Medicare-certified business is somewhat more complicated because of the technicalities involved in the regulations, billing, and cost-reporting parts of the business. For this reason, hospitals may prefer to contract with an experienced provider, and all home care agencies will be vying for this business because hospitals control the feeder system for home care services.

Two other trends demonstrate home care agencies' growing awareness of the need for vertical integration. First, on the supply side, both proprietary and voluntary home care agencies are beginning to establish some type of relationship with durable medical equipment suppliers. Although many agencies may have enjoyed informal relationships with suppliers in the past, the emergence of hi-tech home care has created a new interdependence between the service and supply industries. The durable medical equipment (DME) companies can handle large inventories of stock and prompt deliveries without difficulty, but their ability to provide skilled nursing services over broad geographic areas is more restricted. In contrast, the service agencies have no trouble producing the skilled nursing manpower but have little capacity to stock and deliver supplies. Thus, joint ventures between home care agencies and DME suppliers have become increasingly common.

The other major trend among home care agencies is their increased awareness of the need to formalize a link with their major feeder system, the acute care hospital. The non-hospital-based agencies, whether proprietary or nonprofit, all have a stake in cementing a relationship with as many hospitals as possible. As mentioned earlier, in order to increase their attractiveness to hospital discharge planners, home care agencies are beginning to stress the breadth of their service offerings in order to provide the convenience of one-stop shopping to the discharge planner. Thus, a broader spectrum of service offerings, ranging from hi-tech care to Medicare-certified skilled care, private-duty chore, housekeeping, and homemaker services, and respite care, will probably be more common in the near future. The offering of multiple services in this case not only benefits the referring agency but can substantially increase access and continuity of care for consumers.

Service Integration Options (How to Do It)

Whether for a nursing home or hospital, the options for expansion of long-term care service offerings are the same. Essentially, hospitals and nursing homes can do nothing: develop referral contracts; lease, buy, merge, or build facilities; or joint venture with another provider to lease, build, or buy. Those who opt to do nothing will be least equipped to deal with the increasingly competitive nature of the health care industry. Figure 6–3 summarizes some of the advantages and disadvantages associated with vertical integration as outlined by Stephen Holt.[18] Nursing homes that build or acquire retirement centers and home health care agencies and enter into contracts with acute care hospitals can achieve several things simultaneously. They can increase their potential pool of patient revenues, increase their control over feeder systems, and expand their pool of potential private pay patients, while simultaneously providing needed community services and responding to consumer preferences for a broader array of service options. The same is true for acute care hospitals which can achieve the additional bonus of freeing up Medicare beds to maximize returns from prospective payment.

The advent of prospective payment has caused speculation about the extent to which hospitals might seek to openly compete with nursing homes by converting unoccupied beds to long-term care use or by constructing or acquiring long-term care facilities. Recent rulings by the Health Care Financing Administration indicate that a cooperative versus competitive mode may be more likely. Since the onset of Medicare prospective payment, hospitals have experimented with two types of payments to nursing homes to insure timely access to beds. The first method, the bonus payment, consisted of a separate per diem payment by the hospital to the nursing home for each hospital patient accepted by the nursing home. The second method, the bed-reserve arrangement, consisted of pay-

---

FIGURE 6–3 Vertical Integration: Advantages and Disadvantages

---

Advantages

1. Additional profit margins, increased revenues from more service areas
2. Increased stability of operations
3. Certainty of materials and supplies
4. Quality control of products
5. Prompt revision of production and distribution policies
6. Better inventory control
7. Greater buying power
8. Ability to secure better trained personnel, more opportunity for lateral and vertical career mobility
9. Increased diversity in points of view among persons involved at different stages in vertical arrangements
10. Reduction of administrative overhead and larger span of control
11. Improved technological capacity

Disadvantages

1. Managerial complexity, managerial limitations increased, lack of skilled personnel
2. Inflexibility of operations because spread over diverse operations, less fine-tuned control than a specialist in one
3. Inability of "marginal" firms to operate in a vertically integrated system
4. Risk involved in breaking into a new field
5. Increased inventory holdings and storage and maintenance costs
6. Lack of specialization, leading to decreased efficiency associated with repeated performance of a single function

---

SOURCE: Stephen W. Holt, "Vertical Integration in Home Care—Part I," *Caring,* March 1985, pp. 54–57.

---

ments by hospitals, either in cash or in kind, to nursing homes to ensure that a specified number of beds were always available for the hospital's patients.

Although hospitals have experimented with both approaches, no one has been convinced of the legality of either. However, a recent ruling by the Health Care Financing Administration indicates that bonus payments will not be allowed because they are patient specific and Medicare law does not allow additional payments over and above the Medicare allotment on a patient-specific basis. However, the bed-reserve approach has been approved with payments potentially of either a monetary or technical services nature. Hospitals will not be allowed to claim the cost of a bed-reserve arrangement as an allowable cost on Medicare cost reports. However, payments which the nursing home receives will not be treated as offsets to the facility's allowable operating costs. This new ruling, coupled with constraints on both types of providers regarding capital costs of construction and acquisition, appears to indicate that cooperative, contractual arrangements may be most likely in the future.

Prospective payment is also substantially impacting the home care industry. As described earlier, hospitals are entering the home care business in a major way. In 1983, there were 4,245 Medicare-certified home care providers in the United States. By the end of 1984, this number had increased by 24 percent to 5,247. In 1983, the number of hospital-based, Medicare-certified providers was 579, or 14 percent of all home care agencies. By 1984, this number increased by 54 percent to constitute 17 percent of all home care providers.[19] A 1984 survey of 450 hospitals conducted by *Modern Healthcare* revealed that 60 percent of hospitals with more than 300 beds offered home care and that 79 percent planned to offer it by mid-1985.

The above statistic does not necessarily refer to hospital-owned and operated services, however, and there are still a number of methods that the free-standing home care provider can utilize to survive and possibly thrive in the future. Some of these strategies, as outlined by Nicholas Leone, president of Shared Resource Associates, are displayed in Figure 6–4. These strategies can be used selectively by different home care agencies, depending upon their specific mission, goals, and environment.[20]

The primary strategy for home care agencies is the development of closer ties with hospitals through the negotiation of an "exclusive provider" or "primary provider" arrangement with a hospital. If this is not possible, it still may be possible to increase the volume of hospital referrals by differentiating services (i.e., becoming known as an "expert" provider of enteral or maternal and child health services) or entering a service area that has been underserved. Alternatively, home care agencies can attempt to bypass the hospital discharge planner by marketing directly to physicians and, ultimately, to consumers. Since all Medicare home care referrals must be

---

FIGURE 6–4 Competitive Strategies for Home Care Agencies

---

1. Develop closer ties with hospital referring services
2. Differentiate services and territory
3. Bypass hospital referral policy
4. Provide "private-label" home health services for the hospital entrant
5. Develop a joint venture agreement with the hospital(s)
6. Increase service volume by expanding service territory
7. Increase service volume by expanding service lines
8. Increase service volume and competitive strength through merger or acquisition

---

SOURCE: Nicholas Leone, "Competitive Strategies for a Consolidating Market," *Home Health Line,* vol. IX, October 1, 1984, pp. 248–252.

---

certified by a physician, marketing to the former group should prove useful.

Alternatively, the agency could join forces with the hospital by providing private label services under a division using the hospital's name or develop a legally binding agreement with a hospital to provide the services jointly. A word of caution about joint ventures might be in order here. Because of difficulties in accessing capital, the popularity of the joint venture has soared in recent years. As an organizational arrangement, it has a lot of intuitive appeal. The joint venture allows two different organizations to complement one another's strengths. However, it is a legal arrangement encompassing shared investment, risk, and return in a predetermined activity. The legal arrangement can assume a variety of forms including partnership, limited partnership, or corporation. As Leone points out, before entering into joint venture negotiations, home health agencies should carefully consider the agreement's implications with respect to organizational survival, mission, autonomy, financial strength, tax status, personnel benefit policies, and geographic service area. The arrangements should then be pursued only in cases in which the venture is compatible with or can optimize a substantial number of these concerns.

Finally, joint ventures in the legal sense have not been around long, making their long-run survival unknown. Two problems with the organizational structure deserve mention.

The first concerns differences in organizational cultures and philosophy. In the case of the shared corporation, there may be some inherent strains involved in competing interests that could complicate staff and board relationships. At least one director of a joint venture program has reported that the arrangement is somewhat akin to being the child of divorced parents. If the partners have competing interests, the service program ends up continually running the risk of pleasing one at the cost of alienating the other, a situation that generates substantial stress for all concerned. The second issue is one of trust. Hospitals may be viewed by home care agencies with some trepidation because of their substantially greater resources. Many home care providers fear that hospitals may utilize a joint venture arrangement to learn the home care business and then dissolve the partnership when ready to "go it alone." However, it seems more likely that hospitals will realize that revenues from home care services are limited and that in those situations in which competent agencies with good community reputations and capacity already exist, cooperation may be in everyone's long-range best interest.

To summarize, as Figure 6–5 demonstrates, in a remarkably short time many of the distinctions between community-based and institution-based parallel systems of care have broken down. Prospective payment has had spin-offs with respect to the organization and delivery of health services that far exceed its originators' intent. As a result of incentives to treat acutely ill patients as efficiently as possible, hospitals may be beginning to utilize nursing homes more appropriately for preadmission testing, postdischarge rehabilitation, or subacute care. As a result, nursing homes may begin to joint venture with home care agencies to provide care before admission or following discharge to ease the transition to the home. Community-based and institution-based care are no longer viewed as antithetical rivals but as compatible caregivers, with most astute nursing home providers joining the home care movement and most astute home care providers developing a continuum of community-based services with good tie-ins to acute and long-term institutional care.[21]

In conclusion, as Figure 6–5 demonstrates, increased vertical integration and the development of a systems approach to

---

FIGURE 6–5   Vertical Integration in Long-Term Care

BACKWARD

Equipment, Supplies, Real Estate
   Durable medical equipment
   Respiratory therapy devices
   Enteral and parenteral equipment
      supplied
   Turnkey development division
Service
   Acute hospital
   Inpatient hospital
   Chronic care hospital
   Rehabilitation hospital   Institutional
   Skilled nursing facility
   Intermediate care facility

   Group home
   Personal care home
   Foster home   Sheltered housing
   Congregate housing
   Retirement villages

   Respite care
   Day care
   Rehabilitation facility
   Sheltered workshop   Community care
   Mental health center
   Senior center/congregate meals
   Geriatric assessment clinics

   In-home hospice
   Intermittent skilled care
   Long-term maintenance care
   Meals on Wheels   Home care
   Lifeline
   Maternal/child health
Research/Education and Financing
   Staff training centers
   Research health care: costs, services, delivery
      mechanisms
   Insurance product

FORWARD

SOURCE: This figure represents a modification of one developed by Stephen W. Holt, "Vertical Integration in Home Care—Part I." Reproduced by permission of the National Association for Home Care from *Caring,* March 1985.

care can optimize several goals of an ideal long-term system of care. First, vertical integration fosters the emergence of new service options as they are identified. Vertical integration also fosters continuity of care through the development of an array of informal to formal referral mechanisms and should prove cost effective insofar as it enables treatment at the level and in the locus of care that is most appropriate to the patient's condition. The development of vertically integrated service-delivery mechanisms and options also has important implications for monitoring the quality and managing the financing of long-term care services. We turn to these important considerations next.

NOTES

1. Jeff Charles Goldsmith, *Can Hospitals Survive?* (Homewood, Ill.: Dow Jones-Irwin, 1981), p. 107.

2. "Update: Multis Saw Continued Growth in 1984: AHA," *Multi's*, February 1, 1985, p. 148.

3. U.S. Veterans Administration, *Summary of Medical Programs*, Office of Information Management and Statistics, September 1984.

4. Cynthia Wallace, "VA's New Aging Plan Downplays Hospitals, Stresses Alternatives," *Modern Health Care*, May 15, 1984, p. 172.

5. Joan F. van Nostrand et al., "The National Nursing Home Survey: 1977 Summary for the United States," *Vital and Health Statistics Series*, 13:13, National Center for Health Statistics, DHEW Pub. no. (PHS) 79–1994, 1979, p. 13.

6. The denominator used to estimate percent of facilities and percent of beds reported in this chapter derive from the latest unpublished figures available from the National Center for Health Statistics 1982 Master Facility Inventory Survey. The denominator represents 1982 data, while the numerator represents 1984 data. Thus percentages cited may err on the side of overstatement. However, since little nursing home construction has occurred in the period 1982–1984, they are probably reasonable estimates.

7. William A. Spicer, "Measuring Long-Term Care's Corporate Sector," *Contemporary Administrator for Long-Term Care*, June 1984, pp. 32–35.

8. Linda Punch, *Modern Health Care*, May 15, 1984, p. 131.

9. U.S. GAO, "Medicaid and Nursing Home Care: Cost Increases and the Need for Services Are Creating Problems for the States and the Elderly," January 1984, DHHS Pub. no. (IPE–84–1).

10. Gary Weiss, "Excellent Prognosis: The Outlook for Nursing Home Chains is Glowing," *Barron's*, May 18, 1984, pp. 6 and 7.

11. John P. Byrne and Robert Rubright, "How Vital are the VNA's?" *Caring*, October 1984, pp. 65–68.

12. "Louise Maberry: First Lady of Texas Home Health Directs Six-State Nonprofit Giant," *Home Health Line*, vol. IX, September 3, 1984.

13. Harold Ting, "New Directions in Nursing Home and Home Healthcare Marketing," *Healthcare Financial Management*, May 1984, p. 68.

14. Karen Sandrick, "Multis Enter the Health Insurance Field," *Multis*, February 1, 1985, p. M16.

15. "Trends: Multi Hospital Systems Target Continuum of Care Strategy," *Hospitals*, March 1, 1985, p. 56.

16. "Interview with the President," *Growing* (Bensenville, Ill.: Bensenville Home Society, Spring 1984), p. 9.

17. Roger C. Nauert, "Building Networks Today, Keeping Pace with Tomorrow," *Contemporary Administrator for Long-Term Care*, November 1984, pp. 42-45.

18. Stephen W. Holt, "Vertical Integration in Home Care—Part I," *Caring*, March 1985, pp. 54–57.

19. Stephanie Tames, "DRGs Spur Hospital Interest in Long-Term Care," *Washington Report on Medicine and Health/Perspectives*, January 28, 1985, p. 3.

20. Nicholas Leone, "Competitive Strategies for a Consolidating Market," *Home Health Line*, 9, October 1, 1984, pp. 248–252.

21. Margaret McDonald, "Home Health Care and Long-Term Care: Growing Together," *Contemporary Administrator*, July 1984, pp. 38–40.

PART THREE

Policy Issues

CHAPTER SEVEN

Quality of Care in a Systems Context

- The evaluation and assurance of high quality long-term care services requires multifaceted approaches that reflect the diverse populations cared for, their varying levels and loci of care, and their multidisciplinary mix of providers.

- Care must be taken to include consumers and families directly in the quality-assessment process.

- Information is needed regarding appropriate outcomes of care, adjusted for case mix, for both institutional and community-care providers.

- To be effective, both a greater range of sanctions and excess capacity are needed, so that facilities or agencies can be closed if necessary without adversely affecting or disrupting care.

- Ending the isolation of the long-term care provider through linkages with hospitals and professional schools holds great potential to enhance the quality of care.

- Ultimately, increased involvement of the public in long-term care programs, the development of consumer guides, and heightened consumer education and purchasing power can do much to encourage competition on the basis of quality, thereby raising standards of care across the board.

In the mind of the public, no other concern is more clearly identified with long-term care than quality. Whether deservedly or not, exposés in the popular press have helped to foster an image of long-term care as something that everyone would like to avoid rather than something that every individual should plan on encountering at some point in life and should be enabled to use in an informed way.

Certainly, great strides have been made since the 50s and 60s in rendering nursing homes more safe, fireproof, and sanitary. However, much work still needs to be accomplished in measuring, monitoring, and ensuring the quality of long-term care services. The increasing array of service options and providers that long-term care now subsumes renders this challenge more complex but also more feasible. This chapter addresses this issue by specifying some of the more pressing quality issues; defining what quality means, how it can be measured, and how it is being monitored; and finally, what can be done to improve those mechanisms in current use.

WHY THE CONCERN?

In almost every town in the United States, in any given year, one reads a newspaper account of an abused or neglected resident of a nursing home. Deaths in nursing homes or old-age homes used to be reported with depressing regularity before the adoption and enforcement of more rigorous life and safety codes in licensed long-term care facilities. However, we still have a long way to go. Consistent with its deregulatory philosophy, the Reagan administration cited reports on improved sanitation and safety in long-term care facilities and halved the federal budget for nursing home inspections in 1982. As a result, many states dismissed inspectors, and annual surveys of all facilities were discontinued. Although there is no hard evidence available to assess the impact of this change on quality, some trends, such as increased reports of abuse in New York, Pennsylvania, and Illinois, suggest that the cutbacks had negative side effects for patient care.[1] In 1984, in New York State alone, 2,200 reports of nursing home abuse were reviewed by the state health department.[2] Reports of abuse in New York are reported to have increased by 15

FIGURE 7-1 Unique Characteristics of Long-Term Care: Challenges for Quality Control

---

1. Structure	Proprietary nature of industry
	Low reimbursement rates
2. Users	Multiple interactive conditions
	Chronic, irreversible conditions with poor prognoses
	Preponderance of mental disabilities
	Communicative disorders
	Under PPS, more heavy-care conditions
3. Length of Service	Indeterminate, few weeks to remainder of lifetime

---

percent annually since 1977, when a patient-abuse law requiring nursing home employees to report suspected cases was enacted. Part of the increase reflects better reporting over time, but about 33 percent of the reports have been consistently substantiated by subsequent investigations. Although 37 percent of cases reported involved physical abuse, the majority of cases (60 percent) involved neglect, which includes failure to adequately feed, clothe, shelter, medicate, or provide appropriate activities for residents. Although cases of flagrant abuse are well publicized, they are relatively rare. As these figures attest, other quality concerns, such as neglect, are more prevalent but less well documented in the public press.

Structural Concerns

What are some of these concerns? Figure 7-1 summarizes three of the most pressing, which we describe in some detail. The first issue concerns the structure of the industry, or the predominance of nursing home beds in the United States which are owned and operated by for-profit organizations. In and of itself, for-profit ownership does not imply poor quality care. However, the nursing home industry is also being affected by the efforts of states to curtail growth in long-term care Medicaid costs. During the recession of the early 80s, states were hit simultaneously with lower tax revenues and with reductions in the federal matching share of their Medicaid programs. As a result, many states were forced to hold reimbursement rates constant over periods of years at a time. Thus, we now have not-for-profit as well as for-profit providers complaining in many states and nationally through their trade organizations that low and unreasonable reimbursement rates prohibit their ability to provide high quality care.

Characteristics of Users

Characteristics of long-term care users also make the definition and standardization of quality uniquely complex. Most users of long-term care suffer from multiple illnesses of a long-term chronic nature. Many patients have poor prognoses for recovery at entry to the system. An increasingly large number of patients receiving institution-based care have primary mental disorders and may engage in abusive or regressive behavior. In 1977, organic brain syndrome was the third leading primary diagnosis at admission to a nursing home, affecting 96,400 or close to 10 percent of nursing home residents.[3] An additional 5 percent and 6 percent of residents suffered from developmental and psychiatric disabilities, respectively. Despite the preponderance of mental illness among nursing home residents, less than 1 percent are estimated to actually receive psychiatric assessment and treatment, and neither nursing homes nor home care agencies provide much psychiatric or psychological diagnostic or treatment services.[4] Increasingly, similar types of patients are also being treated in adult day care centers in the community as well. If we add to this cognitively and psychiatrically impaired group those patients with arteriosclerosis and strokes, we can see that a large percentage of long-term care users may have severe problems communicating. Finally, when one adds to this picture other factors, such as the substantial numbers of patients having no family and those having nonexistent or exhausted financial resources, one is essentially describing an increasingly dependent and vulnerable group, the protection of whose rights is quite problematic.

Further complicating this picture are the combined effects of prospective payment, tighter certificate of need approval, and a decreasing ratio of long-term care beds to aged populations. As a result of these developments, a growing body of evidence suggests that both nursing home and home care providers are now coping with increased proportions of "heavy care" patients. Under the prospective payment system (PPS), the average length of a hospital stay in the United States declined from 9.5 days in fiscal year 1983 to 7.5 days in fiscal year 1984. Some of this decline may be due to a shift to outpatient diagnostic testing and surgery. However, the GAO has interviewed hospital, nursing home and home care providers, patient advocates, and discharge planners in six states regarding the impact of PPS and reports unanimous sentiment across all sites and all respondent groups that patients are being discharged more quickly and in a poorer state of health than prior to PPS.[5] Private pay patients were reported to have little difficulty accessing skilled nursing home care; however, Medicaid patients or those expected to become Medicaid eligible had much greater difficulty accessing an appropriate level of postdischarge care.

Length of Service Use

When we discuss quality of long-term care, the enumeration of health and safety factors simply does not suffice. Increasingly, the public is becoming concerned about the quality of life of patients who may receive care for months, years, or the rest of a lifetime in a given long-term care setting. Because of its extraordinary duration, the social, psychological, and environmental facets of long-term care are viewed as equal in importance to considerations of safety and technical competence of care.

Manpower and Staffing

Given all of the above, the complex medical problems of long-term care patients, their psychological and mental health needs, and the increased technical complexity of the growing heavy care group, is the staffing capacity of our long-term care system sufficient to deal with these patients? The great bulk of care provided in nursing homes (66 percent in 1977) and a substantial proportion of home care visits (42 percent in 1983) are provided by paraprofessional nurses' aides and home health aides.[6] There is nothing wrong with a heavy reliance on paraprofessional manpower. If the staff is appropriately trained and supervised, its use can result in desired efficiencies and lower costs of care. The problem arises when neither of these conditions are well met.

In 1977, there were 33 nurses' aides, 7 licensed practical nurses, and 5 registered nurses available for every 100 residents of nursing homes nationally.[7] Although nurses' aides constituted 66 percent of all staff, it has been estimated that they provide as much as 90 percent of all direct patient care. Given this degree of patient care involvement, both the training and retention of aides are matters of concern.

Data from the National Nursing Home Survey indicate that 33 percent of aides had less than a high school education. Previous studies have reported that the average annual ratio of turnover of nursing home aides ranges from 40 to 75 percent.[8] This means that long-stay patients, in particular, suffer from disruption in their routine source of care. The aide turnover rate also has important implications for costs, because the training and supervising of a new aide has been estimated to be four times as high as the former aide's salary. In a recent study of this issue, Waxman and colleagues interviewed 234 nurses' aides in several Philadelphia proprietary nursing homes to determine whether variability in job turnover was related to (1) wages and benefits, (2) job satisfaction, (3) perceptions of ward atmosphere, or (4) perceived quality of patient care. They found that rates of annual turnover varied from a low of 5.2 percent to a high of 75.8 percent. Interestingly, and paradoxically, homes judged to provide better quality of care experienced higher aide turnover rates. One of the chief complaints voiced by aides was their rare involvement in decision structures such as case conferences, despite their detailed knowledge of the patients involved. Thus, more involvement in decision making could help to retain aides and simultaneously enhance quality of care.

Medical Direction

Despite the complex medical conditions that many long-term care users have, the requirement that medical direction be available is relatively recent. Medical direction has only been required in skilled nursing facilities since January of 1976 when, as a condition of participation for Medicare and Medicaid, skilled nursing facilities were required to have a licensed physician available on a part or full-time basis to develop written policies concerning the responsibilities of attending physicians, be responsible for the execution of patient care policies, and monitor the employees' health status. A survey of medical directors published in 1979 reported that the average physician engaged in this capacity was a physician in solo practice who spent less than five hours a week in medical direction activities.[9] Nursing home administrators ranked the unavailability and unwillingness of physicians to serve in this capacity as a very important barrier to compliance, with the least important barrier to implementation being cost. According to administrators, the presence of a medical director was an aid in dealing with other attending medical staff and provided a single medical consultant for staff, which resulted in an improved medical climate and higher quality medical care.

Medical directors are not required in Medicare-certified home care agencies. A recent survey of Medicare-certified home care agencies, sponsored by the House Committee on Aging and The National Association for Home Care, found that 96 percent of agencies provided no physician visits to patients despite the fact that the type of patient being care for, especially with hyperalimentation techniques, is becoming increasingly medically complex. Interestingly, those expanded home care demonstrations that utilized a physician as a member of the home care team seem to document better results than those without physician input.[10] In fact, one of the most aggravating problems for nurses in community-based versus hospital-based home care programs is the need for timely updating of medical orders over the course of a patient's treatment.

Given the constellations of concerns outlined above, what are the current mechanisms used to monitor quality of long-term care services and how adequately do they meet this objective?

Regulating Quality: Mechanisms Currently Used

Definition. In any discussion of quality assurance, one of the first problems that must be addressed is the definition of quality itself. The definition that is most commonly used was developed by Donabedian to measure the components of quality of health care services. According to Donabedian, good quality care encompasses the conceptual components of structure, process, and outcomes.[11] Any one of the components is insufficient in itself for the attainment of high quality care. Rather, all must be present and interact to produce good patient care.

Structure, for the most part, refers to the condition of the facility's operating plant, the equipment, and the qualifications of staff; in other words, to the inputs that are necessary but not in themselves sufficient for the attainment of high quality care. Processes, on the other hand, are the treatments which staff provide and should be appropriate, adequate, and efficient. Finally, outcomes are the end products of a service or treatment and are expected to be consistent with the state of the art of health care practice and knowledge.

Although Donabedian's conceptualization of the dimensions of quality has intuitive appeal, one of the main disappointments of health services research to date is its failure to empirically buttress this theoretical definition. In other words, although it makes sense to assume that good structure and process must be present to produce good patient outcomes, most studies conducted to date have failed to validate the existence of relationships between these dimensions. Figure 7–2 summarizes a comprehensive analysis of the quality-assurance literature in long-term care conducted by Bettina Kurowski and Peter Shaughnessy.[12] As the figure demonstrates, of six studies of institution-based care that attempted to discover evidence of a consistent and statistically significant relationship between structure and process indicators,

FIGURE 7-2 Institutional Care: Relationships Observed between Structure and Process

	Study	Structure	Process	Link Supported Statistically
1.	Gottesman and Bourestum (1974)	Increased level of aide experience Allowing residents to have and keep personal possessions in rooms	Service hours per patient	Yes
2.	Connelly et al (1977)	Various structural measures	Patient-based quality indexes regarding adequacy of 1. Medical care 2. Nursing care 3. Social services	No
3.	Shaughnessy et al. (1980)	Facility size Level of certification	Unspecified process measures	No
4.	Greenberg (1980)	Various structural characteristics	Number of administrative inspection of care violations	No
5.	Ray et al. (1980)	Characteristics of physicians Facilities (direct care staff to patient ratios)	Use of antipsychotic drugs	Yes No
6.	Shaughnessy, Tynan et al. (1980)	Availability of social services Availability of dental and physical therapy services	Facility level process quality scores Patient level process quality scores	Yes Yes, at patient level

SOURCE: Bettina D. Kurowski and Peter W. Shaughnessy, "The Measurement and Assurance of Quality," Long-Term Care, ed., Vogel and Palmer, U.S., DHHS, Health Care Financing Administration, Pub. no. 82–600609.

three found such a link while three did not. As Figure 7–3 demonstrates, several studies are currently being conducted to test the relationship between process indicators and patient outcomes. It may be that this approach will yield more positive results. Finally, Figure 7–4, which illustrates some work completed to date on community-based care, again reveals little *consistent* relationship between patient outcomes and processes of care. Do these disappointing findings indicate that the quest for quality-assurance mechanisms should be abandoned? Probably not. Rather, these studies indicate the difficulty of operationalizing indicators of these constructs in a field situation in a valid and reliable way.

Before getting into this discussion further, however, it is important to first explain the process that is currently used to monitor quality of long-term care services in both institutional and community-care programs.

Procedures Used to Date

Public. As Figure 7–5 demonstrates, several methods have been used to monitor quality of long-term care services provided in the United States. First, state licensure is required of all nursing homes and home care agencies that receive Medicare and Medicaid reimbursement. Licensure is also increasingly required for adult day care programs and continuing care retirement communities. Increasingly, most states' licensure requirements have become identical to Medicare and Medicaid conditions of participation. All providers who wish to seek Medicare and Medicaid reimbursement for skilled nursing home care must meet conditions of participation or certification requirements. In theory, the Health Care Financing Administration (HCFA) regional offices then monitor compliance with conditions of participation. In practice, however, many state licensure laws are identical to the Medicare conditions. Thus, it is the surveyor from the State Department of Public Health who usually determines, as part of the annual Mandatory Medical Review Inspection of Care (IOC) survey, whether a facility or agency complies with the conditions of participation. If the state surveyor recommends revocation of a facility's license, notification of same is sent to the

FIGURE 7–3 Institutional Care: Relationships Observed between Process and Outcomes

Study	Process	Outcome	Link Supported Statistically
1. Langer and Rodin (1976)	Increased resident choice and control over environment	Change in psychosocial functioning	Yes, stronger relationship than previously detected
2. Linn (1977)	Number RN hours per patient day	Mortality Change in functional status	Yes
3. Chekryn and Roos (1979)	Multidisciplinary patient assessment Specified diagnostic procedures Problem-oriented care plans Contact with patient's family	Change in functional status Change in mental status Change in life satisfaction Length of stay	No, functional, mental, and life satisfaction at admission predict status of same at discharge
4. ABT Associates (1980)	Alternate staffing arrangements	Various outcomes	Study ongoing
5. Shaughnessy and Kurowski (in progress)	Particular types of care provided	Particular outcome (i.e., dehydration over three-month period)	Study ongoing
6. Weissert and Meiners (in progress)	Types and amount of care provided	Improvement in functional status	Study ongoing

SOURCE: Bettina D. Kurowski and Peter W. Shaughnessy, "The Measurement and Assurance of Quality," Long-Term Care, ed., Vogel and Palmer, U.S., DHHS: Health Care Financing Administration, Pub. no. 82-600609.

FIGURE 7–4 Community-Based Care: Relationships Observed between Structure, Process, and Outcomes

Study	Process	Outcome	Statistical Evidence of Link
1. Mitchell (1978)	Service use	Functional status	Yes, in home care group
2. Decker (1979)	Various process measures	120 outcome criteria for 33 different conditions	Very few outcomes achieved, due to "unavoidable and unexpected complications"
3. Kurowski et al. (1979)	Utilization of services	Change in functional status	No, functional status at admission is best predictor
4. Weissert et al. (1980)	Level of use (day care)	Mortality Nursing home and hospital use	No Yes
	Level of use (homemaker)	Mortality Nursing home and hospital use	Yes No
5. Skellie and Coan (1982)	Level of use	Mortality	Yes, in first six months of care
6. Shaughnessy and Kurowski (in progress)	Particular types of care provided	Particular outcomes (i.e., dehydration over three months)	Study ongoing

SOURCE: Bettina D. Kurowski and Peter W. Shaughnessy, "The Measurement and Assurance of Quality," *Long-Term Care*, ed., Vogel and Palmer, U.S., DHHS: Health Care Financing Administration, Pub. no. 82-600609.

FIGURE 7–5 Methods of Quality Assurance

Type	Began	Enforced by	Measure(s) Used
1. Licensure		States	Structure
Nursing homes	1930s	All	
Home care	1982	22	
Adult day care	—	3	
2. Certification			Structure
Nursing homes	1966	DHHS regional offices (Medicare) and states (Medicaid)	
Home care	1966	In 2 of 8 states that reimburse through Medicaid	
Adult day care			
3. Mandatory medical care review	1966	Agencies/providers	Structure and process (record oriented)
4. Voluntary peer review	1940s	Trade organizations JCAH, AHCA NLN	Structure and process (record oriented)
5. Mandatory abuse/neglect reports (nursing homes only)	1977	All states/state departments of public health, and attorney general's offices	Outcome, process
6. Certification of level of care			Utilization review
Nursing homes	1966	DHHS regional fiscal intermediaries re: skilled care for Medicare	
Home care	1966	State departments of public health or human resources for Medicaid	

HCFA regional office which then conducts its own review. If the regional office agrees with the state surveyor's findings and the agency does not comply with the standards within a specific time, the agency or facility is denied the right to continue to participate in or receive future reimbursement from Medicare or Medicaid.

Until recently, the state surveyor inspected facilities on a more or less regular basis (depending upon the availability of federal matching funds) and conducted a very thorough inspection of agency or facility administrative, financial, and patient care records. In nursing homes, the inspection process also included direct observation of standards of cleanliness and some direct observations of patients. In the home care setting, however, the surveyor's impressions of adequacy of care are based on agency records with very little direct patient care observation.

Several problems are inherent in this type of approach to quality assurance.[13] First, this type of procedure is subject to something researchers label "mono method bias." For example, reliance on records as a sole indicator of quality of care may inappropriately reward facilities that keep good records but provide poor care and simultaneously punish facilities that provide competent care but keep poor records. Second, there is very little standardization of norms that must be adhered to. The conditions for Medicare home care participation specify that care must be adequate, efficient, effective, and accessible, but no operational definitions of these attributes are provided. Thus, surveyors enjoy a fair amount of leeway in their judgments regarding a facility or agency's compliance with good standards of care. As a result, the reliability of surveyors' judgments tends to vary considerably. Third, this type of survey is cumbersome and costly. According to this method, 100 percent of the facilities were surveyed regularly with a 500–1,000 item survey instrument regardless of their previous degree of compliance or noncompliance with conditions of participation. Finally, although a range of different citations could be filed against poor quality providers, very few states provided rewards or incentives to those facilities that exhibited consistently high or improved levels of compliance with quality standards.

In addition to IOC licensure surveys, nursing homes and home care agencies are required to conduct their own internal Mandatory Medical Review (MMR) quality-assurance programs. The care of all patients in nursing homes that receive public payments (Medicare or Medicaid) must be reviewed on a regular basis by a multidisciplinary clinical care review committee that monitors and upgrades the facility's clinical care. Medicare-certified home health care agencies are also required to conduct MMRs but allowed to base reviews on samples rather than the universe of patients served. Again, guidelines for the conduct of Mandatory Medical Review programs are vague and lack specificity.

Private. As a result of dissatisfaction with these fuzzy guidelines, some providers have opted to participate in voluntary peer review quality-assurance mechanisms that can be used to supplement the MMR. Both the American Health Care Association and the National League for Nursing offer detailed quality-assurance programs to nursing homes and home care agencies, respectively. These provider organizations argue persuasively that providers can and should evaluate themselves since they know more about the facility or agency and patients than any outside regulator. Since 1966, the Joint Commission on Accreditation of Hospitals (JCAH) has also been accrediting long-term care facilities and hospital-based home care agencies that subscribe to its review process on a voluntary basis. As of 1983, JCAH had accredited 1,400 long-term care facilities, 48 percent of which were hospital-based.[14] A majority of JCAH-accredited facilities (60 percent) had over 100 beds and 54 percent were nonprofit. Thus, the typical JCAH-accredited facility does not really reflect the prototypical proprietary free-standing nursing home provider in the United States.

In 1981, an attempt was made by the Reagan administration to shift the burden of regulating quality assurance from the public sector to the private sector by allowing JCAH-accredited facilities "deemed status." Under this procedure, those facilities already meeting JCAH standards could be exempted from the state survey process, since the JCAH survey is generally regarded as having more rigorous process and structure standards. However, this attempt by the administration to extract government from a regulatory function in long-term care met with tremendous resistance from long-term care patient advocacy groups. As a result of the ensuing fracas, a national study of quality assurance in long-term care was commissioned by Congress to be conducted by the Institute of Medicine. This study took several years to conduct, and its findings have just recently been released.

Although attempts to shift quality assurance to a nonpartisan source such as the JCAH that uses national standards uniformly in all states has some appeal, the IOM report argues that we are not yet ready for this shift because of problems with current measurement. As the previous review indicates, the bulk of the quality-assurance work conducted to date has focused on considerations of structure and process with very little attention paid to outcomes of care. As Figure 7–5 demonstrates, the only outcomes that are monitored are outright negative outcomes such as abuse and neglect, which the nursing home staff is required by law to report in much the same way that other health professionals are required to report suspected cases of child abuse and neglect. These reports are then investigated by state health departments and, if confirmed, referred to the state's attorney general offices for follow-up prosecutory activities if appropriate. Many argue that a more systematic way of tracking outcomes of care is needed for all long-term care providers.

Utilization Review

The last quality-monitoring mechanism listed on Figure 7–5 deals not so much with quality per se as with fraud, or the practice of providing and billing for services to clients who do not actually require the level or amount of care provided. Problems concerning levels of care provided in long-term care facilities will be examined in greater detail in Chapter 8 which deals with reimbursement issues and cost control in greater depth. However, it is worth pointing out that all Medicaid and Medicare admissions to nursing homes must first be certified by a physician as requiring institutional care of either an intermediate or skilled level. A recertification of continued need by residents of that same level of care is then carried out at regular intervals. Thus, all Medicare skilled nursing facility patients must be recertified by the facility's medical director whose claims are then reviewed by the regional Medicare fiscal intermediary. Medicaid patients are generally recertified by state surveyors at regular intervals. Finally, a similar process is followed in home care agencies for Medicare and Medicaid patients. All Medicare-reimbursed patients must be certified by a physician at the point of referral for care as being homebound and requiring specific skilled care treatments. Continued need for this level of care is then reviewed every 60 days, recertified by a physician if appropriate, and reviewed by the regional fiscal intermediary who is empowered to retroactively deny visit charges if the specific type of care or length or volume of service appears unwarranted.

Medicaid procedures are even more problematic for home care agencies since many states require agencies to seek prior approval for care before initiating service or treatments. Many agencies charge that the approval mechanisms, especially those used for Medicaid reimbursement, are so cumbersome and time consuming that it is simpler to completely forego participation in the program. While participation is voluntary and programs have the right to make this type of choice, selective participation in Medicaid creates severe hardships for low-income patients' access to timely, convenient sources of high quality care.

To summarize, a great deal of work remains to be done in developing and testing standardized, reliable, and valid indicators of quality long-term care. The past and current state of the art of measurement has been characterized by the fragmentation of responsibility among different levels and offices of government, leading to inefficiencies, costliness, and ineffectiveness of mechanisms used. The methods used to date have also overly relied on structure and process measures that bear little demonstrable relationship to one another let alone to outcomes of care. Finally, while some important work on the development of quality measures in long-term care facilities has been undertaken, the state of the art of measurement of quality in community-based services is considerably more primitive and cited by many as a major concern given the rapid growth rate of this mode of care.

What Can We Do Better?

While the track record for quality measurement and enforcement in long-term care has not been stellar, we are beginning to see some signs of progress. It is important to understand the relative newness of attempts to define attributes of quality care for the chronically ill. As mentioned in the introduction to this chapter, long-term care presents unique challenges with respect to defining and measuring quality. Since the typical long-term care user has multiple chronic conditions and may require care over an extended period in a restricted environment, it is very important that quality measures address this complexity. Thus, multidimensional, comprehensive ways of measuring quality need to be developed, with the main focus of measurement being patient care and outcomes. While many critics of current mechanisms have been arguing along these lines for some time, a landmark court case has lent new urgency to their case.

Smith v. *Heckler* is a case that has been under review in the courts for several years. The case began as a class action suit against the State of Colorado on behalf of Medicaid nursing home residents. In its defense, the State of Colorado pled that it was using federally sponsored, facility-oriented quality standards, which, if faulty, should be the responsibility of the U.S. Department of Health and Human Services (DHHS). Although the state lost its initial case, a subsequent appeal overturned the district court ruling and required DHHS to revamp its nursing home review and enforcement procedures to ensure more than paper compliance with quality objectives.[15] Plaintiffs in the case argued that less than 6 percent of the more than 500 items on the inspection survey were related to patient care or required the observation of patients by surveyors. The appeals court apparently agreed with this charge and ordered the secretary of DHHS to adopt a patient-oriented enforcement system. As a result, HCFA has recently issued guidelines for the implementation of a new Patient Care and Services (PaCS) survey process for nursing homes.

PaCS was developed by a team of researchers from Brown University who piloted the new system in three states prior to its implementation nationwide. The major goal of the PaCS approach is to make the survey process more client centered and more consistent across surveyors. Thus, for the first time, all surveyors in all states will be using the same forms and checklists during the survey and are mandated to interview a 10 percent sample of residents in each facility. The sample of residents is to be chosen after the surveyor has first walked through the facility and formed some judgment about which patients and what kinds of problems suggest potential areas for inquiry. Although the PaCS system represents an advance over the previous "paper-only" approach to surveys, the authors of the new system are the first to point out that it still falls far short of the ultimate goal of quality assurance because normed outcomes of care are still lacking.[16] Two current inspection processes used by New York and Illinois indicate what new quality-assurance methods based on outcomes and/ or using incentive payments may resemble in the future.

The Sentinel Health Event. The Sentinel Health Event (SHE) procedure for monitoring quality assurance in nursing homes has been in place in the state of New York for several years. According to its originator, Donald Schneider, this approach has several advantages. First, the review process entails determining whether any one of 11 sentinel health events that represent undesirable outcomes has occurred in a given facility.[17] Reasoning that the fundamental goal of a regulatory system is the exclusion of unacceptable care, Schneider argues that the use of the SHE process promotes efficient and effective compliance. The process is implemented as follows. All Medicaid-certified long-term care facilities are reviewed annually to determine whether any of the 11 adverse outcomes have occurred to any resident of the facility. The proportion of residents found to experience SHEs in each facility are then compared to statewide norms. If the norms have been exceeded, the review process is carried to a second stage, which entails a review of the process of care which led to the poor outcome. The purpose of this review is to determine whether the event was caused by poor care or whether it was due to some other influence beyond the control of the facility (for example, a new admission arriving at a facility with a preexisting condition). Using decubitus ulcers as an example, stage II asks whether the problem was identified by the facility and whether efforts were taken to ameliorate, treat, or prevent recurrence of the problem. If the "no" responses to the above questions exceed the number found in state norms, the surveyor concludes that the quality of care provided was poor.

According to Schneider, most nursing home administrators in New York approve of the SHE approach and view it as more relevant, equitable, and efficient than the previous state inspection methods. The SHE procedure is currently being studied by an independent evaluator with funding from HCFA, and findings from this study are due shortly. The SHE methodology is important. It advances the state of the art of monitoring quality insofar as it improves the efficiency of the review process and rationalizes it by employing normative standards of care. However, it is regarded by some analysts as a limited approach to quality enforcement because it waits until an adverse outcome has occurred and then uses sanctions against poor quality providers either to exclude them from providing care or to ensure enhanced future compliance with normative standards of care. Many have argued that the use of sanctions as a method of quality enforcement is limited and fraught with problems in the field of long-term care.

To be effective, sanctions must possess gradations of severity (Figure 7–6). Originally, providers were punished by being excluded from participation in Medicare and Medicaid. However, exclusion is not as simple a measure as it may first appear to be. As a strategy of enforcement, it is predicated on the assumption that the available bed supply is sufficiently large to allow transfer of patients on short notice from decertified to certified facilities. This is not always the case in all areas of the country. As a result, several states have been experimenting with a variety of sanctions that vary from minor fines to appointment of a receiver for a given facility to criminal prosecution of the board of trustees of facilities where poor care has resulted in preventable resident mortality. Although most persons would agree that poor quality providers should be driven from participation or punished for bodily

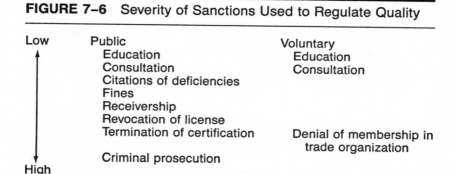

FIGURE 7–6 Severity of Sanctions Used to Regulate Quality

Low	Public	Voluntary
	Education	Education
	Consultation	Consultation
	Citations of deficiencies	
	Fines	
	Receivership	
	Revocation of license	
	Termination of certification	Denial of membership in trade organization
High	Criminal prosecution	

harm to patients, others argue that the imposition of fines serves only to diminish the available facility or program revenues that could be used to enhance patient care. Thus, many argue that rewards or incentives should be given to facilities that provide good care or improve their performance significantly. Illinois is one of many states that is currently experimenting with this alternative incentive-payment approach to ensuring high quality care.

The QUIP Approach. The Illinois Quality Incentive Program (QUIP) was initiated in 1985 as a way to increase the quality of nursing home care for Medicaid patients. The full-fledged program is anticipated to require a staff of approximately 110 nurse case managers statewide, for a ratio of one case manager to approximately 440 residents or an average of 4 to 5 facilities per manager.[18] Under QUIP, the nurses will grade nursing homes on the following five dimensions: (1) facility structural design, (2) involvement of residents in activities, (3) level of integration between the facility and its surrounding community, (4) resident satisfaction with care, and (5) patient care management.

QUIP will award up to $2 per patient day to nursing homes that meet the highest standards of care according to a formula that weighs the five dimensions of quality differently. Under its current formulation, QUIP designates 50 percent of the total $2 award to high quality patient care management with the remaining 50 percent to be divided equally among the other four quality criteria. Thus, the reimbursement formula clearly prioritizes good patient care while simultaneously rewarding other quality of life dimensions as well, albeit at a lower rate. It is estimated that the $2 per patient day bonus for good quality care could net nursing homes as much as $9 million in bonuses in 1985 and $19 million in 1986. This translates to $66,000 in additional revenues for a 100-bed nursing home in 1986.

It is unclear at this early stage of the demonstration whether an incentive of this magnitude will be sufficient to change provider behavior, but the Illinois experience will be an interesting one to watch since QUIP involves several important issues. The instrument used by the case managers is quite subjective, and its measurement properties (reliability and validity) are unknown. Provider responsiveness to the incentive may be nonexistent or variable depending upon the providers' view of the differential costs involved in complying with specific standards. It will be quite interesting to observe their response to the program over time. On balance, it appears that the QUIP approach is promising. This attempt to quantify processes of good patient management and quality-of-life attributes is important, and the QUIP initiative, if carefully evaluated and refined, has the potential to significantly further the state of the art of quality assessment.

Other Nonregulatory Approaches

The foregoing discussion described actions that are being taken, mainly by the states, to enforce and regulate standards of quality. Regulation is not the only route available, however, and several other developments have occurred in the long-term care field in recent years that have important implications for the quality of patient care.

The Role of Research and Teaching. Many analysts working in the area of long-term care have decried the isolation of the nursing home for quite some time. There are some important developments afoot that indicate this isolation may be ending. Both the National Institute on Aging (NIA) and the Robert Wood Johnson Foundation (the nation's largest health-related foundation) have mounted teaching nursing home programs in recent years. The NIA's approach is closely modeled on the teaching hospital and emphasizes affiliations between medical schools and nursing homes that will further basic science research as an aid to our understanding of the physiological and biological processes of aging and chronic disease. The emphasis in this model weighs heavily on the side of biomedical research, consistent with the institute's home in the National Institutes of Health. The teaching nursing home program of the Robert Wood Johnson Foundation differs from the NIA model in fostering relationships between schools of nursing and specific community nursing homes. Reasoning that the bulk of care in nursing homes is provided by nursing staff, the thrust of the program is the development of good nursing care protocols, management, and training and in-service education programs for staff. In addition to the efforts of these organizations to upgrade the standards of care in nursing homes, at least two of the largest proprietary nursing home chains, Beverly and Hillhaven, have developed their own foundations as subsidiary corporations that have the goal of stimulating research and development in long-term care. These are unmistakable signs that the institutional providers are beginning to come of age as mature providers, with research and development beginning to be viewed as major activities. Unfortunately, other actors in the long-term care field, specifically the home care and adult day care providers, are not quite as far along, although approximately two teaching or university-affiliated home care programs are operating at present.

Some might voice concern that the development of a teaching or research and development function might lead to an overly expensive, technology-driven industry that will replicate our nation's experience with acute care hospitals. However, the record of the teaching hospital is also indisputably linked with the high quality of acute care that is taken for granted in American hospitals today. In this light, the development of a research and teaching capacity among long-term care providers can be expected to do much to improve standards of care in the industry.

Staffing. Earlier in the chapter, we discussed the retention of trained aides as a method of promoting continuity of care for long-stay patients and as a strategy for cost containment. Two recently developed strategies for staff retention deserve mention. First, in an article amazingly titled "How I Made Miller's Manors Merrier," Wally Miller, who owns or operates 21 long-term care facilities with 2,386 skilled nursing (SNF) and intermediate care (ICF) beds in Indiana, describes an approach that he developed to set uniform standards across all facilities.[19] First, a comprehensive formal education program was developed for all hourly employees, and second, the intensity of licensed nurse input (RNs and LPNs) was increased. As a result of these reforms, all facilities were subsequently put on a 24-month versus 12-month certification cycle and their status was upgraded by the Indiana Board of Health. Most significant, however, was the drop in turnover rate for aides. In 1978, the rate was 80 percent; by 1982, after initiating this new approach, turnover dropped to 24 percent.

As part of the first initiative (the education strategy), four formal education courses were phased in during 1978 and 1979. The first 40-hour course trained community residents as potential aides. Graduates of this course were hired and encouraged to take a second 30-hour course of geriatric care. Finally, in order to advance along a career ladder, graduates of the second course were encouraged to complete a 60-hour course on medicine followed by the fourth and final step, a 35-hour supervision course. Simultaneously, all facilities increased the intensity of licensed nurse staffing by hiring additional RNs and LPNs. To fund this upgrading of staff, aide staffing levels were reduced, i.e., less well-trained aides were phased out. The target for the increased intensity of licensed nursing care was uniform across all facilities and consisted of one hour of licensed nurse staffing per patient day in SNF facilities and one-half hour per patient day in ICFs.

To evaluate the impact of these quality-enhancement strategies on cost and productivity levels, these outcomes were evaluated for a subsample of eight facilities with records dating back to the year preceding the quality interventions. This analysis revealed that the licensed nurse strategy of staffing fell somewhat short of its goals by 1983 but had increased licensed nurse staffing in SNFs by 7.7 percent and in ICFs by 23 percent. Evaluation of the education intervention revealed substantial education costs and hours in the first year of effort, but these declined as turnover rates dropped and fewer new, untrained aides were hired. The administrative staff concluded that the company succeeded in achieving a productivity improvement of close to 10 percent across all facilities over the seven-year period. Finally, an analysis of total variable costs per year from 1977 to 1983 by level of care was performed. It revealed that both SNF and ICF costs increased by about 5 percent. Much of this increase was attributed to an incentive payment scheme utilized during the same period that rewarded employees in facilities with a low total staffing pattern by increasing their raises by 50 percent. Finally an analysis of total facility staffing by level of care over time showed a reduction of 9 percent in SNFs and 8 percent in ICFs. As a follow-up to this effort, a wage reduction program is now being implemented; this involves continuing the past policy of wage increases for existing employees but reducing the wages for new employees in an attempt to overlay an experience curve on the company's hourly wage structure. With this three-pronged strategic approach, the company is confident that total facility staffing, particularly in SNFs, can be further reduced.

Finally, one other more direct and radical approach to improved retention of staff deserves mention. Charles Greenblatt has recently described an employee profit sharing plan that has been implemented by Residence Nursing Homes, a group of five for-profit nursing homes in upstate New York.[20] Although the Residence Nursing Homes as a group experience low staff turnover rates, some facilities were beginning to experience increased turnover in the late 70s as inflation increased. Administrators were concerned about staff retention but felt across-the-board salary increases were not possible. As a result, they systematically examined other options to enhance employee benefits and finally hit upon a profit sharing strategy as being most direct and least costly to implement. This plan was implemented in the fall of 1981 and consists of the awarding of points to both full-time and part-time employees on the basis of (1) numbers of complete calendar years spent in the company's employment (a reward for long stayers) and (2) number of dollars earned during each year of the plan's operation (one point is given for each $100 earned, a reward for low absenteeism during the year). Each employee thus receives a specific, individualized number of points based on performance. In March of each year, each home's net profit is calculated at which time the board designates the percent of profit which can be distributed back to employees as their profit share. The dollar amount of the profit share per facility is divided by the number of points earned by all employees in the facility and then multiplied by each employee's point total to determine the level of individual awards. Employees can choose to receive their share in a paycheck (with appropriate payroll deductions) or have the gross amount placed in an individual retirement account set up for them.

The limited experience with the plan indicates that management is happy with it because level of benefits are keyed to profit level and not fixed, regardless of facility performance. Additionally, wasteful employee behavior can be impacted since employees can see that these practices are not in their self-interest under profit sharing. One problem of the system is the fact that as staff turnover decreases, staff wages will increase over time, thus requiring larger facility profits as more points are earned across greater numbers of employees. However, management feels that since retraining of new staff will be reduced, facilities will become more profitable over time. A survey of employees found that 90 percent of employees who responded approved of the plan. With 70 percent of beds operated by for-profit owners in the United States at present, a scheme like this seems to have a great deal of potential for successful replication.

Increased Networking and Community Linkages. Other attempts are also being made to end the isolation of the long-term care provider. Nursing homes themselves are becoming aware of the need to improve public relations and involve community organizations in their facilities. Articles in the trade journals now exhort providers to reach out to volunteer groups and Junior Chambers of Commerce to get their side of the story told and enhance their community image. More astute providers are beginning to recognize these activities as good marketing and development techniques.

Several other techniques also hold promise for the development of improved standards of care. The diversification of health care providers as a group into more lines of business, either through ownership, contracting, or networking arrangements, is breaking down barriers between providers and providing more occasions for dialogue among them. Some acute care hospitals, as part of their new agreements with nursing homes, are beginning to assign attending and resident medical staff and nurse practitioners to homes with which they have referral arrangements. These arrangements provide enhanced continuity of care for the hospital's patients, a continuing relationship with the patient, and a greater likelihood that the patient will return to the referring hospital in the future. They also have the important potential to increase standards of care in the long-term care facility overall.

In an earlier section of this chapter, the problem of medical direction in nursing homes and home care agencies was raised. In this regard, one other opportunity for improvement lies in the so-called "doctor surplus." Reports indicate that the number of physicians in the United States increased by 2.5 percent annually from 1970 to 1985.[21] As the pool of physicians grew during 1976–1980, Medicare charges for internist follow-up visits increased by 2.7 percent annually, a figure that is lower than increases in charges for other nonmedical services during the same time period.[22] Finally, total patient visits appear to have peaked in 1982 and have declined since, with a 5 percent reduction occurring between 1983 and 1984.[23] These figures indicate that conditions of medical practice are becoming more competitive. This increased competition, together with continued exposure of medical students to nursing home settings and populations early in their training and the heightened attractiveness of the nursing home as a site for research and education, could do much to draw young physicians into practice and specialization in long-term care.

The development of more options in long-term care services and of more levels of care also has significant potential to reduce the problem of inappropriate placement of patients at either a more or less-skilled level than required. Moreover, the development of these new options also has important implications for quality. As we have already noted, quality standards in home care can stand significant improvement and quality standards in Adult Day Care are virtually nonexistent. The Joint Commission on Accreditation of Hospitals has become involved in quality assurance of Medicare-certified hospices, but many foster, domiciliary, group home, and continuing care retirement community options receive very little scrutiny from outside agencies on a regular basis.

The Role of Informed Consumers

Residents. Finally, in the 80s, we have begun to pay attention to the viewpoint of patients themselves, a very radical departure from approaches in the past. As the earlier discussion of current methods of regulating quality demonstrates, one tends to measure things that are relatively easy to measure, i.e., number of fire extinguishers per square foot and number of full-time equivalent staff by type, all in the name of ensuring safe, high quality patient care. Some structure and process measures are important and should be maintained. We want facilities to be safe and staff to be well trained and available in sufficient numbers. The current mechanisms have erred, however, in focusing exclusively on these types of measures. As mentioned earlier, under pressure from Congress, HCFA has funded a special Committee of the Institute of Medicine to develop recommendations to reform the regulation of quality on long-term care. Anxious that this committee not repeat mistakes of the past and continue to focus on paper surveys, the National Citizens' Coalition for Nursing Home Reform in 1981 issued a "Consumer Statement of Principles for the Nursing Home Regulatory System," which called for the "radical" notion of refocusing surveys to a consumer orientation. Through local ombudsman groups affiliated with its local branches, the coalition organized and conducted group discussions with 455 residents of 107 nursing homes in 15 cities in the fall and winter of 1984.[24]

During the course of 45 discussion sessions, nursing home residents repeatedly ranked staff as the most important component of quality care. According to residents themselves, nursing homes which provide high quality care use carefully selected, qualified nurses and sufficient numbers of well-trained and supervised aides. Residents also identified comfortable and sufficient living space, privacy, safety, security, good lighting, and visible call lights as basic environmental attributes of high quality homes, with quietness, cleanliness, and good temperature controls also mentioned.

Not surprisingly, residents ranked food and meal service as key quality concerns, stressing the importance of variety and choice of foods, proper food preparation, pleasant service, availability of evening snacks, and resident participation in meal planning as key attributes. Residents also valued homes which offered a broad range of activities and special transportation to community events. With respect to medical care, the prompt response of physicians and the need to see physicians privately were mentioned. Finally, with respect to governance, residents stressed the need for participation in decision making through resident councils and the need for laws and regulations that promote adherence to residents' rights.

Interestingly, recent research by Stephen Ullmann suggests that high quality staff, which residents ranked first in importance, can be achieved by facilities with relatively little additional cost. Comparing cost per resident day for New York nursing homes judged to provide different degrees of quality care, Ullmann found that a high-quality physical plant adds $11 per resident day to costs compared to only $1.67 more per resident day for high-quality nursing care.[25]

This pivotal effort of the National Citizens Coalition to involve consumers directly in setting the agenda and defining some of the parameters for ensuring quality is very important. If repeated at periodic intervals, this type of process could significantly improve the relevance of regulatory mechanisms to consumer groups.

Autonomy. This discussion of consumer involvement logically leads to another issue, that of autonomy of long-term care patients, which includes issues of "do not resuscitate," "do not hospitalize," and "do not treat orders." The ethical issues inherent in treating chronically ill patients with severe mental, behavioral, or physical deficits are numerous and complex. Many cases have been described in the press of decisions to tube feed or not tube feed comatose patients. Time and space do not permit exploration of these issues in this chapter in any way which would do them justice since these issues easily warrant a separate volume. However, it is worth pointing out the value of current discussions, reports, and debates as an indication of how far we have come on this issue. Patients with these conditions have been treated in nursing homes for years; now the issues are beginning to surface as subjects of public discussion and debate. Nursing homes are being encouraged to develop in-house ethics committees that can operate as one facet of their quality-assurance process. Administrators and medical directors are being advised to set up mechanisms such as living wills for residents at entry to a facility if possible so that residents' and family members' preferences are a matter of record for future reference.[26] These developments can only serve to increase patient autonomy in the future.

Consumer Groups. Finally, as the summary of the National Citizens' Coalition survey attests, local and national consumer groups can do a great deal to focus attention on quality concerns and upgrade quality of long-term care services. The key ingredient is the involvement of outsiders in caregiving programs from the board level on down in agency or facility activities.

A critical issue involves educating people in the community regarding the importance of long-term care services. Volunteer participation on hospital boards, in auxiliaries, and in patient care activities is a time-honored practice. As hospitals downsize and close and as working-age persons realize the need for quality long-term care services as a result of their personal experiences in trying to arrange care for family members, it seems there is great potential for increased volunteer involvement in long-term care.

To cite a local example, the Chicago League of Women Voters is collaborating with the Five Hospital Program (a long-term home care program) to train volunteers to conduct music therapy for homebound elderly, many of whom live alone in very deprived environments. The therapy will be conducted as part of each client's plan of care, will be individualized, and will relate to the clinicians' therapeutic goals for each client. The Five Hospital Program has run a successful volunteer program for several years with available services including food shopping, letter writing, legal services, and hairdressing; such services would be prohibitively expensive to provide with clinical staff but greatly enrich the clients' quality of life.

All of the measures discussed above have the merit of involving more actors in quality assurance under the theory that multiple, independent observations of long-term care clients and their circumstances and processes of care will serve to enhance quality. As mentioned earlier in this chapter, the most pressing quality issue concerns those clients or patients with psychiatric, behavioral, or communication deficits who have no family spokesperson and rely on public funding for care. The increasing use of local ombudsmen programs, local area offices on aging watchdog committees, and public guardianship programs offer some potential solutions to this problem, but the availability of these mechanisms varies enormously from one location to another. A great deal of work needs to be done in identifying at-risk individuals and enrolling them in some organized, systematic type of advocacy or case management program.

Finally, one other method which has considerable merit to upgrade quality across the board is the publication of consumer guides to long-term care programs or facilities. Publicly available information about fees, services, staff levels, inspection of care citations, and the number of confirmed cases of abuse and neglect could be assembled by such neutral groups as United Way, interdenominational church committees, or the League of Women Voters or developed as a community service by local magazines or newspapers. Dissemination of this type of information could increase the competition among providers to be perceived as four-star programs and do much to enhance quality of long-term care.

As the foregoing attests, the quality of long-term care

FIGURE 7–7   A Multifaceted Approach to Quality

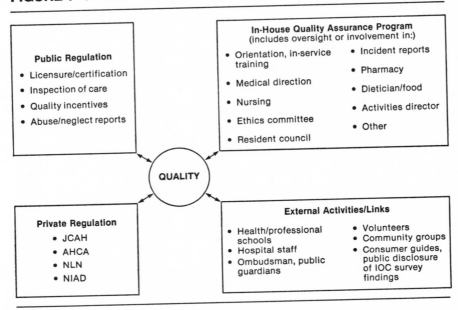

---

services is difficult to define, measure, regulate, enforce, and assure. However, important progress is being made on this front. Figure 7–7 summarizes the methods discussed and demonstrates that the bottom line of quality enhancement is a multidimensional approach. No single attempt to regulate quality will suffice, and the more independent observations of this attribute made, the better patient care will become. However, quality of care is not achieved in a vacuum and good staffing and standards cost money. Can we afford a high quality long-term care system (comprehensively defined) in the United States and can we achieve high quality standards if 50 percent of the cost is supplied by public funds? We turn to these important considerations next.

NOTES

1. Kathleen A. Hughes, "Nursing 'Homes'," Letter to the Editor, *The New York Times,* July 5, 1983.

2. "Abuse Reports Burgeon in New York Facilities," *Contemporary Long-Term Care,* April 1985, p. 16.

3. Joan F. van Nostrand, "The National Nursing Home Survey: 1979 Summary for the United States," *Series 13/43,* National Center for Health Statistics, July 1979, p. 31.

4. "Task Force Report of the American Psychiatric Association," 1981 White House Conference on Aging, 1981.

5. U.S. GAO, "Information Requirements for Evaluating the Impacts of Medicare Prospective Payment on Post-Hospital Long-Term Care Services," Report to Senator John Heinz, Chairman, Special Committee on Aging, February 21, 1985.

6. Al Sirrocco, "Employees in Nursing Homes in the United States: 1979 National Nursing Home Survey," *Vital and Health Statistics,* Series 14, no. 25, 1981, p. 4.

U.S. House of Representatives, "Building a Long-Term Care Policy: Home Care Data and Implications," Select Committee on Aging, Pub. no. 98–484, (Washington, D.C.: Government Printing Office, 1985), p. 25.

7. Sirrocco, "Employees in Nursing Homes."

8. Howard M. Waxman, Erwin A. Carner, and Gale Berkenstuck, "Job Turnover and Job Satisfaction Among Nursing Home Aides," *The Gerontologist,* 24:5, 1984, p. 503.

9. Edmund Ricci and Edward Tessaro, "Medical Direction in Skilled Nursing Facilities," *Research Summary Series,* NCHSR, August 1979, p. 27.

10. Susan L. Hughes, David Cordray, and V. Alan Spiker, "Evaluation of a Long-Term Home Care Program," *Medical Care,* May 1984.

James G. Zimmer, Annemarie Groth-Juncker, and Jane McCusker, "A Randomized Controlled Study of a Home Health Care Team," *American Journal of Public Health,* 75:2, February 1985.

11. Avedis Donabedian, "Evaluating the Process of Medical Care," *Milbank Memorial Fund Quarterly,* 44, July 1966, pp. 166–206.

12. Bettina D. Kurowski and Peter W. Shaughnessy, "The Measurement and Assurance of Quality," in *Long Term Care,* ed. Vogel and Palmer, U.S. DHHS Pub. no. 82–600609.

13. Susan L. Hughes, "Home Health Monitoring: Ensuring Quality in Home Care Services," *Hospitals,* November 1, 1982, pp. 74–80.

14. "JCAH Accreditation for Long-Term Care Facilities: Consider the Benefits," Joint Commission on Accreditation of Hospitals promotional brochure, 1983.

15. Joel M. Hamme, "The Law and Long-Term Care," *Contemporary Administrator for Long-Term Care,* February 1985, pp. 20 and 21.

16. William D. Spector and Margaret L. Drugovich, "PaCS, A Federal Survey Process: What is the Intervention," paper presented at the Annual Meeting of the American Public Health Association, Washington, D.C., November 19, 1985.

17. Donald Schneider, "Nursing Home Quality Assurance in a Changing Regulatory Environment," in *Long Term Care Management,* SRI, Inc., forthcoming.

18. Illinois Department of Public Aid, "New Nurses Ensure Quality Care," *Family,* vol. 2/2 (Spring 1985).

19. Wally Miller, "How I Made Miller's Manors Merrier," *Contemporary Administrator for Long-Term Care,* October 1984.

20. Charles Greenblatt, "Profit Sharing in the Long-Term Care Industry: A Cure for Many Ills," paper presented at the Gerontological Society of America Annual Meeting, San Diego, 1984.

21. U.S., DHHS, *Health United States, 1982,* Pub. no. (PHS) 83–1232, (Hyattsville, Md.: National Center for Health Statistics), p. 113.

22. U.S. Senate Special Committee on Aging, *Medicare: Paying the Physician—History, Issues and Options,* March 1984, p. 24.

23. *SMS Report,* AMA: Center for Health Policy Research, 3:7, October 1984.

24. Elma L. Holder, "Redirecting the Focus from Paper to People," *Contemporary Long-Term Care,* April 1985, p. 78.

25. Steven G. Ullmann, "The Impact of Quality on Cost in the Provision of Long-Term Care," *Inquiry,* 22, 1985, pp. 300–301.

26. Richard W. Besdine, "Decisions to Withhold Treatment from Nursing Home Residents," *Journal of the American Geriatrics Society,* 31:10, October 1983, pp. 602–606.

CHAPTER EIGHT

Medicaid Reforms:
Maximizing Return from the
Public Long-Term Care Dollar

As a result of the various experiments and demonstrations conducted by the states in attempting to constrain increases in Medicaid costs, we have learned the following important lessons with respect to payment for long-term care:

- Prospective payment is associated with a lower rate of increase in reimbursement rates than retrospective payment.

- Case-mix reimbursement can encourage facilities to accept heavy-care patients but must be accompanied by vigorous enforcement of quality-assurance standards.

- Discharge of nursing home residents is possible and should be encouraged but may only apply to a relatively small subset of patients for whom the process must begin early in the nursing home stay.

- Preadmission screening can reduce or delay nursing home admissions by about 15 percent, but can only succeed if community-based services are available for disapproved applicants.

- Community-based care Section 2176 waivers are popular but have not yet been demonstrated to be cost effective. We also need to experiment with different payment mechanisms for community care.

- We need to learn more about the course of long-term care use for various patient subgroups. For example, we need to know which patients have the greatest potential for improvement and discharge, which can be predicted to have long but reasonably stable stays with what type of service, and which are at greatest risk for rapid decline.

The spectre of increased demand for long-term care accompanied by runaway costs has haunted federal and state policymakers for years and has resulted in a dearth of many meaningful new policy initiatives in this field. However, a decade of experimentation with different payment methods for long-term care has yielded significant insights into how the unmanageable can be managed. Virtually everyone agrees that if more disabled individuals will be surviving longer and requiring more long-term care services in the future, more efficient ways of paying the long-term care bill must be found.

Medicaid, the principal source of public funding for long-term care, was initiated as an uncapped, retrospectively reimbursed payment system. We have learned a great deal about reimbursing for health care since the heydays of the Great Society, and this knowledge can significantly inform our future long-term care reimbursement policies. In this chapter, we review some of the Medicaid reforms that have been instituted recently, with emphasis on the more important reimbursement experiments that have been conducted and their implications for the future. Finally, Chapter 9 addresses how the total funding pool for long-term care can be enlarged and the utilization of long-term care services better managed.

As Chapter 3 demonstrated, long-term care costs constitute approximately 44 percent of Medicaid expenditures and are the most rapidly rising component of state budgets. Aggressive state action during the 1981–82 recession reduced the rate of growth in Medicaid expenditures. While the costs of Medicare went up by 34.5 percent from fiscal year 1981 to fiscal year 1983, total federal and state Medicaid expenditure increases were only 17 percent. According to Richard Curtis and Lawrence Bartlett of the National Governors' Association, from 1981 to 1983 state general fund revenues plus reserves increased by only 6 percent, but the state share of Medicaid costs went up by 21 percent.[1] To meet the challenge of increased demand for long-term care with steady or declining resources, states embarked on a number of different experiments to curtail the cost of care. Interestingly, most states did not choose the strategy of cutting back on eligibility. However, a variety of other efforts at cost control have been undertaken. These efforts assume particular importance in view of the likely capping of federal Medicaid funds in the near future, and each is reviewed below.

Closing Loopholes

One of the easier ways of improving the efficiency of Medicaid long-term care payments involved eliminating some of the abuses that were tolerated in the program during its earlier years. According to Curtis and Bartlett, a review of state policy changes undertaken by the National Governors' Association revealed that one third of the 3,400 Medicaid policy changes initiated by the states from 1978 to 1983 involved the denial of Medicaid eligibility to individuals who had recently transferred assets to others at less than full market value. This change in policy makes it more difficult for long-term care users to transfer savings and real estate to relatives and adult children intact in order to meet Medicaid spend-down levels. The elimination of this group thus targets eligibility more accurately to the truly indigent. Changes in mechanisms for calculating levels of depreciation and tax deductible interest allowed on nursing home facilities have also had the effect of curtailing the growth in capital costs associated with long-term care. These changes, however, represent fine tuning rather than radical changes in Medicaid reimbursement policies.

Increased Control of Supply

A far more radical approach than the loophole strategy is the attempt to control growth in costs by regulating the supply of long-term care providers through disapproval of certificate of need (CON) applications. As mentioned earlier, many states adopted this strategy during the late 70s and early 80s as a way to reduce Medicaid outlays. State-imposed moratoria on applications for new nursing home beds peaked during the height of the recent recession. However, even now, despite the fact that states are enjoying increased revenues, 10 states are still enforcing them.[2] While controlling bed supply may work as a short-term strategy, it is not clear that this is a useful long-term strategy. Given the increased number of subacute, heavy-care hospital discharges resulting from hospital prospective payment and the demographic changes described earlier that will increase demand, it seems that the supply of nursing home beds must grow. Although increased use of community-based care can accommodate some of the increase in demand for long-term care, it seems that if the needs of the chronically ill are to be adequately met in the future, both types of care must grow. Although some rather convincing evidence exists that suggests that high occupancy rates are associated with lower costs of care, reports also indicate that a tight bed supply makes enforcement of quality standards difficult.[3] Inspectors are reluctant to close inadequate facilities if no other source of care is available. Thus, if we continue on our current course of relying on public, means-tested funding as a major long-term care financing mechanism, prospects for both increased competition and increased quality of care appear slim.

It is worth noting that community-based care is also affected by state CON criteria. Specifically, as Figure 8–1 demonstrates, 37 (76 percent) of the states have some type of CON review for home care agencies. The majority (56 percent) require CON approval for any new type of home care agency, with some states restricting the criteria to specific types of programs like nursing home, hospital-based, or proprietary agencies. It would appear from these figures that, having been "burned" by hospital and nursing home costs, most states are exercising control over the home care supply.

Whether this type of control is actually warranted is somewhat questionable. Hospitals and nursing homes represent fixed assets. If overbuilt, there is an inherent tendency to fill

---

FIGURE 8–1   States Requiring Certificate of
Need (CON) for Home Care
Agencies by Type

---

*States Requiring
CON—All Types
of HCA (N = 27)*

Alabama
Arkansas
Delaware
District of Columbia
Florida
Georgia
Hawaii
Kentucky
Maine
Maryland
Mississippi
Montana
Nebraska
Nevada
New Jersey
New York
North Carolina
North Dakota
Puerto Rico
Rhode Island
South Carolina
South Dakota
Tennessee
Utah
Vermont
Washington
Wisconsin

*States Requiring CON—
Specific HCA Types*

Institution-based HCA (N = 7)
  Alaska
  Connecticut
  Iowa
  Massachusetts
  Michigan
  Ohio
  Oklahoma

Hospital-based HCA (N = 2)
  Indiana
  Pennsylvania

Proprietary-based HCA (N = 1)
  New Hampshire

SOURCE: William Cabin, National Association for Home
Care, June 1985.

---

them as long as a funding source can be found. The same
imperative does not really exist in home care agencies which
require very little upfront capitalization and can fold up
quietly if insufficient demand exists. Home care staff are also
guests in clients' homes and do not exercise the same control
over client length of stay that institutional facilities do. Thus,
it is possible that the rigid application of CON to home care
could have the perverse effect of impeding access, restricting

supply, and keeping patients in higher cost loci of care longer than a truly competitive approach to the development of home care services that could rely on market forces to control the entry and exit of providers.

Control over Demand

As Chapter 7 demonstrated, the major type of utilization review which occurs in long-term care takes place after admission to a facility. Only physician certification of need for care is required for Medicaid-eligible individuals prior to admission. Over the last decade, a growing body of experience and literature has suggested that the use of a medical screen alone is insufficient for accurate placement decisions. Medical reviews are usually diagnosis and treatment specific and do not consistently address applicants' mental status, degree of social supports, or available community services. Once an individual is admitted to a nursing home and has spent down resources to the point of Medicaid eligibility, it is almost impossible to arrange a discharge back to the community because leases for housing have lapsed and Medicaid patients have no disposable income with which to arrange new housing. As a result of these problems, much more attention is being paid to prevention of the initial admission, with at least half of the states now requiring some form of preadmission screening or prior authorization of Medicaid nursing home admissions. Many states also require preauthorization for Medicaid-reimbursed home care. However, few of these preadmission screening programs have been evaluated carefully.

Two exceptions to this general rule are the Virginia and Massachusetts preadmission screening programs. These are of note not only because they have been evaluated but also because they represent statewide as opposed to county-specific demonstrations.

The Virginia screening program, initiated in 1977, utilized multidisciplinary teams consisting of a public health nurse and physician and a welfare department social worker to screen all persons applying to nursing homes from the community. Rather than focusing on Medicaid recipients only, the Virginia program also applied to non-Medicaid applicants

TABLE 8-1 Outcomes of Virginia Preadmission Screening Program, 1978

	Number	Percent
Total persons screened	2,100	—
Denied certification	420	100.0%
Admitted to nursing home within six months	72	17.2
Approved at rescreen	31	7.4
Appeal upheld	7	1.7
Admitted from a hospital	34	8.1
Total placements avoided at six months	348	83.0
Placements avoided of total screened	348/2,100	16.6%

SOURCE: Elizabeth Bates Harkins, *Study of the Virginia Nursing Home Preadmission Screening Program, Final Report* (Richmond,Va.: Virginia Commonwealth University Center on Aging, March 31, 1982), p. 2.

who were expected to spend down to Medicaid eligible levels within 90 days of nursing home admission. The screening team evaluated applicants using a comprehensive assessment that weighed social, mental, and environmental factors as well as physical health and activities of daily living (ADL) criteria. An appeals procedure was also implemented wherein local screening committee decisions could be reviewed upon request.

By 1978, an average of 2,100 persons per year had been screened, with about 20 percent (420) uncertified for nursing home placement. Analysis of outcomes for this latter group (see Table 8–1) reveals that 31 were rescreened within 6 months, with 50 percent of rescreenings resulting in approval of nursing home placement. Only a very small number of individuals (13) appealed the initial screening decision; of these, 50 percent were certified upon appeal. Finally, a fair number of applicants who were originally denied certification (22 percent) were hospitalized within 6 months of the denial. Half of these individuals returned to their homes following the hospitalization, 14 percent died, and 36 percent were admitted to nursing homes from the hospital. Thus, an additional 17.2 percent of those originally denied admission on the screen were subsequently admitted through appeal, reapplication, or from a hospital, yielding an ultimate net of 16.6 percent deferred nursing home admissions at 6 months.[4]

To determine whether the screen was appropriately placing a more dependent target group, four different groups (each consisting of 100 subjects) were studied: (1) screened applicants who were approved for placement, (2) screened applicants who were not approved, (3) persons admitted to nursing homes who were not screened (admitted from a hospital or income too high), and (4) community-dwelling persons at risk of nursing home admission who did not apply for admission. All four groups were followed for six months to determine their relative consumption of health services and functional status outcomes.

Findings revealed that unscreened nursing home admissions were more advantaged (more were white and were better educated) than screened persons approved for placement. This was consistent with the fact that at least one third of the former group were not screened because their high income made it unlikely that they would become Medicaid eligible within three months of admission. On the other hand, community residents at risk of but not applying for nursing home care were much less likely to be white and more likely to be married than persons who applied but were not approved for placement. With respect to health status, this latter group of screened applicants who were denied certification were only half as impaired in ADL activities as those approved but were more debilitated by their illnesses than community at-risk nonapplicants. Finally, screened applicants denied certification tended to be more in need of companion and home health services than those approved and were also more likely than those approved to have those services available in their community. On the basis of these findings, it appeared that the screening teams were approving appropriate (i.e., more dependent) persons for admission. Analyses of mortality, which controlled for initial ADL functioning, revealed no differences on this outcome across the four groups, and administrative costs of the screen itself were $80 per screen. Based on the 20 percent reduction achieved in nursing home admissions, evaluators concluded that the screen yielded a net savings of $278 per screen in the first six months of operation.

Since a substantial number of the unscreened admissions consisted of persons admitted from hospitals or persons not expected to become eligible for Medicaid within 90 days, the Virginia screening program has recently been expanded to close these two loopholes. Specifically, all community *and* hospital applicants for nursing home care who are anticipated to become Medicaid eligible within *180* days of admission to nursing home care are included now in the screen.[5] Virginia Commonwealth University's Center on Aging is currently studying the impact of the expansion of criteria to this higher income group and is also following up the screening experience over a longer time period (12 versus 6 months). Results of this demonstration will be important since this is one of a few, if not the only program in the country that is controlling the nursing home admissions of persons not already Medicaid eligible. There are many questions about the equity of this process; i.e., if a person wishes to receive nursing home care and is prepared to pay for it for a number of days or months, does a government agency have the right to deny the person access to this type of care?

Reports from the Massachusetts Case Management Screening Program, which was operational in nine sites in Massachusetts in 1982 (covering approximately 35 percent of the state's population), tend to corroborate the Virginia experiences. Of 500 persons screened, 82 percent were approved for the level of care requested, 3 percent were approved for a different level, 8 percent were denied admission, 5 percent were diverted to another source of care, and 2 percent were still awaiting placement in the community.[6]

Both screening programs indicate that approximately 15 to 20 percent of nursing home admissions can be avoided. While not a large number, 15 percent can make a real difference at the margin when nursing home beds are tightly controlled. However, the screening experience to date indicates that at least five conditions must be present for screens to produce good results. As listed in Figure 8–2, these include a multidisciplinary review, an appeals process, the extension of coverage to non-Medicaid eligible persons, and the inclusion of both community and hospital applicants. Finally, the whole screening concept is based on the assumption that the fifth

---

FIGURE 8–2   Conditions under which Preadmission
Screening Works

---

1. Comprehensive multidisciplinary assessment and review
2. Appeals process built in
3. Non-Medicaid eligible persons are included
4. Both community and hospital applicants are included
5. An adequate supply of community-based services exists

---

condition, availability of community support services, is well met. As the Virginia screening program demonstrated, denied applicants are not unimpaired. They are simply comparatively less impaired than persons who have been approved. Denial for these persons may be feasible only if referral to community services is possible. The next Medicaid reform discussed directly addresses this issue.

Shifting the Locus of Care

The Section 2176 waiver authority included in the Omnibus Reconciliation Act of 1981 allowed states to experiment with a variety of home and community-based services as alternatives to costly institutional care. Under the waiver, states were allowed to broaden the array of services covered and to target specific at-risk groups in specific geographic locations.

The response of the states to this waiver, as described in Chapter 1, has been remarkable. As of April 1985, HCFA has approved 95 home and community-based services waivers in 46 states. Approximately half (50) of the requests were targeted to the aged and physically disabled, another 39 focused on the developmentally disabled, and 4 were directed to the mentally ill. An additional 17 "model waivers," predominantly serving children and restricted to no more than 50 individuals per waiver who are not otherwise income eligible for Medicaid, have also been approved. The services most frequently offered through the waiver programs are case management (66), respite care (52), and adult day health services (43).[7]

The main premise behind the Section 2176 waiver is that

the provision of services to at-risk individuals in the community can substitute for institutional care, thus resulting in no additional long-term care expenditures and potentially producing cost savings. In this respect, two issues deserve mention. First, in order to care for persons at risk of nursing home admission while still in the community, states have had to increase Medicaid income eligibility standards to the higher levels allowed for nursing home residents. Several states have also used the waiver to exclude the income of spouses or parents in determining Medicaid income eligibility. Both of these provisions introduce a considerable amount of equity into Medicaid financing of long-term care; however, these changes may also cause an increase in demand for care if a new class of individuals becomes eligible for assistance and overall inpatient bed use does not simultaneously decline. The waivers also make it possible for a new group of Medicaid-eligible patients to use physician services, drugs, and appliances in addition to the case-management and respite services described.

The Office of Management and Budget (OMB) is particularly concerned about the cost-inflating aspect of the 2176 waiver. Consequently, OMB has ordered that waivers will be authorized only if states can assure that no more persons will be served under a combined community and facility-based system than would have been cared for under institutional coverage only. In contrast, the states feel they should be allowed to use any savings derived from more efficient, cheaper community care to expand services to cover more individuals.

As a result of more strict interpretations of the waiver's cost effectiveness requirements by OMB and countervailing desires in congress to see it expand, the waiver program is experiencing "creative tension" at present, and there is some concern that existing state waivers will not be renewed. Very little evaluation of the cost effectiveness of the Section 2176 waivers has occurred. However, the waiver experience is currently being evaluated by HCFA, and it will be interesting to learn whether it has been more successful in targeting high-risk individuals than other community-based care demonstrations conducted to date.

Alternative Reimbursement Methods

In contrast to the efforts described above, which have attempted to curtail demand for institutional long-term care, a great deal of effort has also been expended during the last 10 years on curtailing the rate of increase in cost of care for those individuals already in the system. As states have been forced to pick up a larger share of the long-term care bill over the last 10 years, their interest in reducing the rate of increase in costs has grown commensurately. Section 249a of the 1972 Social Security amendments (discussed in Chapter 1) supported the principle of reasonable cost-related reimbursement for institutional long-term care but gave states considerable leeway in devising particular and unique reimbursement systems. The regulations for this amendment were not actually implemented until 1978 and have since been amended by the Omnibus Reconciliation Act of 1981 to read "reasonable and adequate to meet costs incurred by *efficiently* and *economically* operated facilities."[8] As a result of the latitude allowed by these mandates, the states have enjoyed considerable freedom to experiment with a variety of innovative reimbursement methods.

Prospective Payment. To begin with the most common change, a substantial number of states have moved from retrospective to prospective reimbursement. Under retrospective cost-based reimbursement, long-term care providers were reimbursed retroactively on the basis of the cost that they incurred in providing care during a given year. This reimbursement method was followed in acute care hospitals prior to the onset of prospective payment, with fairly disastrous impact on hospital costs. Under retrospective payment systems, providers have few, if any, incentives to economize since they are reimbursed for what they have spent. This is especially true for Medicare skilled care providers and less true for Medicaid SNF and ICF providers who, in many states, have been paid costs that are capped and that thus more closely resemble flat rates than actual costs. However, in theory, prospective payment encourages all long term-care providers to economize. Since providers know in advance what a payment will be, they can strive to keep costs under this level and will be allowed to retain any difference between cost and payment as profit.

A recent study of state shifts from retrospective to prospective payment systems was conducted by Robert Buchanan.[9] Since proponents of retrospective payment systems have argued that prospective rates could adversely affect quality if set too low, Buchanan was particularly interested in the impact of prospective rates on cost and access to care. His review of cost and utilization data collected from 49 states between 1975 and 1982 revealed that 33 states were using prospective rate-setting mechanisms for skilled care by 1982, and only 12 still used retrospective methods. States using prospective rate setting consistently had lower average Medicaid payments for skilled care, although this difference achieved statistical significance only in 1982. A majority of states (36) also reported the use of prospective rate setting by 1982 for intermediate care. Prospective payments for intermediate care were also lower as was growth in rates, which increased by 79.2 percent over the 8-year period in contrast to a 120 percent increase in payment rates for retrospective reimbursement states. Finally, states using prospective rate setting averaged a significantly greater number of skilled level patients per 1,000 elderly as well as a nonsignificant higher average of intermediate care patients per 1,000 elderly state residents. Medicaid patient days and certified beds were also higher in prospective payment states. Buchanan concluded that prospective payment reduces the rate of increase in cost of inpatient long-term care without decreasing access to care, possibly because prospective payment provides an incentive for administrators to control wage rates, which are the major determinant of costs. Finally, Buchanan recommended that prospective payment be encouraged but linked to a quality of care index; that is, set at the 60th percentile of the previous year's cost with a facility allowed to retain a percentage of the difference between its cost and that rate, based on degree of compliance or noncompliance with inspection of care quality standards, a system not too dissimilar from the Illinois QUIP program described in Chapter 7.

Buchanan's study is somewhat limited because his analysis of these data was univariate. However, a subsequent study by Harrington and Swan using somewhat more sophisticated methods yielded similar findings.[10] Studying the same time period between 1978 (the year that cost-related reimbursement was implemented) and 1982, Harrington and Swan examined the relationship of state reimbursement systems to average reimbursement rates and to changes in rates and expenditures per Medicaid recipient. The Harrington and Swan study also provides additional information with respect to more specific types of prospective reimbursement (see Table 8–2). Their first analysis revealed that states with prospective systems consistently experienced significantly lower per diem rates for both SNF and ICF care than states using retrospective methods, with the facility-class-based type of prospective payment performing best at $14 lower per diem in 1981 for SNF and $16 lower for ICF care, respectively. However, the absolute level of reimbursement rates in any state in a given year is largely a function of rates paid in previous years. Thus, what appears to be a cause-effect relationship between rates and reimbursement systems may more accurately reflect the level of preexisting rates only. To isolate further the effect of prospective payment, observed changes as a function of expected changes in rates by type of reimbursement were also analyzed. Findings revealed that prospective facility-specific payment performed best, experiencing significantly lower (10 percent, on average) expected increases in SNF rates than retrospective systems; however, no differences attributable to payment systems were detected for changes in ICF rates. Finally, analysis of expenditures per recipient by reimbursement system (overall costs versus rates only) revealed that 1981 expenditures per recipient were significantly lower for states using non-facility-specific prospective reimbursement than for states with retrospective payment systems. Further analysis of this issue, controlling for average daily reimbursement rates, revealed no relationship between prospective reimbursement and expenditures per recipient, supporting the hypothesis that prospective payment is effective because it constrains the rate of increase in daily reimbursement rates. The authors conclude, in agreement with the Buchanan study, that prospective payment may allow states to provide more

TABLE 8–2   State Medicaid Reimbursement Systems, 1982

Reimbursement System	Skilled Nursing	Intermediate Care
Retrospective	12	9
Alternative	(38)	(41)
Prospective, facility specific	25	28
Prospective class	6	5
Combination	7	8

SOURCE: Adapted from Charlene Harrington and James H. Swan, "Medicaid Nursing Home Reimbursement Policies, Rates, and Expenditures," *Health Care Financing Review,* 6:1, Fall 1984, p. 42.

days of patient care because it constrains increases in payment rates.

From Levels of Care to Case Mix.   For a substantial period of time, states reimbursed nursing homes largely on the basis of level of care provided (i.e., skilled or intermediate) with some marginal refinements added such as paying on the basis of class membership (i.e., grouping facilities according to geographic location or wage variations, bed size, or occupancy levels). Some states have also adopted ceilings for different cost centers above which charges will not be reimbursed (i.e., percentiles of cost above which payments will not be made). Almost all states use some variations of these methods in computing reimbursement rates. However, the most fundamental change that has occurred over the last 10 years has been a shift from payment on the basis of level of care per se to payments that are variously described as being client-centered or that better control for case mix. In many states, the same surveyors who perform inspection of care quality-assurance surveys also certify levels of care provided. Many have argued and a few studies have found that surveyors who are constantly faced with severe pressures from facility administrators may tend to overrate the level of care required by either certifying a level of care that is no longer required or recertifying care at a higher level.[11] The current two-level SNF and ICF system of reimbursement has also been described as being imprecise and discouraging the acceptance of heavy-care Medicaid residents by facilities. Since a facility can receive the same payment for a light-care as a heavy-care SNF patient, it has no incentive to accept the latter type of patient who, as a result, may remain in a hospital consuming administratively necessary days.[12] As a result of concern over this issue, several other types of reimbursement have been developed.

Client-Centered Reimbursement (The Illinois Point-Count Approach). Client-centered reimbursement attempts to remedy the imprecision and error associated with a two-level reimbursement system by pegging reimbursement to the actual conditions of individual nursing home residents. Illinois was one of the first states to experiment with this type of reimbursement system. The original Illinois point-count system awarded points to patients based on their level of functional incapacity and need for specific nursing procedures. The point-count score was determined by caseworkers from the Department of Public Aid until 1982. At that time, in response to complaints of providers that scoring was not consistent across surveyors and that caseworkers could not validly assess needs for nursing care, the system was revised. Time motion studies were conducted in a sample of facilities to determine the amount of nursing staff time required for 21 various nursing procedures and 7 personal care activities. On the basis of these studies, the number of points awarded to various procedures were revised and licensed RNs were trained to administer a new assessment instrument under the supervision of the Department of Public Health. Under the new system, surveyors base scores on a review of 100 percent of residents in homes with 50 or fewer residents and a review of a 50 percent sample of residents in larger facilities. Reimbursement is made on the basis of the point count and weighted by wage levels for the Health Systems Area in which the care is provided.

There are several problems associated with client-based reimbursement. First, as the above description demonstrates, the reliability of ratings by surveyors can be problematic.

Second, since residents' conditions change, costly and detailed reassessments must be made at regular intervals to insure that the facility is neither underpaid nor overpaid for a specific resident's care. Finally, the worst inherent problem of any client-centered reimbursement policy is the perverse incentive for providers to encourage more dependent conditions in patients to qualify for higher reimbursement rates, assuming that the cost of care for these patients does not exceed the rate of reimbursement.

Since the provider will only lose money if the patient's condition improves, there is no incentive to rehabilitate patients; rather, the exact reverse is true. As a result of concern over this perverse incentive for quality of care, several other experiments have been conducted that sought to retain incentives to accept heavy-care patients while simultaneously encouraging high quality care.

The San Diego Incentive-Reimbursement Experiment. Probably one of the best-known experiments to date is the San Diego experiment conducted by William Weissert and Mark Meiners at the National Center for Health Services Research in the early 80s. The objectives of the experiment were to encourage nursing homes to: (1) admit highly dependent, heavy-care Medicaid residents who otherwise might remain in acute care hospitals, (2) improve residents' outcomes through resident-specific goal setting and care planning, and (3) encourage the appropriate discharge of residents to the community or to lower levels of care to free beds for more-dependent patients.

For two years between April 1981 and April 1983, 36 proprietary nursing homes were randomly assigned to treatment or control conditions. Those in the experimental group were awarded incentive payments based on their ability to achieve any one or a combination of the above goals.

To determine the level of the payments, work sampling studies were conducted on direct patient care activities and other nonpatient care nursing activities by trained RN and LPN teams. Average times for 13 specific categories of patients (type A through DEEE-1-2-3) were identified and assigned specific costs (Table 8–3). Three categories of patients

TABLE 8-3 San Diego Total Admission Incentive Payments per Patient Day

Patient Classification	Minutes of Nursing Care PPD*	Incremental Costs PPD* over Type C	Five Percent Markup on PPD* Costs over Type C	Total Incentive Payment PPD*
Type B	78.03	$ − 2.50	$0.00	$ − 2.50
Type C	104.51	0.00	0.00	0.00
Type D	152.81	4.72	0.24	4.96
Type E-1	121.73	6.93	0.35	7.28
Type E-2	140.18	7.68	0.38	8.06
Type CE-1	121.73	6.93	0.35	7.28
Type CE-2	166.66	10.18	0.51	10.69
Type DE-1	148.21	9.43	0.47	9.90
Type DE-2	214.96	14.90	0.75	15.65
Type DE-3	208.10	10.49	0.52	11.01
Type DEE-1-2	210.36	19.61	0.98	20.59
Type DEE-1-3	203.50	15.20	0.76	15.96
Type DEEE-1-2-3	265.65	25.38	1.27	26.65

*PPD = per patient day.

SOURCE: William G. Weissert, William J. Scanlon, Thomas T. H. Wan, and Douglas E. Skinner, "Care for the Chronically Ill: Nursing Home Incentive Payment Experiment," *Health Care Financing Review*, Winter 1983.

were identified as being ineligible for the payments. Type A patients were excluded because they were likely to be discharged within 90 days and therefore did not require an incentive payment. Type B patients were assigned a negative payment because they actually required a level of care which cost less than the current Medicaid reimbursement rate, and Type C constituted the "break-even" point at which the level of staff time equalled the Medicaid per diem rate. Thus, an incentive reimbursement of zero was paid for Type C patients. Finally, because all homes in the demonstration were proprietary, a 5 percent mark-up for profit was factored in for patients in categories D through DEEE-1-2-3.

To determine whether facilities were eligible for payments, trained RN assessors (members of the research team) were required to approve patients nominated for each type of payment by the nursing home staff. Admission incentive payments were made on the basis of the patient classification scheme shown in Table 8-3, and outcome incentive payments were linked to either a maintenance or improvement goal. When linked to improvement (example, "substantial remission or elimination of multiple Stage III/VI skin ulcers"), the payment was terminated when improvement was achieved. When linked to maintenance (for example, "maintenance of good skin condition of comatose patients"), the payment was "continued only as long as the resident continued to need... maintenance care following an acute episode of illness or injury." [13] Finally, discharge payments for certain patients in the Type B,C,D, and E categories, where appropriate, were made on the basis of $5 an hour for up to 40 hours of staff case management time per discharge and also included an empty bed compensation factor. To receive the full payment, the discharge plan was required to be approved in advance by the research team nurse, achieved within 5 days of its target date, and successful; that is, the patient was required to remain in the lower level of care for at least 90 days without undergoing either a nursing home or hospital admission.

The incentive payments for heavy-care admissions enjoyed mixed success.[14] Specifically, experimental group facilities did admit significantly more Type E patients, experienced significantly reduced admissions of Type B patients, and the overall case mix of experimental facilities became significantly more impaired in activities of daily living (ADL) over time in comparison to controls. However, experimental facilities did not increase admissions of Type D patients who constitute a larger proportion of all backlogged Medicaid hospital long stayers. Two explanations for this finding were advanced by study investigators. First, Type E patients were easier to identify since their nursing care needs were concrete (i.e., tube feeding, decubitus, or comatose care). Second, on average, the payment for Type E patients was 2.5 times as great as that for Type D patients. Thus, facilities acted fairly rationally in targeting patients who were easily identifiable and for whom higher payments were available. In theory, the payment differential would have been absorbed to some degree by the increased nurse staffing time required. However, most homes did not hire increased skilled nursing staff.

Finally, the reduction in hospital length of stay (LOS) for Type E patients was not sufficient in size to underwrite the cost of the incentive payment. To have broken even, the hospital LOS of 57 Type E patients would have to have been reduced from 56 to 26 days at $300 per day. In fact, the net increase in Type E patients admitted to experimental nursing homes during the final phase of the experiment was 13, and compared to controls, 31. Thus, the net effect of the intervention was limited.

Findings were also mixed with respect to discharges to lower levels of care.[15] The nursing home staff in experimental facilities participated in in-service training sessions run by research staff to explain paperwork involved and discuss less intensive care options. The nursing home staff then could nominate specific patients for discharge, and these nominations were required to be approved by the research staff. If approved, the discharge planning process was then conducted by a facility nurse. Table 8–4 lists the number of discharges per group and indicates that the number of persons nominated for discharge in both groups was similar. However, considerably more individuals in the experimental group were ultimately discharged. The study did not monitor the outcomes of discharges for control group residents but found that a substantial number (70 percent) of experimental discharges remained at a lower level of care for the prescribed 90 days. However, the majority of discharges (70 percent) were made to lower levels of institutional care (ICF or board and care) than to private homes in the community. Rates of successful discharge were also found to vary with the length of residents' nursing home stay, with the highest rate of success (81.8 percent) found among residents with lengths of stay of under 180 days. In both groups, the movement from nomination of appropriate individuals for discharge to the creation of a discharge plan appeared to be a major stumbling block. Researchers speculate that the required paperwork may have been too complex. It is also possible, since social workers were not involved in this process, that skills necessary to implement successful discharge planning for this group of multiply impaired individuals were simply not available.

Perhaps more fundamentally, these findings also suggest that the number of residents with any potential for discharge to the community may be rather small and that discharge

TABLE 8–4 Impact of Incentive Payments on Discharges

	Experimental	Control
Nominated for discharge	128	137
Approved by research nurse	113	132
Discharge plan submitted	48	—
Discharged	47	30
Remained at lower level at least 90 days	33	—
Lower level institutional care	24	—
Home	11	—

SOURCE: Brenda J. Jones and Mark Meiners, "Nursing Home Discharges: The Results of an Incentive Reimbursement Experiment," (Hyattsville, Md.: National Center for Health Services Research and Technology Assessment, April 26, 1985).

planning should concentrate on the early months of a nursing home stay. Further, with the increased availability of sophisticated skilled home health care services, this pool of patients may continue to shrink as more of these patients are discharged from hospitals to skilled care in the home. While discharge planning in the nursing home should be available and encouraged, it probably should be targeted to residents with the most potential to benefit from it, and policymakers should not expect to generate substantial cost savings through getting people out of nursing homes but concentrate instead on preventing the initial admission.

The results of impact on functional status are not yet available and appear to be the most problematic of the outcomes studied. As described earlier, functional status improvement incentives were one-time payments, linked to the attainment of a specific goal. In contrast, maintenance payments were "continued only as long as the resident continued to need maintenance care following an acute episode of illness or injury." If a patient suffered an acute exacerbation of an existing condition, payments would be made for staff efforts which resulted in restoring the individual to his or her pre-acute episode level of functioning. Results are not yet available from this portion of the study, but the approach raises some interesting questions. First, and most importantly, we have very little understanding regarding the potential of select groups of nursing home patients to improve, remain stable, or decline over time. Evidence suggests that as more patients have been discharged from hospitals to home care and as the nursing home bed supply has remained constant, nursing homes have been admitting sicker patients. We have no knowledge about what proportion of nursing home residents with which set of characteristics have most potential for improved or maintained functional status. It appears that this question must be addressed before a payment system geared to these outcomes is developed. If very few patients fall into this category, incentive payments would have little impact. One other study which explicitly addressed the issue of payments for maintenance care deserves mention in this regard.

Outcome-Based Reimbursement. At the same time that the San Diego experiment was being conducted, another study focusing on outcome-based reimbursement was being conducted by a team of researchers headed by Robert Kane, then of the Rand Corporation in Los Angeles. Similarly concerned over the perverse incentives of client-centered point-count reimbursement schemes, this group tested the question of whether it would be possible to prognose the outcome of each nursing home resident and pay facilities based on the degree of success or failure experienced in achieving prognosed outcomes of care. To hone in more closely on reimbursement based on achievable results, Kane and his colleagues first concentrated on developing an instrument that could validly and reliably assess residents' functional status.[16] Building on already existing assessment methods, they identified six domains of functioning, developed a series of scales which could measure each, and tested these scales on successive waves of residents of four Los Angeles skilled nursing facilities. The original six domains included were physiologic, ADL, affective, cognitive, social interaction, and satisfaction with care and environment. Four of the six scales were found to have good interviewer reliability scores (0.8 Pearson's R), and for the most part, stable factors were also identified across successive cohorts of residents with respect to their responses to the instrument. The assessment was particularly noteworthy insofar as scores were based on performance rather than self-reported capacity whenever feasible. Finally, the whole process required less than one hour of interviewing time per resident.

Having established that the instrument was reliable and valid, the research team then investigated the potential of using scores at a given point in time to predict resident-specific functional status in the future.[17] Using the assessment instrument described above, three waves of functional status data were collected at three-month intervals on approximately 250 patients. Regression analyses of status scores revealed that the best predictor of any single scale score was the same scale score from a previous wave (i.e., wave one scores predicted wave two scores best and so on and so forth), with the total amount of variance explained ranging from a low of 0.51 to a high of 0.93. Using multiple waves of measurement yielded very minor improvements in amount of variance explained by two waves only.

Although functional status scores were quite stable and predicted the course of functional status quite well, efforts to predict changes in residents' status (discharged improved, discharged worse, discharged dead) were less successful. Kane et al. attribute this to the fact that recent admissions were very different, that is, less stable and therefore more likely to experience status changes than long-stay residents. However, they felt that continued observation of recent admissions with a larger sample size could yield the ability to model status changes for this group more accurately. Since functional status scores from an earlier interview predicted future scale scores quite well, the authors concluded that unexpectedly large deviations from previous scores have the potential to reflect true changes in residents' status. However, the causes of large scale changes would need to be determined since some might include unforeseen events that might not be under the facility's control. In this case, exceptions to the reimbursement could be negotiated.

The next step in Kane's outcome-based reimbursement methodology is the transformation of scale scores to a single aggregated measure which could be used in computing payment. At this point, the weighting of the scales becomes quite complex. For example, whose values will be used in assigning weights, the state Medicaid department's, the taxpayer's, or the resident's? An additional problem with the concept of outcome-based reimbursement is the fact that most clients in long-term care facilities may not change much over time. Thus, the stability that makes accurate measurement possible also may indicate that very few patients are capable of achieving anything better than their prognosed "stable" outcome. The main value of the payment mechanism appears to lie in its ability to detect and penalize those instances of poor quality care when more patients deteriorate than would be expected and its ability to dissuade homes from encouraging dependency in hopes of generating a higher case mix or point-count score. On the negative side, this system is largely untested to date and results reported are based on close (every three months) measurement of the total universe of patients receiving care. Thus, the system in its current form appears too costly for practical implementation on a wide-scale basis.

Case-Mix: The RUGS Approach. Approaching the same goals of enticing facilities to accept heavy-care patients because they will be paid a fair rate for them, Schneider and colleagues at Rensselaer Polytechnic Institute in Troy, New York, have come up with a DRG-like prospective reimbursement system entitled Resource Utilization Groupings (RUGS).[18] Working closely with the New York State Department of Health, Schneider and colleagues have developed a system which classifies patients into discrete categories based on their pattern of clinical characteristics and related resource consumption. The second iteration of this classification system (RUGS II) went into effect as a reimbursement method for all New York State Medicaid-reimbursed nursing home patients in January of 1986, and a revised version is currently being tested for use with Medicare patients at several different sites across the country.

Using a similar approach to the studies described earlier, the RUGS research team collected patient assessment information (277 data elements) on over 3,400 residents of 52 New York State facilities chosen to represent all relevant strata (region, size, ownership, staffing levels, etc.) and prescreened to eliminate facilities with quality of care deficiencies. Simultaneously, data on RN, LPN, and aide utilization were collected through a 24-hour study of time spent with each patient. Indirect care time was also measured and apportioned either proportionately to specific residents when appropriate or attributed equally to all residents in the case of routine activities. Data on care provided by other professionals were also obtained on the patient assessment instrument, as were data on ancillary costs by type.

The patient assessment instrument covered several types of data including administrative and patient demographic data, general medical evaluation, activities of daily living, psychological or behavioral conditions, services and treatments, social support available (for those admitted within six months), comments on special patient cases, and a scale that measured the attitudes of nursing staff toward the patients. Staff time data were then translated to costs by multiplying each type of staff time by facility-specific salary and fringe benefit factors to account for differences in costs as a function of staff mix.

The objective of the study was to identify a set of discrete resident groupings that could most efficiently explain variance in staff time. Using AUTOGRP, the same statistical procedure used to derive DRGs, and working closely with an advisory group of researchers and clinicians, a "special population" clinical approach to the data analysis was developed. This approach yielded the five hierarchical groups shown in Figure 8–3. These groupings are both clinically different from one another and statistically distinct with respect to resource consumption. A secondary split within the hierarchical groups based on ADL functioning (summed responses to the items eating, transferring, and toileting) yielded the 16 discrete patient reimbursement categories shown in Figure 8–3.

These three ADL items were chosen because they were considered to be activities over which facilities exercised little control. For example, according to Schneider, bathing and dressing are activities which may reflect the policy of the facility as much as the functional capacity of residents. The items chosen were thought to be less vulnerable to "gaming" by facilities once reimbursement based upon them was initiated. This classification revealed that the majority of patients

FIGURE 8–3 RUGS II Classification System

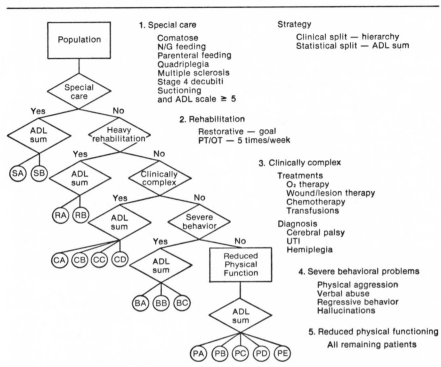

SOURCE: Donald Schneider, "New York State Long-Term Care Case-Mix Reimbursement Project Executive Summary: Derivation of RUGS-II, New York State Department of Health and Rensselaer Polytechnic Institute, December 1984.

assessed (55 percent) were placed in the reduced physical-functioning group, with 25 percent of all patients falling in the A or minimally impaired group. This finding indicates that if a RUGS-II type of reimbursement encourages facilities to accept more heavy-care patients for whom reimbursement would be higher and discourages the acceptance over time of light-care, reduced physical-functioning patients, the case-mix composition of nursing home residents could shift substantially toward a heavy-care emphasis over time.

The RUGS-II classification system has a higher variance reduction (42 percent) than DRGs and is reputed to be far less complex to operationalize. Attempts are currently under way to assess the stability of the classification scheme by monthly monitoring of functional status over 12 months for one original resident and four new admissions for each sampling unit studied. Discharge and hospitalization data are also being collected on patients three months after admission. The reimbursement methodology is also being developed, and a shorter, more efficient assessment instrument tested.

As Schneider points out in his description of the RUGS-II approach, however, two important elements must be present to maximize patient well-being while simultaneously achieving cost-effective care through a case-mix reimbursement approach. First, light-care patients are light in the sense that they do not require decubitus, nasogastric, or suctioning care and have only one ADL impairment. These same individuals may, however, have multiple instrumental ADL impairments with respect to cleaning, shopping, meal preparation, etc. Although skilled or intermediate care placement may be inappropriate, sheltered care or personal, chore, or homemaker care in the community may be sorely needed to prevent "dumping" light-care individuals back to the community in a way that is analogous to the mental health deinstitutionalization experience of the 70s.

Finally, all prospective payment systems run the risk of undercutting quality of care if reimbursement levels are set too low. Many analysts have recommended that quality-incentive payments be built into reimbursement systems. Others argue that reimbursement for care and quality assurance are separate, distinct issues that should not be fused. Schneider recommends that RUGS-II can work where it is supplemented (1) by an extensive community-care network of services similar to the one that exists in New York State and (2) by a quality-assurance program like the Sentinel Health Event approach, which can ensure a minimum level of quality across all facilities statewide.

Community-Based Care

The examples above have been limited to experiments undertaken to manage the cost of institutional care. Serious activity with respect to cost control is also occurring on the community-based side of the long-term care system. Schneider will be adapting the RUGS-II approach to home health care reimbursement in late 1985, and two other HCFA-sponsored demonstrations in home care reimbursement are currently in progress.

Medicare home health outlays are projected to exceed $3 billion by 1990, durable medical equipment projections are similar, and hospice care is projected to reach $815 million. To control these expenditures, HCFA currently has two demonstrations in prospective payment and competitive bidding in the field.

The prospective payment demonstration is just beginning and is targeted to enroll 120 agencies in 10 states in three different payment methods: rate per visit (the existing Medicare-reimbursement methodology), rate per period of time, and rate per episode of illness. The rate per visit method sets a rate schedule based on the six types of visits (RN, physical therapy, occupational therapy, speech, etc.) that are eligible for Medicare reimbursement.[19] The rate per period of time method is a per patient-month payment (similar to a monthly capitation rate) that would pay for the total period of care regardless of type or volume of services provided. Finally, the rate per episode of illness method pays a flat rate per episode and is similar to DRG payments but not based on diagnosis. The prospective rates for agencies will be individualized, based on each agencies' base rate in the year prior to the inception of the demonstration.

The demonstration is being conducted by ABT Associates with a research team headed by Judith Williams. All participating agencies (N=120) will be matched and randomly assigned to one of the three experimental payment methods (40 agencies per group) or to control group conditions, i.e., customary Medicare reimbursement. A contract for its evaluation was slated to be negotiated by HCFA by late 1985. HCFA is particularly concerned to learn which payment method is most successful in restraining the rate of increase in rates while simultaneously retaining a base level of quality of care standards. The experiment will be interesting to watch, but findings may be difficult to interpret if HCFA simultaneously freezes or caps Medicare rates for home care. If the rates are frozen or capped for control group home care agencies, it will be very difficult to assess the cost effectiveness of alternative reimbursement methods and an important opportunity to acquire important new information could be lost.

Shifting the Payment Source: Family Copayments

During recent years, some attempts have been made to reduce the role of public financing of long-term care by either encouraging or requiring families of long-term care patients to contribute to the costs of care. In 1983, HCFA issued guidelines which for the first time explicitly informed states that they were entitled to require adult family members to support adult relatives. Although a number of states enacted such family responsibility laws for their Medicaid programs, only Idaho has attempted to enforce it. Idaho's attorney general has since found the law to be inconsistent with federal Medicaid guidelines, and the issue has been floundering in Idaho courts for more than a year.[20]

At present, the Reagan administration is still encouraging the concept of family responsibility and is proposing that spouses of Medicare-supported nursing home residents who have incomes equal to or above twice the level of the government's official poverty line be required to contribute 20 percent of their income for nursing home care. At present, the administration is lobbying for legislation that would require states to implement this provision in return for increased flexibility in use of federal Medicaid funds for long-term care. However, this measure is quite unpopular politically. Most observers of long-term care believe that families have been bearing the burden of informal care for extended periods of time and that, if anything, tax incentives for continued care rather than disincentives are an appropriate policy route. There is an additional problem of implementation and enforcement associated with responsibility laws. With respect to adult children, are out-of-state adult children responsible for payments in the state where a parent is receiving care? How could payments in this case be enforced? What would happen in cases in which the parent receiving care has divorced and is remarried? Which parent do adult children have responsibility for in these situations? Because of its inherent unpopularity and the implementation problems described, most observers do not believe that family responsibility "deeming" will yield much relief from Medicaid long-term care expenditures.

What We Have Learned and Where We Are Heading

To summarize, we have learned a great deal about how not to pay for long-term care, but it is not clear that reducing the increase in cost at the margin will yield sufficient dollars to underwrite projected future increases in the demand for long-term care services. In 1965, Medicare legislation turned on a faucet of health care funding that led to unprecedented growth in costs of acute care. As a result of these cost increases, better ways of managing and paying for health care services have been sought. As the experiments described in this chapter attest, better ways of paying the long-term care bill have emerged over the last 20 years. However, long-term care faces a different challenge than acute care. There is virtually unanimous agreement among health care providers that growth in acute hospital care is nonexistent or negative. In contrast, all agree that growth in long-term care services must occur and that savings derived from more efficient payment methods and incentives are insufficient to finance the scope of services required in the future. Indeed, there is some anecdotal evidence that suggests that if demand for nursing home care exceeds supply (a condition generally believed to be true at present and predicted to become worse in the future), heavy-care Medicaid patients will experience severe problems accessing needed nursing home care.[21] Nursing homes are currently marketing heavily to private pay clients and sometimes requiring contracts at entry that mandate the availability of private funding for one to two years or more. To deal with this problem and ensure that individuals who need it can achieve access to care in a timely and efficient manner, it is imperative that new and possibly very different financing mechanisms for long-term care be developed in the future. We turn to this important issue next.

NOTES

1. Richard Curtis and Lawrence Bartlett, "High Cost of LTC Squeezes State Budgets," *Generations,* Fall 1984.

2. Richard Merrill, personal communication, Intergovernmental Health Policy Project, Washington, D.C.

3. Steven G. Ullmann, "Cost Analysis and Facility Reimbursement in the Long-Term Health Care Industry," *Health Services Research,* 19:1, April 1984.

4. Elizabeth Bates Harkins, *Study of the Virginia Nursing Home Preadmission Screening Program, Final Report* (Richmond, Va.: Virginia Commonwealth University Center on Aging, March 31, 1982), p. 2.

5. Greg Arling, John A. Capitman, and Angela Smith, *Findings from the Virginia Long-Term Care Tracking System Project* (Richmond, Va.: Virginia Commonwealth University Center on Aging, December 1, 1984).

6. Jackson Knowlton, Steven Clauser, and James Fatula, "Nursing Home Preadmission Screening: A Review of State Programs," *Health Care Financing Review,* 3:3, March 1982.

7. Carol O'Shaughnessy and Richard Price, *Medicaid "2176" Waivers for Home and Community-Based Care* (Washington, D.C.: Congressional Research Service, June 21, 1985).

8. Philip G. Cotterill, "Provider Incentives under Alternative Reimbursement Systems," *Long Term Care,* ed. Vogel and Palmer, U.S. DHHS, Health Care Financing Administration, no. 82–600609, 1982.

9. Robert J. Buchanan, "Medicaid Cost Containment: Prospective Reimbursement for Long-Term Care," *Inquiry,* 20, Winter 1983, pp. 334–342.

10. Charlene Harrington and James H. Swan, "Medicaid Nursing Home Reimbursement Policies, Rates, and Expenditures," *Health Care Financing Review,* 6:1, Fall 1984.

11. V. L. Greene and D. Monahan, "A Comparison of the Level of Care Predictors of Six Long-Term Care Patient Assessment Systems," *American Journal of Public Health,* 70:11, November 1980.
David H. Gustafson, Richard van Koningsveld, and Robert W. Peterson, "Assessment of Level of Care: Implications of Inerrater Reliability on Health Policy," *Health Care Financing Review,* 6:2, Winter 1984.

12. Christine E. Bishop, Alonzo L. Plough, and Thomas R. Willemain, "Nursing Home Levels of Care: Problems and Alternatives," *Health Care Financing Review,* Fall 1980, p. 33.

13. William G. Weissert, William J. Scanlon, Thomas T. H. Wan, and Douglas E. Skinner, "Care for the Chronically Ill: Nursing Home Incentive Payment Experiment," *Health Care Financing Review,* Winter 1983, p. 48.

14. Mark R. Meiners, Phyllis Thorburn, Pamela C. Roddy, and Brenda J. Jones, "Nursing Home Admissions: The Results of an Incentive Reimbursement Experiment" (Hyattsville, Md.: National Center for Health Services Research and Health Care Technology Assessment, May 31, 1985).

15. Brenda J. Jones and Mark Meiners, "Nursing Home Discharges: The Result of an Incentive Reimbursement Experiment" (Hyattsville, Md.: National Center for Health Services Research and Health Care Technology Assessment, April 19, 1985).

16. Robert L. Kane, Robert Bell, Sandra Riegler, Alisa Wilson, and Rosalie A. Kane, "Assessing the Outcomes of Nursing Home Patients," *Journal of Gerontology,* 38:4, 1983.

17. Robert L. Kane, Robert Bell, Sandra Riegler, Alisa Wilson, and Emmett Keeler, "Predicting the Outcomes of Nursing Home Patients," *The Gerontologist,* 23:2, 1983.

18. "New York State Long-Term Care Case Reimbursement Project Executive Summary: Derivation of RUG-II," New York State Department of Health and Rensselaer Polytechnic Institute, December 1984.

19. "Home Health PPS Demo Will Be Organized by ABT Associates," *Hospitals,* March 16, 1985, p. 47.

20. Ed Lewis, "Reagan Plan Shifts Costs to Families," *Contemporary Long-Term Care,* July 1985.

21. U.S. GAO, *Medicaid and Nursing Home Care: Cost Increases and the Need for Services Are Creating Problems for the States and the Elderly,* DHHS Pub no. (IPE–84–1), January 1984.

PART FOUR

The Future

CHAPTER NINE

Expanding the Funding Pool and Improving the Management of Care

- Projected increases in the costs of long-term care require that pooled financing mechanisms be used in the future.

- The pooling of public funds already earmarked for long-term care may achieve efficiencies in operations and thereby enable a marginal increase in the number of people cared for at current cost, but it is insufficient to meet the needs of the increased numbers of long-term care users in the future.

- The investment of private funds in pooled risk-sharing, private insurance policies holds great promise of enabling the currently catastrophic cost of long-term care to be more affordable in the future.

- To maximize the scope of benefits offered through long-term care insurance policies, case management or co-payments may be necessary.

- Although the conversion of housing equity into cash income might enable more elderly to purchase long-term care insurance premiums, the popularity of this approach is untested.

- A preferred strategy could entail long-term care insurance wraparounds of Medicare risk-based HMOs that would feature pooled funding, risk sharing, group marketing, and strong case management of both acute and long-term care.

Many analysts of long-term care policy options have painted a picture of gloom and doom regarding the future. It is true that the number of individuals requiring care will increase substantially in the future and that new sources of funding for long-term care need to be identified, but the picture is hardly one of unmixed gloom. The good news is the fact that we have learned a considerable amount during the Medicaid years (1965–85) about how and how not to finance and deliver health care. The bad news is that we still have not developed a viable method of financing and managing catastrophic care for those who need it. However, several very promising developments are being tested at present, of which this chapter provides an overview.

To continue with more specifics about the good news, growth in overall health expenditures is expected to moderate considerably during the remainder of the 80s. From 1973–83, spending for all health care tripled, increasing from $103 billion to $355 billion. Expenditures during 1983–1990 are anticipated to less than double from $355 to $660 billion.[1] It is widely believed that the period 1965–1975 was marked by an expansion of services and access to care. In contrast, the late 70s and 80s have witnessed the realization that care must be better managed if it is to be affordable.

The acute care sector has undeniably experienced the greatest amount of innovation aimed at the control of costs. As a result of the combined effects of Medicare prospective payment, increased growth of HMOs, PPOs, and employer coalitions, a significantly lower rate of increase in acute care hospital costs is projected, from $147 billion in 1983 to $277 billion in 1990. Nursing home expenditures, which grew at a rate of 16 percent annually from 1950 to 1983, are also expected to moderate to a 10 percent annual rate of growth over the same period, increasing from $29 billion in 1983 to $35 billion in 1990. The projected increase in the number of elderly is expected to account for most of the increase in nursing home expenditures, with the increase in noninstitutional care options accounting for the deceleration in rate of growth.

Certain recent developments in the financing and management of long-term care are especially significant with respect to their potential impact on access to, supply of, and cost of long-term care services in the future. This chapter examines a variety of these developments that are aimed at expanding the funding pool for long-term care and simultaneously promoting the efficient use of long-term care services. All options are examined with respect to the policy criteria described in Chapter 1; that is, with respect to their impact on access, equity, quality, affordability, and continuity of care.

POOLED PUBLIC FUNDING

Many analysts have suggested that the effectiveness of public dollars for long-term care could be maximized if existing, fragmented public funding streams were pooled to finance a coordinated array of long-term care services. As Chapters 2 and 3 demonstrated, several different funding sources now pay for specific types of long-term care services using different criteria for service eligibility. Many argue that both the financing and delivery of care could be improved and made more efficient if these funding streams were pooled at the state level with greater state control over the discretionary use of funds. If all funds targeted for long-term care in 1983 (institutional and noninstitutional) had been pooled, states could have accessed approximately $19 billion for long-term care. While this option sounds sensible, and two states (California and Oregon) are currently experimenting with this pooled financing strategy, there are several inherent problems with the approach.

First, this approach assumes that public monies spent for long-term care services are known when, in fact, the portion of Title XX services spent for long-term care and the part of Medicare home care funds spent for acute versus chronic conditions is not easily identifiable. Second, the programs which fund long-term care services have been in existence for several years and have built up constituencies over time. Title XX and the Older Americans Act monies essentially fund social services, whereas Medicare and Medicaid fund medical and nursing care. While many critics argue that separate and parallel systems of medical and social services are inefficient at best and futile at worst, it is not clear who would win in a merged system. Would such a merger further medicalize long-term care? The amount of funding for medical services clearly swamps comparable outlays for social services ($14.2 billion versus $4.8 billion), and the piper with the most dollars usually calls the tune. On the other hand, such a move might foster coalition building among what are now competing constituencies.

A merged system would also require integrated data management and a fairly substantial bureaucracy that could screen candidates for eligibility and coordinate and monitor continued eligibility for services authorized. Although a strategy of this type may be necessary to curtail the rate of growth and maximize the efficiency of current public spending for long-term care, it may simply be insufficient as a single policy option with respect to future demand for long-term care services. The pooled funding strategy might be budget neutral or cost saving with respect to its impact on the federal deficit. However, the strategy assumes that only already existing funds are necessary and does not substantially expand the total pool of available dollars for long-term care. In a study of this issue, Palley and Oktay have reported that the six states that have utilized pooled-funding have found that less than half of the potential for community-based care can be met by it.[2] Finally, if we continue to use a means-tested approach to eligibility, we will perpetuate the current method of requiring impoverishment and generating dependency before eligibility for care could begin. This would certainly appear to be a counterproductive policy for curtailing the cost of long-term care. As a result of dissatisfaction with this strategy, many have argued that a greater emphasis on the development of private versus public financing of long-term care is in order.

Increased Private Financing

As tables in Chapter 3 demonstrated, a rather astounding amount of long-term care is already financed with private funds. Specifically, the elderly finance 50 percent of institutional and community-based long-term care services directly out of pocket, with Medicare and private insurance funding less than 3 percent of the cost of care. Medicare was originally developed and funded as an insurance program to protect the elderly from the costs of health care. It has done a reasonable job with respect to acute care expenditures, insofar as elderly now pay only 15 percent of these costs out of pocket. With respect to long-term care expenditures for those with truly catastrophic conditions, the record is quite poor. It is a cruel irony that 20 years after the passage of Medicare, the elderly are even more vulnerable to indigency as a result of extraordinary health care expenditures than they have been in the past. At the same time, the federal government is coping with an annual budget deficit of unprecedented size, and recent voting records suggest that the public is unreceptive to new taxes aimed at creating a new health care entitlement.

Given the confluence of these events, increased attention has been paid to the possibility of expanding the role of private financing of long-term care, yet enabling this role to be affordable. Private insurance for long-term care in the last five years has come to be a very serious option that is not only being discussed but is actually being implemented by several major insurance companies.

In a recent analysis of the private long-term care insurance market, David Kannell and associates at ICF, Incorporated (ICF, Inc.) have reviewed the major plans which currently exist and have identified two current models of private insurance.[3] Both are summarized below.

Individual Long-Term Care Insurance Plans. Approximately 48 percent of individuals over age 65 had some form of private insurance coverage in 1979.[4] In most instances, these were medigap policies that paid Medicare deductibles and coinsurance rates for the 21st to 100th days in a skilled nursing facility (SNF). Mark Meiners at the National Center for Health Services Research has identified a number of companies that truly offer an extended care (three to four years of protection) benefit.[5] He has estimated that 16 companies presently offer long-term care insurance policies. The ICF, Inc. analysis of the offerings of four of these plans for the Assistant Secretary's Office of Planning and Evaluation (DHHS) was completed in January 1985 and revealed that all four plans (see Table 9–1) shared striking similarities.

Specifically, all plans offer indemnities ranging from $10–$50 per day for extended nursing home stays of from three to four years, all offer some type of intermediate or custodial care as well as a skilled nursing care benefit, and all use age-related premiums at the time of purchase of care as well as deductibles and prior hospitalization requirements as ways of discouraging adverse selection and excess utilization. Of the four plans, only Fireman's Fund and Kemper offer a substantial home care benefit; however, in both cases the benefit applies only to individuals who are first hospitalized and subsequently enter a skilled home nursing facility. Thus, both plans attempt to provide an alternative home care option for individuals who are already nursing home users. This restriction on home care benefits reflects insurers' concerns about potential excess use of a home care benefit if it were more generously structured. However, somewhat ironically, most research on elderly consumers' preferences for long-term care insurance reveals that consumers would be much more willing to purchase a policy with a generous home care benefit.[6] The addition of a more liberal benefit might considerably enhance the marketability of existing policies, thereby spreading risk over a greater number of policyholders and bringing premium costs down. However, insurers are stressing caution above all other concerns and appear reluctant to expand the home care benefit until more information about probable utilization and cost is available.

To further control the degree of potential adverse selection (i.e., the possibility that only those most in need of and likely to use care will enroll), all four plans use medical screens and exclude certain preexisting medical conditions from coverage for periods of six months to one year after the initial purchase

TABLE 9–1   Approximate Annual Premiums by Age at Issue for Major Long-Term Care Insurance Plans*

	Age 65	Age 75
Fireman's Fund†	$600	$870
Kemper‡	305	461
United Equitable§	265	615
Pacific Benefit ‖	290	440

*Caution should be used in comparing these figures. Plans vary with respect to the level of indemnity provided.

†Provides $50 daily indemnity for skilled or custodial care for up to four years following 20-day deductible; also $25 daily for home health care if the individual leaves nursing home after a stay of 180 days or more.

‡Provides $20 per day for first 100 days and $40 per day for days 101 to 1,095 (up to three years) for skilled care; provides $10 daily for 60 days of custodial care after 20 days of SNF care.

§Provides $50 daily indemnity for SNF care for up to 4 years, $25 daily for ICF or custodial care for up to six months, following 20-day deductible.

‖Provides $30 daily indemnity for SNF care or ICF care (for a condition which first required skilled care) after a 20-day deductible.

SOURCE: ICF Incorporated, *Private Financing of Long-Term Care: Current Methods and Resources. Phase I Final Report,* submitted to the Office of the Assistant Secretary for Planning and Evaluation, U.S. DHHS, January 1985, pp. 19–21.

of coverage. Fireman's Fund, which has been offering its product since 1976, has found that the medical screen rejects only 8 percent of applicants, most of whom are under age 65 and have disabling conditions which clearly predict need for catastrophic care.

As Table 9–2 indicates, very little is known about the experience or characteristics of private long-term care insurance beneficiaries because the plans are new and benefits are not used until several years following the initial date of enroll-

TABLE 9–2   Fireman's Fund Long-Term Care Insurance: Characteristics of Enrollees and Beneficiaries

Years of experience	9
Total number of enrollees	7,000
Average age at enrollment	78
Average age of beneficiary	83
Average length of stay (days)	256

SOURCE: ICF Incorporated, *Private Financing of Long-Term Care: Current Methods and Resources. Phase I Final Report,* submitted to the Office of the Assistant Secretary for Planning and Evaluation, U.S. DHHS, January 1985, p. 23.

ment. For example, the experience of Fireman's Fund indicates that policyholders enrolled at age 78 on average, but did not begin to use the benefit until age 83. Their 256-day average length of stay reported to date is thus artificially low since it reflects only those beneficiaries who have been discharged from care to date. Thus, the average number of days used can probably be expected to increase over time.

Finally, all the plans described have been sold on an individual basis, which precludes the economies of scale of mass marketing and involves costly screening to control risk. Several factors have undermined the development of a mass marketing approach that underwriters would prefer and that could reduce the cost of insurance premiums. First, state insurance regulations differ substantially, necessitating the tailoring of policies to individual state conditions. Second, given the relative newness of this type of insurance and the lack of experience associated it, companies are mainly concerned about reducing adverse selection. Therefore, they emphasize individual screening as a way of controlling access to benefits.[7] Despite these drawbacks, within a relatively short five-year period, we have seen a substantial degree of increased interest, activity, experience, and competition in the individual long-term care insurance market. As a result, individuals with an average age of 75 can now purchase a variety of long-term care insurance plans from 16 different companies at premium costs ranging from $400–$700 per year. However, the growth potential of individually marketed policies may be low compared to that of mass-marketed policies. Therefore, the development of group policies may offer significant advantages to the individual insurance approach.

Group Long-Term Care Insurance Plans. According to the ICF, Inc. analysis, most group long-term care insurance offered by employers is extremely limited and strongly resembles the Medicare SNF benefit of 100 days of skilled nursing home care following an acute care hospitalization. The expansion of coverage to three to four years of care for younger workers who experience a work-related disability requiring long-term care is thought to require very little additional expense, given the infrequent occurrence of such an event. However, employer groups explain that most employees do not express demand for a catastrophic long-term care benefit. Employers are currently struggling to reduce outlays for acute care coverage and are reluctant to add a new benefit.[8] One notable exception to this general rule, as described by the ICF report, is the Blue Cross of Michigan/United Auto Workers (UAW) Plan. This plan is significant for a number of reasons, including its age and the scope of its enrollees and coverage. The plan has been in existence for 12 years, covers 800,000 workers and their dependents (2.2 million individuals), and includes skilled nursing and home health benefits for both active and retired UAW workers.

As Figure 9–1 demonstrates, the plan offers an explicit incentive to policyholders to substitute less expensive nursing home or home care for acute hospital care by reducing available benefits by a factor of 2 or 3, respectively, for each hospital day used. The UAW plan is also notable for the generosity of its coverage. More than 1,000 home care visits of both a medical and social services (homemaker, chore) type are allowed with no copayment or deductibles required. Since the plan covers so many enrollees, the monthly premium is also very low at fifty cents per member per month. Although one

---

FIGURE 9–1   Group Long-Term Care Plan for United Auto
Workers/Blue Cross of Michigan

Years of Operation	12
Enrollees	2.2 million
Coverage	730 skilled nursing care days (reduced by 2 days for every day of prior hospital care used up to a total of 365 hospital days)
	1,095 medical and social service home health care visits (reduced by 3 visits for each prior hospital day), first dollar coverage, no copayment, deductibles
Utilization	Low
Monthly Cost	$0.50 per member

SOURCE: ICF Incorporated, *Private Financing of Long-Term Care: Current Methods and Resources. Phase I Final Report,* submitted to the Office of Assistant Secretary for Planning and Evaluation, U.S. DHHS, January 1985.

would expect that benefits of this scope would be extensively used, ICF reports that utilization has been quite low. Two explanations are offered. First, physicians have little awareness of the plan's existence and therefore rarely prescribe the services covered. Second, although the plan covers retirees, the majority of individuals enrolled are active workers and their families, a group that is not at high risk of using long-term care because of their relative good health and independent functional status. Finally, until 1983, those (mainly retired) enrollees who were Medicare eligible were required to use Medicare benefits first whenever possible. The 1983 Medicare amendments now mandate the exact opposite, i.e., that any private insurance sources be used first for individuals aged 65 to 69. This change in the regulations is probably too recent for its impact to be detectable.

One other plan that is currently being test marketed but which should prove noteworthy in the future is the American Association of Retired Persons (AARP)/Prudential plan. This plan will be offered to a large group of 250,000 potential purchasers and is reported to include a more innovative home care benefit. Since the home care option has been treated very gingerly to date, the AARP/Prudential experience will be watched with great interest by both the health policy and the insurance communities.

Meiners' Prototype Policy

In order to answer several questions about the potential costs of long-term care policies, Mark Meiners and Gordon Trapnell have recently developed a prototype long-term care insurance policy that they have analyzed under a variety of alternative assumptions.[9] Their analyses purposely varied many of the key characteristics of different policies, such as age at purchase, amount of benefit paid per day, years of coverage, generosity of home care coverage, and alternative risk assumptions, in order to learn the relative effect of changes in these parameters in increasing policy costs.

Their basic prototype policy provides a fixed daily benefit for skilled and intermediate nursing home care for up to three years. The policy allows home health care to be substituted for nursing home care at the rate of three visits per week of unused nursing home benefit. A 90-day elimination period is required, and the annual premium rate is fixed at time of purchase.

Findings from their analyses indicate that increased age at purchase and the enrollment of groups rather than individuals (i.e., no use of a screening procedure to control adverse selection) had the greatest effects on increased premium costs. The group premiums differed only slightly from screened premiums at age 65 and 70, a fact which the authors attribute to the lower expense of mass marketing the group policy. By age 75, however, the lack of selection begins to dominate, increasing premiums for group policyholders by 13 percent at age 75 and by 23 percent at age 80. The home health benefits added little to the premium cost and actually reduced premium cost if used as a substitute for nursing home care. Given the absence of observed longitudinal utilization data, this prototype offers very useful parameters to benefits managers and insurers who are struggling to develop new long-term care insurance products. Its usefulness is limited, however, by the fact that it reflects 1976 data on national nursing home use. A revised prototype based on the 1985 National Nursing Home Survey would be of considerable interest since prospective payment and other forces may have changed some of the assumptions used to derive this model.

Impediments to Expansion

Although the plans described above provide evidence of the potential for private long-term care insurance, several obstacles exist that have the potential to retard the development of this promising financing strategy. First, many elderly individuals mistakenly believe that they already have good coverage for long-term care.[10] By the time they discover the limitations of their Medicare benefits, it is usually too late. Generally patients do not appreciate the paucity of their Medicare long-term care benefits until they are already applying for a nursing home admission. Similarly, younger workers are generally unaware ahead of time of the potentially devastating economic consequences of a catastrophic illness, accident, or congenital anomaly. For both groups of younger and older consumers, a considerable educational effort that could be undertaken by government, unions, and other relevant vested interest groups is necessary.

The government could also play a substantial role in promoting the growth of private insurance policies. At the state level, more flexibility in regulation would help. At the federal level, the options range from tax exemptions for purchase of insurance to making the purchase of coverage compulsory. In the latter case, universal long-term care insurance could be required, utilizing private carriers. Finally, the government's recent decisions to have Medicare payment used as a last resort could have negative effects on the development of employer-sponsored, private long-term care insurance benefits. Employer coalitions have been struggling for some time to reduce health care costs of working-age employees. If they become increasingly responsible over time for the acute health care costs of retirees, they would be loathe to institute a new health care benefit. Thus, a strategy developed to bolster the Medicare trust fund could have negative consequences on Medicaid expenditures in the future.

To summarize, there is no question that the private long-term care insurance financing strategy requires more development. At present, the benefits are narrowly defined, indemnities are not indexed for inflation, and marketing costs are high. What's important, however, is that the concept of pooled risk sharing for a catastrophic event like long-term care, makes inherent sense and that insurance companies are no longer just talking about the option but acting and sometimes even directly providing case management services. Although no one knows the perfect formula, it's important to remember that the early days of life insurance were marked by similar uncertainties but ultimately spawned an industry of considerable wealth that simultaneously filled a real and pressing social need.

Combining the Financing and Management of Care

The S/HMO.   Private insurance for long-term care is one method of spreading risk and pooling funds to ensure that long-term care is affordable in the future for the growing number of people needing care. The Social/Health Maintenance Organization (S/HMO) that has been developed and implemented by the Brandeis Health Policy Center with foundation funding and Health Care Financing Administration (HCFA) waivers, represents another pooled financing, risk-spreading mechanism that is currently being tested at four sites across the country. In contrast to private insurance, the S/HMO entails a considerably more powerful approach since it combines both the financing and management of acute and long-term care. As Jay Greenberg's list of the essential feature of an S/HMO (Figure 9–2) demonstrates, the S/HMO approach emphasizes the development of a full spectrum of vertically integrated service options.[11] Because S/HMOs, like the private insurance carriers, are concerned about potential adverse selection or the increased enrollment of individuals at risk of being high service users, they also screen applicants who

---

FIGURE 9–2 Features of a Social/Health Maintenance
Organization (S/HMO)

---

1. Sponsoring agency assembles full range of acute and chronic care services into a specific system.
2. Agency enrolls a membership reflecting community distribution (includes healthy and impaired individuals).
3. Enrollees pay agreed upon premiums in advance for services. All enrollees pay some "capitation" rate and premiums are pooled.
4. Sponsoring agency is then at risk for costs of service which cannot exceed funding pool.

---

apply for membership. The S/HMOs are committed to serving some high-risk, impaired users but only in proportion to the distribution of these individuals in the community. They therefore set admission quotas based on prevailing community rates of impairment/unimpairment, and once accepted, members pay fixed monthly fees for services. The S/HMO, like any other HMO, is obligated in return to provide care to all members without exceeding the level of funding available. The S/HMO differs from regular HMOs insofar as it offers a greater degree of coverage for long-term care services, including both home health and social service benefits. The S/HMO demonstration sites are still marketing their plans at present but report steady enrollment to date. The demonstrations began marketing in early 1985 and are funded for three and a half years of service, with an evaluation being conducted by HCFA to determine the impact of the S/HMO experience on Medicare and Medicaid expenditures.

Critics of the S/HMO have charged that the demonstrations offer a somewhat limited long-term care benefit in comparison to the private insurance policies described earlier. S/HMO proponents agree that the benefits are circumscribed at present but argue that caution dictates a prudent initial course that can be expanded in the future. Part of the S/HMO's current difficulties stem from the fact that the same year that the S/HMOs began marketing, HCFA encouraged all HMOs to enroll Medicare beneficiaries. Thus, in order to have premiums that are competitive with those of Medicare HMOs, the

TABLE 9–3 Private Premiums and Chronic Care Benefits of S/HMO Demonstration Sites

Site	Monthly Premium	Annual Chronic Care Benefit	Renewability of Institutional Benefits
Kaiser	$49	100 days nursing home; $1,000 per month home/ community	Only for new "spell of illness"
Metropolitan Jewish Geriatric Center	29	6,500 in any setting	Fully renewable
Ebenezer	29	6,250 in any setting	$8,000 lifetime
Senior Care Action Network	40	7,500 in any setting	Fully renewable

SOURCE: Jay Greenberg et al., "The Social/Health Maintenance Organization and Long-Term Care," *Generations,* Summer 1985.

S/HMOs are being forced to keep benefit packages modest at a cost ranging from $29 to $49 a month (see Table 9–3). A second, and more fundamental, potential problem of S/HMOs is the fact that although case-managed care may produce economies for providers, it may not be consistent with consumer preferences. One of the main goals of long-term care reform is increased consumer autonomy, access, and choice regarding care options. It is not clear how the S/HMOs will reconcile potential differences of opinions between enrollees and case managers regarding what constitutes appropriate care. Therefore, drop-out and reenrollment rates for S/HMOs as well as the new Medicare HMOs will bear scrutiny in this regard. It will also be important for the S/HMO to be viewed as a significant but not sole solution to financing long-term care, since this option may not be suitable for or preferred by everyone. Perhaps most importantly, the S/HMOs constitute four diverse living laboratories from which much can be learned in the next few years about the utilization and cost of an unprecedentedly broad span of acute and long-term care services. This information can be extremely useful in modeling demand for care in the future. It can reduce uncertainties currently associated with use of community-based care to known risks of use that can be translated to premium costs and pricing. As such, the S/HMO demonstrations and their evaluation constitute a very important breakthrough and benchmark in the development of long-term care policy in the United States.

Other Capitated Approaches As mentioned above, competition among HMOs and other prepaid competitive medical plans (CMPs) is heating up with respect to the Medicare market. Until 1984, HMOs could enroll Medicare beneficiaries but were discouraged from doing so by two factors. First, Medicare reimbursed HMOs only 80 percent of their cost, leaving it up to the HMO to bill the beneficiary for the remaining 20 percent. Second, under the less competitive conditions that prevailed prior to PPS, HMOs did not have much interest in the Medicare market and viewed it as being somewhat risky because older persons are known to be higher acute care users. Both conditions have since changed. Under new HCFA regulations issued in January 1985, HMOs and CMPs can now receive flat rates from Medicare for each enrollee signed up. Medicare pays the HMO or CMP either 95 percent of the adjusted area per capita cost (AAPCC) for each beneficiary or the adjusted community rate (ACR), the premium which the HMO would charge the general public for the Medicare benefit package, if it is lower. In return, the Medicare HMO/CMP is obliged to provide the full benefit package of services to which Medicare beneficiaries are entitled with the exception of end-stage renal dialysis. Thus, HMOs/CMPs must provide or contract for all physician, hospital, skilled nursing home, or home care services that Medicare customarily reimburses.

As a result of this increased level of payment, more direct reimbursement, and the increased level of competition among HMOs for market share, the new Medicare HMOs are marketing aggressively and constitute an important new entrant to the long-term care marketplace. It is estimated that 364,000 persons are currently enrolled in 65 Medicare risk-based HMO/CMPs, with another 91 risk-based contracts pending. HCFA currently predicts an enrollment of 700,000 Medicare beneficiaries under Tax Equity and Fiscal Responsibility Act contracts by the end of fiscal year 1986 and 1.5 to 2 million enrollees by fiscal year 1987. This rapid penetration of the Medicare marketplace by HMOs may have important implications for long-term care. With their interest in low cost per case and armed with large numbers of Medicare enrollees, the Medicare HMO/CMPs will be in an ideal position to negotiate discounted rates from a whole array of long-term care providers ranging from day care to home care to institutional long-term care providers.

One important element to watch in this whole process will be the selection criteria used by the HMOs. It is commonly believed that most capitated delivery systems thrive not only because they manage care efficiently but also because enrollees who self-select into these plans differ from others of similar age and sex who do not enroll. It is possible that a chronically ill person who is at most risk of high health care use might not join an HMO because of reluctance to disturb a long-standing relationship with a particular physician or because he or she wants to be assured that care will be provided in a specific setting when needed.

The On-Lok Model The capitation models described above all used pooled funding to finance care for a broad range of individuals with excellent to poor health status. To avoid adverse selection, they have used incentives to screen out or otherwise limit the enrollment of the high-risk user. In marked contrast, On-Lok, a community-based long-term care program in San Francisco, has embarked on an experiment to provide risk-based, prepaid long-term care to an exclusively high-risk elderly population. At enrollment, all On-Lok enrollees must be age 55 or older and meet California state SNF nursing home admission criteria with respect to their level of ADL impairment. Since all enrollees are eligible for SNF care, On-Lok receives a Medicare frailty-adjusted AAPCC rate that is twice the normal AAPCC rate, or equal to the amount which Medicare would normally pay for SNF care. These payments are made until the enrollee's 100th day of care, at which point the enrollee shifts over to a Medicaid reimbursement rate or pays approximately $1,000 per month for care until the Medicaid spend-down level is reached. The benefit package provided by On-Lok is extremely comprehensive, covering nursing home, hospital, medical and specialty care, and home health services with a heavy emphasis on day care. Richard Zawadski, director of research, estimates that On-Lok's average per person cost of maintaining an enrollee in fiscal year 1985 was $1,490 per month, of which private funds paid about 7 percent, Medicare 33 percent, and Medicaid the remaining 60 percent.[12] On-Lok currently cares for an enrolled population of 300 individuals and reports very little disenrollment after the first month of care. This capitalized approach to the care of an exclusively high-risk group is extremely interesting and would benefit from replication elsewhere in order to learn more about its generalizability.

Continuing Care Retirement Communities

The Continuing Care Retirement Community (CCRC) described in Chapter 4 is still another method of using pooled funding to cover the risk of need for long-term care services. In most instances, applicants to a CCRC pay a substantial initial entry fee that is supplemented by monthly payments. The initial fee covers the capital and financing payments of the CCRC and the monthly fee offsets operating expenses. The monthly fee is usually adjustable to allow for inflation. While some CCRCs offer guaranteed life care with on-site health care services (a fully integrated model), some offer only on-site residential services with arrangements in place to access health care services as needed. For example, a "residential only" model might contract with an outside home health care agency or a nursing home of good repute in the neighborhood to arrange a special discounted fee for its residents as needed. Most fully integrated CCRCs report that only about 20 percent of all residents actually use nursing home care during their stay; yet all residents are willing to make substantial up-front payments in case they may need that care in the future. Most established CCRCs also have long waiting lists for admission, which indicates that despite relatively high prices, demand for care exceeds supply. Most residents apply in their early 70s (some CCRCs refuse applications from individuals over age 75) but are 75 by the time they enter a facility. According to the ICF report cited earlier, current entrance fees range from $25,000 to $100,000, with monthly fees of from $583–$1,140. In CCRCs operated by religious groups, if residents are unable to afford increased monthly payments, the facility will subsidize care from its endowment funds.

Like the HMO, the CCRC is financially at risk for providing care and has a vested interest in maintaining residents' optimal health and functional status. However, the substantial up-front payments coupled with not insignificant monthly fees restricts this pooled financing option to that group of elderly who are mainly well educated, upper-income individuals who plan ahead for contingencies. Unfortunately, this is probably not the same group that is at greatest risk of needing long-term care services, that is, the single or widowed female with little or no family and moderate to low income. However, the CCRC is certainly a significant long-term care financing option. It seems reasonable to expect that if housing values continue to increase, greater numbers of elderly may be empowered through the sale of real estate to access what formerly was exclusively an option of the very well-to-do.

Other Options

The ICF, Inc. report referred to above also describes a few other options for financing long-term care that are currently being discussed. These include single premium annuities, combined life and long-term care insurance, long-term care IRAs, and pension benefit options. These options vary in the extent to which they can be implemented and in their degree of likely success, but they are of interest insofar as they reflect the range and creativity of current thinking on this topic.

Single premium annuities could be purchased by an elderly person at entry to a nursing home or retirement community. The purchase price would be based on life expectancy at time of purchase and the value of the monthly payment. The annuity would then furnish a monthly fixed payment until death. Since the payment would not be restricted to reimbursing a specific type of care (i.e., SNF days only), it could provide an incentive for nursing home users to return to community living. The annuity could also be offered by many types of organizations including the nursing home itself. According to the ICF, Inc. report, this option could prevent spend down and transfer to Medicaid coverage and could place nursing homes at risk for financing care. However, given the quality of care problem in some facilities, this financing mechanism might also provide an incentive for some facilities to allow persons whose actual life expectancy is longer than predicted to deteriorate and die quickly.

In contrast, combination life and long-term care insurance seems more workable. The concept here is that the value of life insurance declines with advancing age, whereas the need for long-term care insurance increases. If a life insurance policy could gradually be reduced to zero between ages 65 and 75 and converted to a long-term care benefit of increasing value over the same time period, individuals would have much better protection from financial risk. While this solution appears workable, especially for single individuals who have few concerns about the needs of beneficiaries, it probably would not be that attractive an option for married couples. In the case of married couples, husbands are at higher risk of predeceasing their wives, who can be expected to survive for several years. Given this scenario, most couples might prefer to retain a full life insurance benefit and supplement it with a long-term care insurance policy.

Long-term care IRAs are another option that involve the targeting of an IRA specifically for the financing of long-term care services. Therein lies the rub. Since individuals now invest in IRAs that can be used for any purpose, including but not limited to payment for long-term care, it is difficult to see why one would choose this option. There are ways in which the government could increase the utility of a long-term care IRA by making the period of investment longer and the total amount that could be accumulated greater and by raising the mandatory age of use from 70.5 to 75. These steps would allow more reserves to be accumulated and would ensure that they would be available during the period of highest risk.

Flexible pension benefit options also offer intriguing possibilities for financing long-term care. This method would allow individuals to reduce the amount of a yearly pension in order to be able to draw upon a special lump sum in any given year. For example, reduction of a $13,000 per year pension to $12,000 would enable the use of a $12,000 additional cash payment in any year chosen. This approach has the virtue of working with existing pension funds; however, a sum of this size would cover only relatively short-term nursing home stays.

Finally, the private insurance plans discussed previously all suffer from the problem of limited knowledge regarding risk of extraordinarily long use of care. Although current data suggest that approximately 90 percent of individuals who use nursing homes do not exceed four years of use, it may not be possible to easily predict the small 10 percent minority who may be very long stayers (six to eight years or more).[13] A government reinsurance program which would pay full cost of care for this group could protect insurance companies, reduce the cost of premiums, encourage the purchase of long-term care insurance and thereby potentially reduce government outlays for Medicaid. This suggests that even if private long-term care insurance policies become more common, some residual government program like Medicaid might be necessary to provide financing for extreme long stayers and for those unable to purchase insurance policies.

In this vein, it is worth noting that one common theme which runs through all of these options is an assumption that long-term care insurance premiums can be affordable and that most consumers can pay the price. We examine this issue next.

Availability of Private Funds

It seems reasonable to assume that the majority of individuals under age 65 could have their needs for long-term care insured through some type of catastrophic care policy which could be financed through the workplace. Such a plan would cover the employee as well as his or her spouse and dependents under age 21. Since the need for long-term care is relatively rare in this age group but economically devastating for individual families to finance when it does occur, risk sharing not only makes sense but should also be affordable. The question of financing long-term care insurance for the elderly is not quite as simple but may still be feasible.

Income. Most available information concerning income of the elderly derives from the decennial census, which is generally believed to underreport real wealth of the elderly since the information is self-reported and the elderly as a group are believed to underreport financial information. Thus, estimates obtained tend to err on the conservative side. Table 9–4 demonstrates that the income of elderly persons varies considerably depending upon sex, age, and marital status. All other things being equal, males have more income than women, couples are better off than single persons, and younger elderly have greater income than older elderly.

According to recent articles on these issues by Torrey and Atkins, there are several reasons why these differences exist.[14] First, men in general have worked longer and at higher wages than women and thus retire with higher social security benefits and pensions. Couples benefit from the potential availability of two incomes. The young elderly as a group appear to have benefited from a full working career under social security, increased availability of private pensions, continued participation in the work force (more young old than old-old continue to derive income from earnings) and the fact that their spouse is more likely to still be alive. In contrast, the old-old depend to a larger extent on social security as a primary source of income, no longer generate income from earnings, generally rely on pensions that are not indexed for inflation (which thus decline in real value over time), and are more likely to be single. Very old widowed and single women appear to be the most economically disadvantaged elderly subgroup and also constitute the highest numbers of institutional long-term care users.

Some evidence suggests, however, that the situation of elderly women might improve in the future. Currently, surviving widows who never worked (a large number of the current cohort of very old women age 85 and older) are allowed only two thirds of the social security income that they enjoyed while their husbands were alive. Similarly, in many instances, pensions provided to very old men do not include joint

TABLE 9–4 Median Income of Aged Units by Age, Sex, and Marital Status, 1982

Marital Status and Sex	Age of Aged Unit			
	65–67	68–72	73–79	80+
Married couples	$17,930	$16,210	$13,900	$11,070
Unmarried men	8,840	7,400	7,160	6,250
Unmarried women	6,210	6,150	5,530	5,180

SOURCE: S. Grad., *Income of the Population 55 and Over, 1982*, U.S. DHHS, Social Security Administration, Pub. no. 13–11871, Washington, 1984, Table 11.

and survivor benefits. The pensions thus cease upon their deaths, further complicating the economic plight of surviving widows. While these facts characterize the current cohort of very old women, the economic characteristics of future cohorts of very old women may be quite different since they should reflect the greater labor force participation and higher incomes earned by women during recent years.

The main point of current statistics on income of the elderly is that private insurance using age-based premiums that are fixed at the time of enrollment is much more affordable if purchased while one is still employed or during the early years of retirement. In this case, premiums are lower and more income is available for their payment. If purchased later, when real income is smaller, premiums are higher and the likelihood of needing care is greater.

Assets. It has become fashionable of late to describe the elderly's economic situation as being a cash-flow problem. As Table 9–5 illustrates, the major asset possessed by substantial numbers of the elderly is real estate; specifically a home that in most instances is wholly owned and has increased substantially in value since the time of its purchase. Rational economic theory suggests that as persons age, they accumulate assets which they can spend during retirement to provide needed services. As a result of the substantial real estate equity which elderly homeowners possess, another method of financing long-term care through home equity conversion has received a considerable amount of attention.

TABLE 9-5 Home Equity of the Elderly	
Value of Home	Percent of Elderly
none	26
$ 1— 4,999	20
5,000— 9,999	5
10,000— 19,999	7
20,000— 24,999	7
25,000— 49,999	22
50,000— 74,999	11
75,000 or more	3
Total	100

SOURCE: Adapted from Table 21, ICF Incorporated, *Private Financing of Long-Term Care: Current Methods and Resources. Phase I Final Report,* submitted to the Office of the Assistant Secretary for Planning and Evaluation, U.S. DHHS, January 1985.

Home Equity Conversion

Nearly 75 percent of people age 65 and older owned their own homes in 1980. Of these, 80 percent owned their homes free and clear.[15] As Table 9–5 demonstrates, in 1981, 49 percent of all elderly aged 65 and older possessed at least $10,000 in home equity and 42 percent had more than $20,000 tied up in a home. Bruce Jacobs and William Weissert have done some pioneering research on the possibility of converting this illiquid asset to an annuitized cash income that could be used for a variety of purposes, including the purchase of long-term care.[16] For those elderly at the lower end of the home equity scale, the conversion of equity to income could mean the difference between living below or above the poverty level; for 5 percent of all elderly, home equity conversion will still not allow the purchase of much beyond life's necessities. For approximately 60 percent of elderly, substantial cash income could be annuitized through one of two mechanisms which are currently available.

RAMs. The Reverse Annuity Mortgage (RAM) allows the elderly homeowner to borrow against accrued home equity in order to generate monthly income payments that vary in size according to the amount of home equity borrowed against, the interest rate, and the length of the loan. RAMs have been offered in three locations in the United States: California, New Jersey, and Wisconsin. Most RAMs are made for a fixed time period of from 5 to 10 years, and the amount of the loan is usually based on 60–80 percent of the home's appraised value at the time the loan is made. Thus, banks are protected to some degree from possible declines in property values and owners continue to have a vested interest in maintaining the property in order to protect their investment. Although RAMs have been in existence for several years, they tend to suffer from the major problem of fairly low consumer interest. Two major stumbling blocks which inhibit increased use of this mechanism appear to be the symbolic value of home owner- ship to the current cohort of elderly retirees and their fears about risks involved in this type of financial arrangement. RAMs generally work best for persons over age 75 or 80 because this group generally has a shorter life expectancy and is not likely to outlive a loan covering a period of 5 to 10 years. Additionally, since the loan is only needed for a relatively short time, the monthly payments are higher and thus provide larger income supplements at the time when health care expenditures are greatest. However, a large number of current elderly aged 80 and above are survivors of the Great Depres- sion and as a consequence are a very risk-aware group who value security above all else, especially in their extreme old age. The value of a house as a symbol of one's lifetime savings and as an estate that can be passed on intact to heirs also undoubtedly constrains others from using this option. As the composition of future elderly cohorts changes to include indi- viduals with different attitudes toward borrowing and if more moderately priced retirement housing becomes available, more elderly may be able to finance an increased portion of their long-term care through the sale of homes or through their conversion to an annuity. Certainly, it appears that the payment of private long-term care insurance premiums could be afforded by a substantial portion of the elderly through this mechanism.

Grannie-Mae's. Another approach to the use of home equity that may meet with more success is the Grannie-Mae approach, according to which adult children can purchase an elderly parent's home but guarantee the parent life tenacy plus a monthly annuity or monthly mortgage payments. This sale lease-back approach has several advantages for families. Adult children as buyers can depreciate the property for tax purposes while elderly sellers can take advantage of the one-time capital gains deduction of up to $125,000 on the sale that is available to homeowners over age 55. In contrast to the RAM, the loan in this case is not limited to a fixed, relatively short period of 5 to 10 years at the end of which an elderly person would be devoid of both assets and housing. Instead, the Grannie-Mae covers an extended period of time and allows property to stay within the family where it can continue to increase in value. However, the approach assumes family goodwill and trust as well as a certain dependency by the elderly on children that some older persons may find unpalatable. Finally, given the young age of both of these home equity conversion strategies, their appeal is largely untested to date.

Summary

As the foregoing discussion attests, considerable creativity is being directed toward the discovery and analysis of new approaches to the financing of long-term care. Of the strategies reviewed in this chapter, the private insurance option would definitely appear to hold the greatest amount of promise. As mentioned earlier, the pooling of public funds which could be used as state block grants for the financing of long-term care would involve substantial investment in new data management systems and a new bureaucracy that could assess eligibility and monitor and manage care plans but would not substantially expand the total pool of dollars available for care.

The CCRCs, while offering a secure haven for the well-to-do elderly, appear to be beyond the means of most elderly people. The S/HMO offers considerable advantages over the regular Medicare/HMO with respect to the scope and variety of its long-term care benefits. However, the popularity of a directly case-managed approach to care with the elderly remains to be seen.

In contrast to the above approaches, private insurance for long-term care offers several advantages. First, it is more affordable than the CCRC option and therefore more accessible to greater numbers of the elderly. Phase II of the ICF, Inc. report referred to previously estimates that 21 percent of all individuals aged 67–69 in 1980 who had at least $3,000 in assets would purchase a long-term care insurance benefit assuming premiums were less than 5 percent of their income, while 49 percent of this cohort would purchase the insurance, assuming a premium cost less than 10 percent.[17] Furthermore, as Table 9–6 illustrates, substantial benefits are predicted to accrue to both the Medicaid program and to premium holders under a long-term care insurance benefit. Specifically, Medicaid costs over a 25-year period are predicted to decline by 8 percent under the 5 percent of income scenario and by 23 percent or $9 billion under the 10 percent option. Furthermore, these savings pale in comparison to reductions in the level of out-of-pocket payments predicted. Under the 5 percent scenario, out-of-pocket payments would decline by 37 percent and under the 10 percent scenario, by 59 percent. Alternatively, under our current Medicaid funding strategy, 39 percent of this cohort would be expected to enter a nursing home at some point, 50 percent of whom would use Medicaid to finance all or part of a stay averaging over 800 days.

According to this analysis, private long-term care insurance can do a great deal for the estimated 9 million middle- to upper-middle income elderly individuals who are currently at risk of spending down income and assets due to catastrophic long-term care expenditures. The wealthy would be relatively unaffected by the development of an insurance option since they can already finance care. So, unfortunately, would the lower-income elderly unless premiums could be reduced in

---

TABLE 9–6   Effect of Long-Term Care (LTC) Insurance on
Cumulative Medicaid Costs for Nursing
Home Patients in the Age 67–69 Cohort*

		With LTC Insurance	
Source of Payment	No LTC Insurance	5 Percent Assumption†	10 Percent Assumption†
Medicare	$ 1.9	$ 1.9 (0%)	$ 1.9 (0%)
Medicaid	37.6	34.7 (−8)	28.9 (−23)
Out of Pocket	47.4	29.9 (−37)	19.6 (−59)
Insurance	0	20.6 (N/A)	39.5 (N/A)
Total	$86.9	$87.2 (+1%)	$90.0 (+4%)

*This table reflects the cumulative nursing home expenditures (in billions of nominal dollars) for all individuals in the age 67–69 cohort who enter a nursing home through the entire 35-year period.

†The 5 percent assumption assumes that individuals and couples will purchase long-term care insurance if its annual premiums are less than five percent of their income and they have $3,000 or more in financial assets. The 10 percent assumption is similar except that it assumes individuals and couples will purchase the insurance if its premiums are less than 10 percent of their income and they have $3,000 or more in financial assets.

SOURCE: ICF Incorporated, *Private Financing of Long-Term Care: Current Methods and Resources. Phase I Final Report,* submitted to the Office of the Assistant Secretary for Planning and Evaluation, U.S. DHHS, January 1985, Table 24.

size through more efficient marketing techniques or better knowledge regarding the risk associated with the benefit plans provided.

One very promising way to combine the best of both worlds (private long-term care insurance and the case-management expertise of Medicare HMOs) would entail linking the two approaches in a joint venture or wraparound of some type. At present, long-term care insurance premiums may be higher than necessary due to the inefficiencies of (1) marketing policies on an individual basis, (2) screening individuals to avoid adverse selection, and (3) lack of a case management function to monitor benefit use. In contrast, Medicare HMOs enroll large groups of elderly and case manage their care but are limited to current Medicare and Medicaid reimbursement with respect to their ability to finance the service benefits provided. Thus, their long-term benefits are quite limited. If a marriage of private long-term care insurance and Medicare HMOs could be arranged through joint ventures or wrap-arounds, both parties could potentially reap substantial benefits which could be passed on to consumers.

As a result of such a merger, economies of scale could be achieved in marketing policies and savings could accrue from the case management of benefits. The cost of an individual premium could be lowered, and Medicare HMOs could provide a far more meaningful long-term care benefit than is currently the case. Ultimately, it might also be possible to expand the type of benefit provided to include more community care options, consistent with the preferences of most older consumers.

This strategy appears to offer the most realistic solution to the problem of simultaneously maximizing protection from risk of catastrophic expense and maximizing care options for the greatest number of elderly people without further taxing public expenditures for long-term care. Theoretically, if lower cost premiums could be provided under this scenario, the number of elderly enrollees who could be enfranchised under this option would grow.

However, the problem of including the very low income group would remain. Two methods of handling this problem have been considered. First, Rosalie and Robert Kane have argued that a new Title XXI long-term care insurance benefit, similar to that provided by the Canadian government, be offered in the United States.[18] In this case, just as about 100 percent of all elderly have access to social security benefits, there would be universal entitlement to a long-term care benefit. An alternative approach which deserves some analysis would use the government as purchaser of last resort of private insurance policies for those individuals who are unable to finance premiums from their own income.

The latter strategy has several virtues. First, the government could essentially provide a voucher for these individuals who could then shop for the benefit plan with the greatest appeal. This prudent shopping would, in theory, stimulate competition among insurance plans that, in turn, should encourage variety in design of benefit options and decreases in price. Second, since individuals' income and assets would remain intact, they would be able to shop across providers. In other words, if an individual or family became dissatisfied with care in a given nursing home or care from a particular community care agency, transfer to another provider should be possible. More competition among providers with respect to quality and price of care might result. This strategy might also entail certain efficiencies since no huge government bureaucracy would be required to process claims for care. Rather, insurance coverage could be made mandatory with tax breaks given to employers to induce compliance. The strategy would have the rather compelling advantage of empowering more persons to purchase care of their choice, as opposed to our current policy of generating dependency in order to qualify for care. The strategy is discussed at greater length in the chapter to follow.

NOTES

1. Ross H. Arnett III, Carol S. Cowell, Lawrence M. Davidoff, and Mark S. Freeland, "Health Spending Trends in the 1980s: Adjusting to Financial Incentives," *Health Care Financing Review*, 6:3, Spring 1985.

2. Howard Palley and Julianne Oktay, "The Chronically Limited Elderly: The Case for a National Policy for In-Home and Supportive Community-Based Services," *Home Health Services Quarterly*, 4: Special Issue, 1983.

3. ICF Incorporated, *Private Financing of Long-Term Care: Current Methods and Resources. Phase I Final Report*, submitted to the Office of the Assistant Secretary of Planning and Evaluation, U.S. DHHS, January 1985.

4. Marjorie Carroll and Ross Arnett, "Private Health Insurance Plans in 1978 and 1979: A Review of Coverage, Enrollment, and Financial Experience," *Health Care Financing Review*, September 1981.

5. Mark R. Meiners, "The State of the Art in Long-Term Care Insurance," in Patrice Feinstein, Marian Gornick, and Jay Greenberg, *Long-Term Care Financing and Delivery Systems: Exploring Some Alternatives*, Conference Proceedings, Washington, D.C., January 24, 1984.

6. Mark R. Meiners and A. Tave, *Consumer Interest in Long-Term Care Insurance: A Survey of the Elderly in Six States* (Hyattsville, Md.: National Center for Health Services Research, 1984).

Bernard Friedman, "Private Insurance for LTC: How Large are the Unmet and Potential Demands of the Elderly?," *Working Paper 104* (Evanston, Ill.: Northwestern University, Center for Health Services and Policy Research, 1983).

Bill Jackson and Joyce Jensen, "Home Care Tops Consumers' List," *Modern Healthcare*, May 1, 1984.

7. ICF, *Phase I Final Report,* 1985.

8. Regina Herzlinger and Jeffrey Schwartz, "How Companies Tackle Health Care Costs: Part 1," *Harvard Business Review,* July–August 1985.

Regina Herzlinger, "How Companies Tackle Health Care Costs: Part II," *Harvard Business Review,* September–October 1985.

9. Mark R. Meiners and Gordon R. Trapnell, "Long-Term Care Insurance: Premium Estimates for Prototype Policies," *Medical Care,* 22:10, October 1984.

10. Stephen A. LaTour, Bernard A. Friedman, and Edward F. X. Hughes, "Medicare Beneficiary Decision Making about Health Insurance: Implications for a Voucher System," *Medical Care,* June 1986.

11. Jay N. Greenburg, Walter Leutz, Sam Ervin, Merwyn Greenlick, Dennis Kodner, and John Selstad, "The Social/Health Maintenance Organization and Long-Term Care," *Generations,* 9:4, Summer 1985.

12. Richard Zawadski, personal communication.

13. *Home Health Line,* 10, October 21, 1985, p. 295.

14. Barbara Boyle Torrey, "Sharing Increasing Costs on Declining Income," *Milbank Memorial Fund Quarterly: Health and Society,* 63:2, 1985.

G. Lawrence Atkins, "The Economic Status of the Oldest Old," *Milbank Memorial Fund Quarterly: Health and Society,* 63:2, 1985.

15. Ibid., pp. 406–407.

16. H. Bruce Jacobs and William Weissert, "Home Equity Financing of Long-Term Care for the Elderly," in Patrice Feinstein et al., *Long-Term Care Financing and Delivery Systems: Exploring Some Alternatives* (Washington, D.C.: U.S. Government Printing Office, January 24, 1984).

17. ICF, *Phase II Final Report,* January 1985.

18. Rosalie A. Kane and Robert L. Kane, "The Feasibility of Universal Long-Term Care Benefits: Ideas from Canada," *New England Journal of Medicine,* 312:21, May 23, 1985.

CHAPTER TEN

Summary: Maximizing Options

Long-term care is finally assuming a major role on the nation's social and health agenda. Policymakers are recognizing that the problem of long-term care will not go away, will increase in size if left unattended, is directly linked to our acute care costs, and may not be insurmountable.

This chapter summarizes what is known about long-term care in the United States and argues that a radically different method of financing long-term care is pivotal to achieving the overarching policy goals described in Chapter 1. The increased availability of private long-term care insurance, coupled with other advances in long-term care reimbursement and management, can do much to advance increased access, equity, affordability, quality, and continuity of care.

James Callahan has done some pathbreaking work in applying systems theory to the analysis of long-term care policy options. According to his framework, choices between "closed" and "open" systems approaches are possible. Under the closed system approach, all applicants for care would enter the system through a designated single entry point. Alternatively, an open system would allow multiple access points to care. It is important to emphasize at the outset of this summary that we do not argue here for the development of a single closed system of long-term care in the United States for two reasons.[1] First, from a practical standpoint, a unified national system of care is probably politically unattainable given the wide range of cultures, preferences, and geographical and regional differences that we as a nation subsume. Second, and perhaps more fundamentally, a single system approach to care, like the Local Area Management Organizations advocated by Ruchlin and his colleagues, may be undesirable.[2] This approach could be monolithic and uniform in scope and inefficient and unresponsive to consumer preferences. While a nationally funded and operated long-term care system might achieve equity through reducing care for all to a common denominator, it would not provide the diversity of service options which could foster consumer autonomy and increased competition, which, in turn, could increase the quality and reduce the cost of long-term care. Instead, we argue for multiple service options, or a cafeteria benefit approach, to long-term care that could encompass and foster competition among service options and promote consumer choice and continuity of care by increasing the availability of services, their loci, and levels of care provided.

History. The history of long-term care policy has been marked by fragmentation and is a textbook case of the "disjointed incrementalist" approach to public policy. As a result of this piecemeal approach, long-term care services are organized into two or three separate delivery systems that infrequently interact, have different criteria for eligibility, and use different funding mechanisms. As a result, consumers and families who are faced with the overwhelming implications of catastrophic illness have little knowledge about and frequently little control over service options. The average American is ill prepared to deal with the fact that he or she or a family member has a risk of experiencing a chronic disabling disease that could be financially devastating to all but the very poor, who have public protection, and the very well to do. The government and unions or professional organizations could play an enormous role in educating groups about their limited coverage for long-term care expenditures and their potential risk of experiencing them.

Cost. During the major part of the 20th century, acute care has occupied a center-stage position on our nation's health care agenda. We have first focused on keeping acute care providers afloat (the Blue Cross movement of the 30s), building our acute care capacity (Hill-Burton construction activities of the 40s, 50s, and 60s), and removing economic barriers to access to acute care in various ways for different population subgroups; i.e., through tax deductions for insurance coverage of working persons, Medicare for the elderly and permanently disabled, and Medicaid for the indigent. Increased access, reimbursed on the basis of uncapped, retrospective cost in an age of startling technological development, has fostered both an abundant supply of acute health care services of unexcelled quality and rapid inflation in their cost. Rapid increases in cost, in turn, have led to changes in reimbursement methods and the development of prospective case-mix reimbursement and capitated delivery systems. Finally, recent examinations of high acute care costs have begun to identify small subsets of high users as the source of a disproportionate share of these costs.[3] In many instances, these individuals suffer from chronic conditions for which they experience multiple acute care hospitalizations which often increase in number, intensity, and duration during an individual's last year of life.

We are beginning to recognize the contribution of chronic disease to acute care hospital expenditures and to better appreciate the need for links between the acute and long-term care sectors. According to Anderson and Steinberg's recent analysis of acute hospital expenditures, 23 percent of Medicare beneficiaries who were discharged from a short-stay hospital more than once over a four-year period accounted for 80 percent of Medicare inpatient hospital expenditures during that period, with 60 percent of Medicare expenditures attributable to 12.5 percent of the beneficiaries who were discharged three or more times during the same four-year period.[4] Similarly, Rice and LaPlante have reported that 14.6 percent of the noninstitutionalized population who are limited in activities because of at least one chronic condition account for 40 percent of short-stay hospital discharges, 58 percent of total short-stay hospital days, and 50 percent of all restricted activity and bed disability days nationally.[5]

Leaving the acute care costs of the chronically ill aside, institutional long-term expenditures alone have increased from $2 billion in 1965 to $27 billion in 1982. Medicaid, a shared state and federal program, is the current principal public funding source for long-term care. The states have shared directly in the increased cost of long-term care and, as a result, a broad constituency that has a vested interest in the reform of long-term care financing has developed across the country. Costs of institutional long-term care, although moderating during the last few years, have constituted as much as 40 percent of the states' Medicaid budgets, leaving very little funding remaining for acute care services and markedly constraining the undertaking of needed health promotion initiatives. Under the current Medicaid solution, indigency and dependency are fostered and access to care for the less advantaged is becoming increasingly limited as our supply of beds remains constant, the population in need of care grows, and providers target their services to private pay populations.

Demand. There is no question that the number of people in need of long-term care will increase in the future. Although healthier life styles, increased use of seat belts, and medical breakthroughs like hip replacements and lens implants may combine to reduce the morbidity and impairment caused by trauma and chronic disease, the increased survival of the very old and our increased technical ability to sustain life under very impaired circumstances indicate that the numbers of people in need of long-term care will grow substantially from 1990 to 2040. Figure 10–1, a letter written by an elderly retiree of a major Chicago corporation, speaks eloquently to this point.

Although the elderly constitute a greater proportion of those needing long-term care, they are not the only group in need. Demand for long-term care cuts across age groups and is an intergenerational issue. Specifically, while two thirds of those in need of long-term care services are age 65 or older, it is estimated that one third are under age 65.[6] Ideally, an

---

FIGURE 10–1 Letter from Elderly Retiree to Benefit Department

---

> Benefit Dept
>
> I am 82 years - live in my apartment.
> Have to have help -
> Cleaning bathroom -
> transporation to Doctor
> vacum cleaning - etc.
> Is there any way I ?
> Can get reimbursement
>
> I can get my own
> meals - Cannot shop
> for food -
>
> Please advise me
> Thank you

---

improved open system of long-term care would not be based on age, but instead on functional status or need for sustained help in activities of daily living as a criterion for care.

Available evidence also indicates that future consumers of long-term care services will be better educated, have strong preferences concerning the locus and mix of services received, and have more disposable income with which to purchase or finance care. In other words, although certain long-term care users (especially those with cognitive deficits who are without family advocates) will continue to need special protection, most long-term care users or their families can be expected to be active versus passive consumers of care. This is especially likely to be true if needed educational campaigns regarding long-term care services are undertaken in the future.

Providers. Providers are acutely aware of the growth potential of the long-term care market. Technological advances that make it possible to provide skilled treatments safely in the home, efforts to constrain acute care costs, and consumers' preferences for a wide variety of service options have combined to greatly expand the number of providers, the places in which care can be provided, and the levels and combinations of long-term care services that are possible. Some critics have argued that the array of services is confusing and may inhibit the long-term care user from using care appropriately. It seems more likely, however, that our fragmented financing mechanisms and eligibility criteria cause the confusion than the multiplicity of service options per se. Thus, if the financing of care could be streamlined, the increased array of providers and services could be expected to greatly improve consumer autonomy, thereby increasing competition among providers, who might ultimately be forced to compete on the grounds of quality or price of care offered.

Systems Integration. Just as the number and types of long-term care services have increased, changes have also occurred in the way that services are organized and delivered. Long-term care is a young growth industry and is experiencing the horizontal and vertical integration common to young industries. Although the predominance of investor-owned nursing home chains in the industry has been cited as an unmixed bane, the development of brand-name recognition of long-term care providers might have consumer benefits. Consumers have a pretty good idea of what they will be getting for their money when they stay at a Holiday Inn or buy ice cream at Howard Johnson's. In the not too distant future, they may also associate certain values with care from a Manor Care nursing home or from a VNA or Quality Care home care agency.

It is at least theoretically possible that nursing home and home care chains, irrespective of ownership type, could reduce the cost of long-term care through purchasing, marketing, and other administrative efficiencies. However, it is important to be careful in using the term "chain." For example, HCFA uses the term to include any agency having a separate administrative office or branch. It is not at all clear that the term chain should be used to refer to the corporate restructuring currently occurring at an epidemic rate among what are otherwise single, free-standing home care providers. This restructuring is not intended in most cases to achieve the economies of scale associated with horizontal integration. Rather, it is occurring in response to current Medicare step-down, cost accounting methods that force agencies to protect non-Medicare funds from subsidizing the legitimate costs of providing Medicare services and allows them to develop other lines of business in anticipation of increased competition.

While true horizontal integration may lower the cost of care by providing economies of scale and may standardize levels of care by fostering brand-name recognition, vertical integration in the industry is also increasing rapidly and has the potential to increase both access to care and its continuity. Since more providers are providing multiple levels of care, possible entry points to care are multiplied, and since levels of care are offered in a systems context, transfers from one level to another are facilitated.

Quality.   The increased availability of providers and services is both a long-term boon and a short-run problem with respect to quality of care. Increased service options can improve the quality of long-term care in the sense that better matches ought to be possible between services offered and an individual's changing needs for care over time. Theoretically, an increased array of options should heighten consumer satisfaction and facilitate the utilization of appropriate levels or intensity of care. On the other hand, the increased number of providers and services is described as a short-term problem because useful quality standards and norms take time to develop. As a consequence, they are largely absent at present in some of our newer forms of community-based care like high-tech home care, homemaker and chore services, and adult day care. We do not wish to imply that community-care services are inferior in quality to institutional services. Rather, we are simply stating that these services are new and that time will be required before appropriate standards of care can be developed for them. The increased multiplicity of services and providers (assuming that care can be financed) should also heighten the quality of long-term care insofar as consumers will increasingly be able to choose among alternatives. As a result of increased consumer autonomy, competition on the basis of quality can be expected to increase across long-term care providers.

Finally, the growing recognition of the need for multiple measures and observers of quality, that is, increased involvement of the public in long-term care services, increased availability of physicians, and the long-overdue recognition of the importance of consumer satisfaction with care, can lead to new definitions of and possibilities for improving the quality of long-term care services.

Reimbursement Reforms. We have learned a great deal about better ways to pay for publicly and privately financed health care services over the last 20 years. The states, in particular, as bulk purchasers of care have come to recognize their ability to manipulate the supply, demand, price, variety, and loci of long-term care services. As a result, nursing home admissions of potential Medicaid eligibles are being screened for prior approval, and these persons are increasingly offered community care alternatives when possible. Similarly, both the rate of increase in and the supply of long-term care providers are being more carefully regulated. These efficiencies in the Medicaid program are important and noteworthy, but they ultimately raise the question of how much can be wrung from the Medicaid dollar before those whom the system is supposed to benefit begin to suffer. Specifically, as the level of Medicaid reimbursement declines, nursing homes increasingly target their services to private pay customers. Since this latter group is predicted to increase in size while our bed supply is remaining relatively constant, it appears that access to care among Medicaid patients can only become more acute. Thus, the Medicaid reimbursement reforms and their resulting efficiencies may ultimately help to cement in place a two-tiered, inequitable system of long-term care. One way to solve this dilemma would be to minimize, if not dismantle, the role of Medicaid in financing long-term care in favor of mandatory long-term care insurance of either a public or private nature. In the latter case, just as diagnosis-related groups and other Medicare reimbursement reforms are being adopted by the private insurance industry, so RUGS II and other long-term care case-mix reimbursement methods could be adopted by the insurance industry.

The Pivotal Role of Financing

We argue that improvements in our current methods of financing long-term care are central to achieving the overarching policy goals of increased access, equity, affordability, quality, and continuity of care as outlined below.

Access.   Neither Medicare nor private supplementary insurance policies cover long-term care expenditures to any meaningful degree. Medicaid, our only public insurance program, requires the depletion of personal assets. At present, individuals are required to pay all long-term care costs out of pocket to the point of indigency before Medicaid becomes available to underwrite total costs of care. This "all or nothing" solution to financing care creates several severe problems with respect to access. First, as long as we have a shortage of long-term care beds or services, Medicaid patients whose care is reimbursed at a lower rate will be unattractive to providers who will preferentially admit private paying patients. Second, once a private pay patient spends down to the point of Medicaid eligibility, he or she has no resources left to use for discharge planning or to purchase care from another facility or provider. Thus, the patient essentially becomes the provider's captive. States could attempt to solve this problem through a variety of regulatory methods. For example, states could provide preferential certificate of need approvals for providers who admit a minimum number of Medicaid patients. The states could also reimburse according to intensity of care required or factor in special bonus payments for providers who care for a specific proportion of Medicaid patients. These approaches would facilitate Medicaid admissions; however, Medicaid transfers or discharges would be much more difficult under a regulatory approach. Long-term care insurance, in contrast, would render the patient sought after by providers and would enable the beneficiary or his family or advocate to pick and choose across a variety of services.

Equity. Under our current system of financing care, financial status rather than needs and preferences determine eligibility for care. The Medicaid Section 2176 waivers discussed in Chapter 7 redress to some extent the current imbalance in our public spending for institutional versus community-based long-term care. Private insurance could carry this approach even further by directly encouraging conscious trade-offs by consumers in the decision to use home versus inpatient care. Chronically impaired users of long-term care usually suffer from multiple deficits and have lost control over a number of important functions. It is particularly important that they, as a group, be enabled to exercise choice and autonomy to the maximum extent feasible. A private long-term care insurance policy with a comprehensive benefit structure could do a lot to further this important policy goal.

Affordability. Long-term care is not needed by everyone. Even among the highest risk group of persons over age 80, only one in five use institutional long-term care services. Yet if one should be unlucky enough to need it, the cost of care is catastrophic. At present, nursing home care averages $27,000 a year. Table 10–1 displays figures from a recent analysis of the elderly's risk of spend down to Medicaid coverage under alternative scenarios. The analysis was conducted by Larry Branch and colleagues using longitudinal data from the Massachusetts Panel Study and Framingham data sets and demonstrates that startling proportions of the elderly, if institutionalized, will become Medicaid eligible within three months of admission. The numbers range from 63 percent of all elderly over age 65 who live alone to 37 percent of married couples. Even costs of home care are shown

TABLE 10-1 Risk of Spend Down to Medicaid Eligibility among Different Elderly Subgroups

	Percent of Elderly Meeting Spend-Down Criteria over Time (Weeks)					
	0	13	26	39	52	104
75 years and older*						
Live alone and institutionalized	7	46	59	66	72	85
Married couple, one of whom is institutionalized	2	25	41	43	57	82
Married couple, one of whom requires extensive home care due to Alzheimers†	2	11	25	30	41	52
66 years and older						
Live alone and institutionalized	8	63	74	80	83	91
Married couple, one of whom is institutionalized	4	37	47	53	57	80
Married couple, one of whom requires extensive home care due to Alzheimers‡	4	16	33	39	47	55

*Based on data from the Massachusetts' Health Care Panel Study, a longitudinal investigation of the health and social needs of the elderly. Institutional costs are based on an estimated $75 per diem cost of care.

†Based on estimated 6.28 hours of homemaker or home health aide service/day as per findings of Hu, Huang, and Cartwright and calculated at the rate of $5.69 per hour (prevailing charge in Massachusetts).

‡Based on data from the Framingham longitudinal study.

SOURCE: Lawrence G. Branch, Daniel J. Friedman, and Elinor Socholitzky, testimony before the House Select Committee on Aging, July 30, 1985.

to be potentially economically devastating, with 50 percent of married couples who receive home care services for the care of an Alzheimers-impaired spouse spending down to Medicaid in one year. At present, these catastrophic expenditures are funded out of pocket until the point of medical indigency is reached. There must be a better way to distribute these costs so that care can be affordable when needed. Long-term care insurance would achieve this goal by spreading risk across a large group of enrollees who would encompass both the well and the sick. It would also eliminate the spend down of income and assets by middle-income users and would produce substantial savings for Medicaid, which could be used as a reinsurance program for extreme long stayers as well as a means of financing or purchasing insurance premiums for the indigent.

Quality. As mentioned earlier, long-term care insurance has the potential to improve the quality of care insofar as it can increase the autonomy of the long-term care consumer and increase competition among providers and service options. Armed with knowledge about the available array of service options and empowered to purchase care of his or her choice, consumers or their families could pick and choose among providers at will, in the same way that individuals shop among primary and acute care providers today.[7] There would still be a role for oversight and quality-assurance standards but whether this role would be most effectively played by public or private regulators or some combination of the two remains to be seen. The protection of the cognitively impaired who lack family advocates will continue to require special attention and more experimentation with different models of guardianship and ombudsman activities. Ultimately, however, increased public knowledge about quality standards for long-term care and increased purchasing power could go a long way to improve quality standards in the industry.

Affordability. The development of pooled risk-sharing financing methods for long-term care would constitute an improvement over our current Medicaid spend-down approach in making care affordable for the individual consumer. If lessons learned from the long-term care reimbursement and capitation experiments described earlier are transferred, the cost-inflating spiral associated with long-term care in the past can also be better managed in the future. The increased availability of private long-term care insurance could also help to reduce Medicaid expenditures, thus reducing outlays for publicly financed care at both the state and federal level. The creation of a private insurance market estimated to be ultimately worth $5 billion would also create new income and tax revenues which could be used to offset rather than augment the federal deficit.[8]

At least two issues require further consideration, however, in the attempt to use long-term care insurance as a vehicle to increase the affordability of care. First, some creative thinking and research needs to be devoted to the whole issue of mandatory catastrophic care insurance that would cover all United States citizens, including the estimated 30 million who are currently uninsured. A second issue concerns the role of federal tax policy in encouraging the development of private long-term care, catastrophic insurance plans. Jeff Goldsmith has written recently about the erosion that has occurred in the acute care health insurance line of business among the nation's largest insurance companies.[9] According to Goldsmith, the combined inroads of alternative delivery systems and self-funded insurance plans among employers have substantially eroded the acute care health insurance market share which the major insurers enjoyed in the past. Insurers may have learned from their losses and may be ready to assume a more assertive posture concerning cost control and premium increases. Alternatively, employers may wish to develop their own long-term care benefit plans to maximize their cash flow and more closely monitor beneficiary use. In either case, federal tax policy in allowing employer and employee deductions for long-term care or catastrophic insurance can play a critical role in encouraging the development of this financing option. At present, the magnitude of public cost savings resulting from tax incentives for the development of insurance options is unknown but constitutes an important area for future research.

Continuity. We have also argued that the availability of a comprehensive catastrophic long-term care insurance benefit can positively impact continuity of care by enabling the purchase of a variety of service options. Under our current Medicaid versus out-of-pocket financing system, individuals are encouraged to hoard resources against the possibility of eventual medical indigency caused by institutional care expenditures. In all fairness, the private long-term care insurance policies that currently exist do little to facilitate a continuum approach to such care insofar as the community-care benefits now offered are very narrowly defined. However, the S/HMO, On-Lok, and AARP/Prudential initiatives now in place can be very instructive in documenting patterns of community-care use over time and in establishing predictors of use and cost that can be used to structure more generous and simultaneously more affordable community-care options in the future.

Issues Requiring Further Research

Three major trends which have as yet unknown consequences for long-term care will be important to monitor in the future.

Capitation. As discussed earlier, the increased availability of Medicare risk-based HMO/CMPs and the S/HMO demonstrations will have important implications with respect to the continuity and affordability of future long-term care services. The fact that providers will be at financial risk for providing cost-effective care should improve the efficiency with which care is delivered and increase its affordability. Similarly, efforts of the capitated systems to contain costs should result in searches for least costly alternatives, which in theory should stimulate the development of vertically integrated systems of care. However, the impact of case-managed, capitated delivery systems on consumer autonomy and access to services of choice is less well known and will be very important to monitor in the future

Consolidation. The impact of the current trend toward the increased consolidation of long-term care providers into a handful of multiunit systems is unknown but has potentially serious implications with respect to issues of cost, quality, and access to long-term care services in the future. Very little is known about the comparative effects of system versus nonsystem membership on these attributes of care at the individual provider level. Our current research on multiunit hospital systems indicates that these organizations are becoming much more involved in long-term care than they have been in the past.[10] Eight multiunit hospital systems were recently asked to rank the strategic importance of 15 different health care services. As Figure 10–2 demonstrates, home health care and long-term care were ranked among the top five. This configuration of top five choices differs substantially from that which we would have observed three to four years ago, prior to the implementation of prospective payment, and it speaks eloquently to the intentions of the multis with respect to long-term care activities in the future. The increased consolidation of nursing homes and home care agencies will also be impor-

FIGURE 10–2 Services Viewed as Most Important to Systems' Goals/Strategic Plans (N = 8)

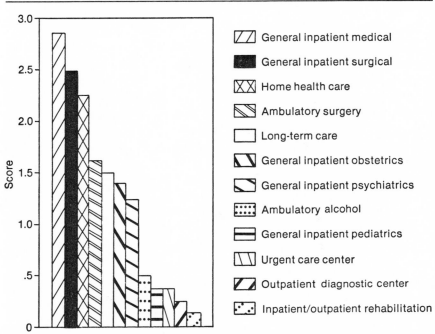

tant to monitor and to assess with respect to both positive and negative effects on quality and cost of care.

Community Care. As we repeatedly stressed throughout this book, low-tech community-care services are underfunded in the United States despite the fact that consumers consider them to be the first option of choice.

In our view, community and institutional care do not compete but rather complement one another. Given the increase in the number of people needing long-term care in the future, both types of care will be sorely needed. At present, public funding for institutional care clearly surpasses that available for community care. However, if our current institutional bed supply remains constant, the need for community care may increase rapidly. As a result of Medicare prospective payment for hospital care and Medicare and Medicaid case-mix reimbursement for nursing home and home care, the case mix of both nursing home and Medicare home care providers may shift to include heavier proportions of subacute patients in the future. As a result of this shift, lighter-care, lower-income patients who formerly received long-stay sheltered or intermediate nursing home care may be left in a no-care zone. As we stated in Chapter 8, these people are not without needs; they simply do not require sophisticated or intense medical or nursing care. Estimates of the size and characteristics of this population and their service patterns and cost are needed in order to develop viable public or private financing strategies for their care.

Importance of Health Services Research

Finally, in closing, it is important to note the critical role that research and development have played and will continue to play in long-term care. From the community-based care experiments to the development of the S/HMOs, from RUGS II to estimates of demand for long-term care insurance and of active life expectancy, health services research has played a critical role in informing decision makers about the complexity and trade-offs involved in long-term care policy options. As a result of these research and development activities, as a society we can confront the crisis and opportunity of long-term care with better knowledge and understanding regarding the degree to which issues like access and quality interact. We can now approach new policy options with greater appreciation of the need for a comprehensive systems approach to care. Herzlinger and Schwartz have recently characterized health care costs as a "lump of rubber: (wherein) pushing down on one part will only cause a rise in another."[11] As a result of research undertaken over the last decade, we are acutely aware of this need for a comprehensive systems approach to the development of new long-term care delivery and financing options. Not only do we understand the complexity and interplay of the issues better, we also now have new tools and a new armamentarium of strategies and techniques with which to attack them. As a result of this progress, and if such activities continue to be invested in the future, we can welcome the problem of long-term care for what it really is—the opportunity to structure better and more affordable catastrophic care for all.

NOTES

1. James J. Callahan, "A Systems Approach to Long-Term Care," in *Reforming the Long Term Care System,* ed. Callahan and Wallack, 1981.

2. H. S. Ruchlin, J. N. Morris, and G. H. Eggert, "Management and Financing of Long-Term-Care Services," *New England Journal of Medicine,* 306, January 14, 1982, pp. 101–106.

3. C. J. Zook and F. D. Moore, "High Cost of Medical Care," *New England Journal of Medicine,* 302:18, May 1, 1980.

J. Lubitz and R. Prihoda, *Use and Costs of Medicare Services in the Last Years of Life,* National Center for Health Statistics, DHHS Pub. no. (PHS) 84–1232, December 1983.

Stephen T. Fleming, Edward J. Kobrinski, and Michael J. Long, "A Multidimensional Analysis of the Impact on High-Cost Hospitalization," *Inquiry,* 22:178–187, Summer 1985.

4. Gerard F. Anderson and Earl Steinberg, "Hospital Readmissions in the Medicare Population," *New England Journal of Medicine,* 311:21, November 22, 1984, pp. 1349–1353.

5. Dorothy Rice and Mitchell LaPlante, "The Burden of Multiple Chronic Conditions," paper presented at the Annual Meeting of the American Public Health Association, Anaheim, Calif., November 12, 1984.

6. William G. Weissert, "Size and Characteristics of the Noninstitutionalized Long-Term Care Population," *Urban Institute Working Paper,* 1466–20, September 1982.

7. Jeff Charles Goldsmith, "Death of a Paradigm: The Challenge of Competition," *Health Affairs,* 3:3, Fall 1984, p. 11.

8. Milton Freudenheim, "Business and Health: Nursing Home Insurance," *The New York Times,* October 30, 1985, p. 34.

9. Goldsmith, "Death of a Paradigm."

10. Susan Hughes, Stephen Shortell, Ellen Morrison, and Bernard Friedman, "A Study of the Strategies, Structures, and Performance of Multi-Unit Hospital Systems: Implications for Long-Term Care," presentation at the National Center for Health Services Research and National Institute on Aging Workshop, Bethesda, Md., September 29, 1985.

11. Regina E. Herzlinger and Jeffrey Schwartz, "How Companies Tackle Health Care Costs: Part I," *Harvard Business Review,* July–August 1985, p. 69.

BIBLIOGRAPHY

"Abuse Reports Burgeon in New York Facilities." *Contemporary Long-Term Care,* April 1985.

American Hospital Association. *Hospital Statistics.* 1981.

American Hospital Association. *Hospital Statistics.* 1982.

American Medical Association. *SMS Report.* AMA: Center for Health Policy Research, 3:7, October 1984.

ANDERSON, GERARD F., and EARL STEINBERG. "Hospital Readmissions in the Medicare Population." *New England Journal of Medicine,* 311:21(November 22, 1984), 1349–1353.

ARLING, GREG; JOHN A. CAPITMAN; and ANGELA SMITH. *Findings from the Virginia Long-Term Care Tracking System Project.* Richmond, Va.: Virginia Commonwealth University Center on Aging, December 1, 1984.

ARNETT, ROSS H. III; CAROL S. COWELL; LAWRENCE M. DAVIDOFF; and MARK S. FREELAND. "Health Spending Trends in the 1980's: Adjusting to Financial Incentives." *Health Care Financing Review,* 6:3, Spring 1985.

ATKINS, G. LAWRENCE. "The Economic Status of the Oldest Old." Milbank Memorial Fund Quarterly: *Health and Society,* 63:2, 1985.

BALDWIN, CARLISS Y., and CHRISTINE E. BISHOP. "Return to Nursing Home Investment: Issues for Public Policy." *University Health Policy Consortium Working Paper DP-50,* January 1983.

BASSUK, ELLEN, and SAMUEL GERSON. "Deinstitutionalization and Mental Health Services." *Scientific American,* 238:2, February 1978, pp. 46–53.

BERK, MARC L.; GAIL LEE CAFFERATA; and MICHAEL HAGAN. "Persons with Limitations of Activity: Insurance, Expenditures and Use of Services." *NCHES Data Preview 19,* PHS, 84–3363.

BESDINE, RICHARD W. "Decisions to Withhold Treatment from Nursing Home Residents." *Journal of the American Geriatrics Society,* 31:10, October 1983, pp. 602–606.

BISBEE, GERALD, JR., and DONNA J. MELKONIAN. "Hospitals: Major Focus of Medical, Social Services." *Generations,* November 1980, pp. 22–34.

BISHOP, CHRISTINE E.; ALONZO L. PLOUGH; and THOMAS R. WILLEMAIN. "Nursing Home Levels of Care: Problems and Alternatives." *Health Care Financing Review,* Fall 1980.

BLUM, STEPHEN R., and MEREDITH MINKLER. "Toward a Continuum of Caring Alternatives: Community-Based Care for the Elderly." *Journal of Social Issues,* 36:2, 1980.

BRODY, HOWARD, and JOANNE LYNN. "Sounding Board: The Physician's Responsibility Under the New Medicare Reimbursement for Hospice Care." *New England Journal of Medicine,* April 5, 1984.

BREMNER, R. H. *From the Depths.* New York: New York University Press, 1956.

BUCHANAN, ROBERT J. "Medicaid Cost Containment: Prospective Reimbursement for Long-Term Care." *Inquiry,* 20, Winter 1983, pp. 334–342.

Bureau of the Census. *Projections of the Population of the United States: 1982–2050,* (Advance Report). Current Population Reports, Population: Estimates and Projections, Series P-25, no. 922, Washington, D.C.: U.S. Department of Commerce, 1982.

BYRNE, JOHN P., and ROBERT RUBRIGHT. "How Vital are the VNA's?" *Caring,* October 1984, pp. 65–68.

CALLAHAN, JAMES J. "A Systems Approach to Long-Term Care." In *Reforming the Long Term Care System,* ed. Callahan and Wallack. 1981.

CAMPION, EDWARD; AXEL BANG; and MAURICE T. MAY. "Why Acute Care Hospitals Must Undertake Long-Term Care." *New England Journal of Medicine,* 308:2, January 13, 1983, pp. 71–75.

CARROLL, MARJORIE, and ROSS ARNETT. "Private Health Insurance Plans in 1978 and 1979: A Review of Coverage, Enrollment, and Financial Experience." *Health Care Financing Review,* September 1981.

CHERRY, LAWRENCE, and RONA CHERRY. "New Hope for the Disabled." *New York Times Magazine*, February 5, 1984, pp. 52–55, 59, and 60.

COLLINS, GLEN. "Increasing Numbers of Aged Return North from Florida." *New York Times*, March 15, 1984, pp. 1 and 10.

CONNOR, MICHAEL J.; and SANDRA B. GREENE. "Should Extended Care Following Hospitalization Be Encouraged?" *Inquiry*, Fall 1983.

COTTERILL, PHILIP G. "Provider Incentives Under Alternative Reimbursement Systems." In *Long Term Care*, ed. Vogel and Palmer. U.S. DHHS Health Care Financing Administration, no. 82–600609, 1982.

CURTIS, RICHARD, and LAWRENCE BARTLETT. "High Cost of LTC Squeezes State Budgets." *Generations*, Fall 1984.

DEMING, MARY BEARD, and NEAL E. CUTLER. "Demography of the Aged." In *Aging: Scientific Perspectives and Social Issues*, ed. Diana S. Woodruff and James E. Birrin. Monterey, Calif.: Brooks/Cole Publishing, 1983.

DOLAN, MICHAEL, ed. *Long Term Care Management*, Washington: McGraw Hill: 15:4 February 27, 1986.

DONABEDIAN, AVEDIS. "Evaluating the Process of Medical Care." *Milbank Memorial Fund Quarterly*, 44:SUPPL, July 1966, pp. 166–206.

DONLAN, THOMAS G. "No Place Like Home: That's Increasingly True These Days for Health Care." *Barron's*, March 21, 1983, pp. 6, 7, and 32.

EVASHWICK, CONNIE. "Long-Term Care Becomes Major New Role for Hospitals." *Hospitals*, July 1, 1982, pp. 50–55.

FIELD, M., and B. SCHLESS. "Extension of Medical Social Services Into the Home." *Social Casework*, March 1948, pp. 22–25.

FLEMING, STEPHEN T.; EDWARD J. KOBRINSKI; and MICHAEL J. LONG. "A Multidimensional Analysis of the Impact of High-Cost Hospitalization." *Inquiry*, 22, Summer 1985, pp. 178–187.

FREELAND, MARK S., and CAROL ELLEN SCHENDLER. "National Health Expenditure Growth in the 1980s: An Aging Population, New Technologies, and Increasing Competition." *Health Care Financing Review*, 4:3, 1983.

FREUDENHEIM, MILTON. "Business and Health: Nursing Home Insurance." *The New York Times*, October 30, 1985, p. 34.

FRIEDMAN, BERNARD. "Private Insurance for LTC: How Large are the Unmet and Potential Demands of the Elderly?" *Working Paper 104*: Evanston, Ill.: Northwestern University, Center for Health Services and Policy Research, 1983.

FRIES, JAMES. "The Compression of Morbidity." *Milbank Memorial Fund Quarterly: Health and Society,* 61:3, Summer 1983.

FROST and SULLIVAN. *Home Healthcare Producers and Services Markets in the United States.* New York 1983, Report A1120.

GLICK, PHYLLIS ET AL. "Pediatric Nursing Homes." *New England Journal of Medicine,* 309:11, September 15, 1983.

GOLDSMITH, JEFF CHARLES. *Can Hospitals Survive?* Homewood, Ill.: Dow-Jones Irwin, 1981.

GOLDSMITH, JEFF CHARLES. "Death of a Paradigm: The Challenge of Competition." *Health Affairs,* 3:3, Fall 1984.

GREENBERG, JAY N.; WALTER LEUTZ; SAM ERVIN; MERWYN GREEN-LICK; DENNIS KODNER; and JOHN SELSTAD. "The Social/Health Maintenance Organization and Long-Term Care." *Generations,* 9:4, Summer 1985.

GREENBLATT, CHARLES. "Profit Sharing in the Long-Term Care Industry: A Cure for Many Ills." Paper presented at the Gerontological Society of America Annual Meeting, San Diego, 1984.

GREENE, V. L., and D. MONAHAN. "A Comparison of the Level of Care Predictors of Six Long-Term Care Patient Assessment Systems." *American Journal of Public Health,* 70:11, November 1980.

GUSTAFSON, DAVID H.; RICHARD VAN KONINGSVELD; and ROBERT W. PETERSON. "Assessment of Level of Care: Implications of Inerrater Reliability on Health Policy." *Health Care Financing Review,* 6:2, Winter 1984.

HAMME, JOEL M. "The Law and Long-Term Care." *Contemporary Administrator for Long-Term Care,* February 1985, pp. 20 and 21.

HARKINS, ELIZABETH BATES. *Study of the Virginia Nursing Home Preadmission Screening Program, Final Report.* Richmond, Va.: Virginia Commonwealth University Center on Aging, March 31, 1982.

HARRINGTON, CHARLENE, and JAMES H. SWAN. "Medicaid Nursing Home Reimbursement Policies, Rates, and Expenditures." *Health Care Financing Review,* 6:1, Fall 1984.

HARRIS, RICHARD. *A Sacred Trust.* New York: The New American Library, 1966.

HELBING, CHARLES. "Medicare: Participating Providers and Suppliers of Health Care Services." *Health Care Financing Notes,* 1981.

HERZLINGER, REGINA. "How Companies Tackle Health Care Costs: Part II." *Harvard Business Review,* September–October 1985.

HERZLINGER, REGINA E., and JEFFREY SCHWARTZ. "How Companies Tackle Health Care Costs: Part I." *Harvard Business Review,* July–August 1985.

HILL, JENNIFER BINGHAM. "High-Tech Home Health Care Is Showing Promise, But Some Big Problems Remain." *Wall Street Journal,* April 14, 1984.

HINES, WILLIAM. "Many Newborns Expected to Live to 100." *Chicago Sun-Times,* June 21, 1984.

HING, ESTHER. "Characteristics of Nursing Home Residents, Health Status, and Care Received: National Nursing Home Survey, United States, May–December 1977." *Vital and Health Statistics,* Series 13:51, April 1981.

HOLDER, ELMA L. "Redirecting the Focus from Paper to People." *Contemporary Long-Term Care,* April 1985.

HOLT, STEPHEN W. "Vertical Integration in Home Care—Part I." *Caring,* March 1985, pp. 54–57.

Home Health Line. Vol. X, October 21, 1985, p. 295.

"Home Health PPS Demo Will Be Organized by ABT Associates." *Hospitals,* March 16, 1985, p. 47.

HUGHES, KATHLEEN A. "Nursing 'Homes.'" Letter to the Editor, *The New York Times,* July 5, 1983.

HUGHES, SUSAN L. "Home Health Monitoring: Ensuring Quality in Home Care Services." *Hospitals,* November 1, 1982, pp. 74–80.

HUGHES, SUSAN L.; DAVID CORDRAY; and V. ALAN SPIKER. "Evaluation of a Long-Term Home Care Program." *Medical Care,* 22:5, May 1984.

HUGHES, SUSAN. "Apples and Oranges? A Review of Community-Based Long-Term Care Demonstrations." *Health Services Research,* 20:4, October 1985.

HUGHES, SUSAN; LARRY MANHEIM; PERRY EDELMAN; and KENDON CONRAD. "Impact of Long-Term Home Care on Hospital and Nursing Home Use and Cost." *Working Paper,* Evanston, Ill.: Northwestern University, Center for Health Services and Policy Research, March 1986.

HUGHES, SUSAN; STEPHEN SHORTELL; ELLEN MORRISON; and BERNARD FRIEDMAN. "A Study of the Strategies, Structures, and Performance of Multi-Unit Hospital Systems: Implications for Long-Term Care." Presentation at the National Center for Health Services Research and National Institute on Aging Workshop, Bethesda, Md., September 29, 1985.

ICF Inc. *Private Financing and Long-Term Care: Current Methods and Resources. Phase I Final Report.* Submitted to the Office of the Assistant Secretary of Planning and Evaluation, U.S. DHSS, January 1985.

Illinois Dept. of Public Aid. "New Nurses Ensure Quality Care." *Family,* 2:2, Spring 1985.

International Center for Social Gerontology. *Report on Congregate Housing.* Washington, D.C., 1978.

"Interview with the President." *Growing,* Bensenville, Ill.: Bensenville Home Society, Spring 1984.

JACKSON, BILL, and JOYCE JENSEN. "Home Care Tops Consumers' List." *Modern Healthcare,* May 1, 1984.

JACOBS, BRUCE H., and WILLIAM WEISSERT. "Home Equity Financing of Long-Term Care for the Elderly." In Patrice Feinstein et al. *Long Term Care Financing and Delivery Systems: Exploring Some Alternatives,* Washington, D.C., U.S. Government Printing Office, January 24, 1984.

"JCAH Accreditation for Long-Term Care Facilities: Consider the Benefits." Joint Commission on Accreditation of Hospitals promotional brochure, 1983.

JONES, BRENDA J., and MARK MEINERS. "Nursing Home Discharges: The Result of an Incentive Reimbursement Experiment." Hyattsville, Md.: National Center for Health Services Research and Health Care Technology Assessment, April 19, 1985.

KANE, ROBERT L.; ROBERT BELL; SANDRA RIEGLER; ALISA WILSON; and EMMETT KEELER. "Predicting the Outcomes of Nursing Home Patients." *The Gerontologist,* 23:2, 1983.

KANE, ROBERT L.; ROBERT BELL; SANDRA RIEGLER; ALISA WILSON; and ROSALIE A. KANE. "Assessing the Outcomes of Nursing Home Patients." *Journal of Gerontology,* 38:4, 1983.

KANE, ROSALIE A., and ROBERT L. KANE. "The Feasibility of Universal Long-Term Care Benefits: Ideas from Canada." *New England Journal of Medicine,* 312:21, May 23, 1985.

KATZ, SIDNEY ET AL. "Active Life Expectancy." *The New England*

Journal of Medicine, 309:20, November 19, 1983, pp. 1218–1224.

"Kids Who Live in ICUs: HHS Will Send Some Home." *Medical World News,* October 10, 1983.

KNOWLTON, JACKSON; STEVEN CLAUSER; and JAMES FATULA. "Nursing Home Preadmission Screening: A Review of State Programs." *Health Care Financing Review,* 3:3, March 1982.

KRAMER, ANDREW; PETER SHAUGHNESSY; and MARY PETTIGREW. "Cost-Effectiveness Implications Based on a Comparison of Nursing Home and Home Health Case Mix." *Health Service Research,* 20:4, October 1985, p. 387–406.

KUROWSKI, BETTINA D., and PETER W. SHAUGHNESSY. "The Measurement and Assurance of Quality." In *Long Term Care,* ed. Vogel and Palmer. U.S., DHHS, Pub. no. 82–600609.

LATOUR, STEPHEN A.; BERNARD A. FRIEDMAN; and EDWARD F. X. HUGHES. "Medicare Beneficiary Decision Making about Health Insurance: Implications for a Voucher System." *Medical Care,* June 1986.

LAVE, JUDITH. "Medicare: Use of Skilled Nursing Facilities, 1980." *Health Care Financing Notes,* September 1983.

LEONE, NICHOLAS. "Competitive Strategies for a Consolidating Market." *Home Health Line,* vol IX, October 1, 1984, pp. 248–252.

LEVIT, KATHARINE R.; HELEN LAZENBY; DANIEL R. WALDO; and LAWRENCE M. DAVIDOFF. "National Health Expenditures, 1984." *Health Care Financing Review,* Fall 1985.

LEWIS, ED. "Reagan Plan Shifts Costs to Families." *Contemporary Long-Term Care,* July 1985.

LIU, KORBIN, and YUKO PALESCH. "The Nursing Home Population: Different Perspectives and Implications for Policy." *Health Care Financing Review,* 3:2, December 1981.

LIU, KORBIN, and KENNETH G. MANTON. "The Characteristics and Utilization Pattern of an Admission Cohort of Nursing Home Patients." *The Gerontologist,* 23:1, 1983, pp. 92–98.

Long-Term Care Management. Ed. Michael Dolan. N.Y.: McGraw-Hill, February 27, 1986.

"Louise Maberry: First Lady of Texas Home Health Directs Six-State Nonprofit Giant." *Home Health Line,* vol. IX, September 3, 1984.

LUBITZ, J., and R. PRIHODA. *Use and Costs of Medicare Services in the Last Years of Life.* National Center for Health Statistics, DHHS Publication no. (PHS) 84–1232, December 1983.

MAHESHWARAN, D.; SUSAN HUGHES; and RUTH SINGER. "Marketing Survey of Upper Income Elderly." *Working Paper,* Evanston, Ill.: Northwestern University, Center for Health Services and Policy Research, December 2, 1983.

MANTON, KENNETH G., and KORBIN LIU. "Projecting Chronic Disease Prevalence." *Medical Care,* 22:6, June 1984, pp. 511–526.

McCAFFREE, KENNETH ET AL. "Profits, Growth and Reimbursement Systems in the Nursing Home Industry." *Health Care Financing Grants and Contracts Report,* April 1981.

McDONALD, MARGARET. "Home Health Care and Long-Term Care: Growing Together." *Contemporary Administrator for Long Term Care,* July 1984, pp. 38–40.

MEINERS, MARK R. "The State of the Art in Long-Term Care Insurance." In Patrice Feinstein, Marian Gornick and Jay Greenberg, *Long Term Care Financing and Delivery Systems: Exploring Some Alternatives,* Conference Proceedings, Washington, D.C., January 24, 1984.

MEINERS, MARK R; PHYLLIS THORBURN; PAMELA C. RODDY; and BRENDA J. JONES. "Nursing Home Admissions: The Results of an Incentive Reimbursement Experiment." Hyattsville, Md.: National Center for Health Services Research and Health Care Technology Assessment, May 31, 1985.

MEINERS, MARK R., and A. TAVE. *Consumer Interest in Long-Term Care Insurance: A Survey of the Elderly in Six States.* Hyattsville, Md.: National Center for Health Services Research, 1984.

MEINERS, MARK R., and GORDON R. TRAPNELL. "Long-Term Care Insurance: Premium Estimates for Prototype Policies." *Medical Care,* 22:10, October 1984.

MERRILL, RICHARD. Personal communication. Intergovernmental Health Policy Project, Washington, D.C.

MILLER, WALLY. "How I Made Miller's Manors Merrier." *Contemporary Administrator for Long Term Care,* October 1984.

MUSE, DONALD N., and DARWIN SAWYER. "The Medicaid and Medicare Data Book, 1981." *Health Care Financing Program Statistics,* April 1982.

NAUERT, ROGER C. "Building Networks Today, Keeping Pace with Tomorrow." *Contemporary Administrator for Long-Term Care,* November 1984, pp. 42–45.

"New York State Long-Term Care Case Reimbursement Project Executive Summary: Derivation of RUG-II." New York State Department of Health and Rensselaer Polytechnic Institute, December 1984.

NEWACHECK, PAUL; PETER BUDETTI; and PEGGY MCMANUS. "Trends in Childhood Disability." *American Journal of Public Health,* 74:3, March 1984.

O'SHAUGHNESSY, CAROL, and RICHARD PRICE. *Medicaid "2176" Waivers for Home and Community-Based Care.* Washington, D.C.: Congressional Research Service, June 21, 1985.

PALLEY, HOWARD, and JULIANNE OKTAY. "The Chronically Limited Elderly: The Case for a National Policy for In-Home and Supportive Community-Based Services." *Home Health Services Quarterly,* 4: Special Issue, 1983.

PARINGER, LYNN. "Economic Incentives in the Provision of Long-Term Care." In *Market Reforms in Health Care,* ed. Jack Meyer. Washington, D.C.: American Enterprise Institute, January 1983.

PARINGER, LYNN. "The Forgotten Costs of Informal Long-Term Care." *Urban Institute Working Paper 1455–28,* June 1983.

PUNCH, LINDA. *Modern Health Care.* May 15, 1984, p. 131.

RANGASWAMY, ARAVINDAN, and SUSAN HUGHES. "Marketing Long-Term Home Care Services to the Elderly, A Survey." Center for Health Services and Policy Research, Working Paper 88, Evanston, Ill.: Northwestern University, 1982.

"Regulatory Round-up: Final Hospice Regulations Published." *Caring,* February 1984, pp. 5–8.

RICCI, EDMUND, and EDWARD TESSARO. "Medical Direction in Skilled Nursing Facilities." *Research Summary Series,* NCHSR, August 1979.

RICE, DOROTHY P., and JACOB J. FELDMAN. "Living Longer in the United States: Demographic Changes and Health Needs of the Elderly." *Health and Society,* Summer 1983, p. 384.

RICE, DOROTHY, and MITCHELL LaPLANTE. "The Burden of Multiple Chronic Conditions." Paper presented at the Annual Meeting of the American Public Health Association, Anaheim, Calif., November 12, 1984.

RICKER-SMITH, KATHERINE, and BRAHNA TRAGER. "In-Home Health Services in California: Some Lessons for National Health Insurance." *Medical Care,* March 1978.

ROSSMAN, I.; S. D. EAGER; and M. CHERKASKY. "The Treatment of Cardiac Patients on a Home Care Program." *Modern Concepts of Cardiovascular Disease,* 14:7, 1950.

RUBENSTEIN, LAWRENCE; K. R. JOSEPHSON; G. D. WIELAND, P. A. ENGLISH; J. A. SAYRE; and R. L. KANE. "Effectiveness of a Geriatric Evaluation Unit." *New England Journal of Medicine,* 311:26, 1984, pp. 1664–70.

RUCHLIN, H. S.; J. N. MORRIS; and G. H. EGGERT. "Management and Financing of Long-Term-Care Services." *New England Journal of Medicine,* 306: 101–106, January 14, 1982.

SANDRICK, KAREN. "Multis Enter the Health Insurance Field." *Multi's,* February 1, 1985, p. M16.

SCANLON, WILLIAM J., and JUDITH FEDER. "The Long-Term Care Marketplace: An Overview." *Health Care Financial Management,* January 1984.

SCHNEIDER, DONALD. "Nursing Home Quality Assurance in a Changing Regulatory Environment." In *Long Term Care Management,* SRI, Inc., forthcoming.

SIRROCCO, AL. "Employees in Nursing Homes in the United States: 1979 National Nursing Home Survey." *Vital and Health Statistics,* Series 14:25, 1981.

SIROCCO, AL. "Nursing and Related Care Homes." *Vital and Health Statistics,* Series 14, no. 29, 1983, p. 1.

SKELLIE, F. A.; G. M. MOBLEY; and R. E. COAN. "Cost-Effectiveness of Community-Based Long-Term Care." *American Journal of Public Health,* 72, 1982.

SMYTH-STARUCH, KATHRYN; NAOMI BRESLAU; MICHAEL WEITZMAN; and STEVEN GORTMAKER. "Use of Health Services by Chronically Ill and Disabled Children." *Medical Care,* 22:4, April 1984.

SOLDO, BETH J. "In-home Service for the Dependent Elderly: Determinants of Current Use and Implications for Future Demand." *Research on Aging* 7:2, June 1985, pp. 281–304.

SOLDO, BETH J., and KENNETH G. MANTON. "Health Service Needs of the Oldest Old." *Health and Society,* 63:2, 1985.

SOMERS, ANNE, and FLORENCE M. MOORE. "Homemaker Services: Essential Options for the Elderly." *Public Health Reports,* 91:4.

"Special Adults: New Challenge to Primary Care MDs." *Medical World News,* February 24, 1986, pp. 68–81.

SPECTOR, WILLIAM D., and MARGARET L. DRUGOVICH. "PaCS, A Federal Survey Process: What is the Intervention." Paper presented at the Annual Meeting of the American Public Health Association, Washington, D.C., November 19, 1985.

SPICER, WILLIAM A. "Measuring Long-Term Care's Corporate Sector." *Contemporary Administrator for Long-Term Care,* June 1984, pp. 32–35.

STEVENS, ROBERT, and ROSEMARY STEVENS. *Welfare Medicine in America; A Case Study of Medicaid.* New York: The Free Press, 1974.

TAMES, STEPHANIE. "DRGs Spur Hospital Interest in Long-Term Care." *Washington Report on Medicine and Health/Perspectives,* January 28, 1985.

"Task Force Report of the American Psychiatric Association." White House Conference on Aging, 1981.

TING, HAROLD. "New Directions in Nursing Home and Home Healthcare Marketing." *Healthcare Financial Management,* May 1984.

TORREY, BARBARA BOYLE. "Sharing Increasing Costs on Declining Income." *Milbank Memorial Fund Quarterly: Health and Society,* 63, no. 2, 1985.

TOWNSEND, PETER. "The Effects of Family Structure on the Likelihood of Admission to an Institution in Old Age: The Application of a General Theory." In *Social Structure and the Family,* ed. E. Shanas and G. F. Streib. Englewood Cliffs, N.J.: Prentice-Hall, 1965, p. 175.

"Trends: Multi Hospital Systems Target Continuum of Care Strategy." *Hospitals,* March 1, 1985, p. 56.

U.S. DHHS. *Health United States, 1982.* Pub. no. (PHS) 83–1232, Hyattsville, Md.: National Center for Health Statistics.

U.S. DHHS. *Report on Activities Following the Surgeon General's Workshop on Children with Handicaps and Their Families.* Bureau of Health Care Delivery and Assistance, Division of Maternal and Child Health, Public Health Service, April 1984.

U.S. DHHS. Health Care Financing Administration. "Evaluation of the Home Health Agency Prospective Payment Demonstration." Request for Proposals, May 1985.

U.S. GAO. "Medicaid and Nursing Home Care: Cost Increases and the Need for Services Are Creating Problems for the States and the Elderly." DHHS Pub. no. (IPE–84–1), January 1984.

U.S. GAO. "Information Requirements for Evaluating the Impacts of Medicare Prospective Payment on Post-Hospital Long-Term Care Services." Report to Senator John Heinz, Chairman, Special Committee on Aging, February 21, 1985.

U.S. House of Representatives. "Building a Long-Term Care Policy: Home Care Data and Implications." Select Committee on Aging, Pub. no. 98–484, Washington, D.C.: Government Printing Office, 1985.

U.S. Senate Special Committee on Aging. *Medicare: Paying the Physician-History, Issues and Options.* March 1984.

U.S. Veterans Administration. *Summary of Medical Programs.* Office of Information Management and Statistics, September 1984.

ULLMAN, STEVEN G. "Cost Analysis and Facility Reimbursement in the Long-Term Health Care Industry." *Health Services Research,* 19:1, April 1984.

ULLMANN, STEPHEN G. "The Impact of Quality on Cost in the Provision of Long Term Care." *Inquiry,* 22, 1985.

"Update: Multis Saw Continued Growth in 1984: AHA." *Multi's,* February 1, 1985, p. 148.

VAN NOSTRAND, JOAN F. ET AL. "The National Nursing Home Survey: 1977 Summary for the United States." *Vital and Health Statistics Series,* 13:13, National Center for Health Statistics, DHEW Pub. no. (PHS), 79–1994, 1979.

VLADECK, BRUCE C. *Unloving Care: The Nursing Home Tragedy.* New York: Basic Books, 1980.

WALDMAN, SAUL. "A Legislative History of Nursing Home Care." In *Long-Term Care: Perspectives From Research and Demonstrations,* ed. Ronald J. Vogel and Hans C. Palmer. Washington, D.C.: U.S. Department of Health and Human Services, Health Care Financing Administration, 1983.

WALLACE, CYNTHIA. "VA's New Aging Plan Downplays Hospitals, Stresses Alternatives." *Modern Health Care,* May 15, 1984.

WAXMAN, HOWARD M.; ERWIN A. CARNER; and GALE BERKENSTUCK. "Job Turnover and Job Satisfaction Among Nursing Home Aides." *The Gerontologist,* 24:5, 1984.

WEICHERT, BARBARA G. "Health Care Expenditures." *Health: United States, 1981,* Hyattsville, Md.: U.S. Department of Health and Human Services, Office of Health Research Statistics and Technology, 1981.

WEISS, GARY. "Excellent Prognosis: The Outlook for Nursing Home Chains is Growing." *Barron's,* May 18, 1984, pp. 6–8.

WEISSERT, WILLIAM G. "Seven Reasons Why It Is So Difficult to Make Community-Based Long-Term Care Cost Effective." *Journal of Health Services Research,* 20:3, October 1985.

WEISSERT, WILLIAM G. "Size and Characteristics of the Noninstitutionalized Long-Term Care Population." *Urban Institute Working Paper 1466–20,* September 1982.

WEISSERT, WILLIAM G.; WILLIAM J. SCANLON; THOMAS T. H. WAN; and DOUGLAS E. SKINNER. "Care for the Chronically Ill: Nursing Home Incentive Payment Experiment." *Health Care Financing Review,* Winter 1983.

WEISSERT, WILLIAM G.; T. H. WAN; and B. LIVIERATOS. "Effects and Costs of Day Care and Homemaker Services for the Chronically Ill: A Randomized Experiment." Hyattsville, Md.: National Center for Health Services Research, 1979.

WILLIAMS, MARK E.; T. FRANKLIN WILLIAMS; JAMES G. ZIMMER; W. J. HALL; and C. A. PODGORSKI. "Report of a Randomized Trial Evaluating the Effectiveness of an Ambulatory Geriatric Consultation Service." Paper presented at the American Public Health Association Annual Meeting, Washington, D.C., November 1985.

WINKLEVOSS, HOWARD E., and ALWYN POWELL. *Continuing Care Retirement Communities: An Empirical, Financial and Legal Analysis.* Homewood, Ill.: Richard D. Irwin, 1984.

WINSLOW, R. E. A. *The Evolution and Significance of the Modern Public Health Campaign.* New Haven: Yale University Press, 1923.

ZAWADSKI, RICHARD. Personal communication.

ZIMMER, JAMES G.; ANNEMARIE GROTH-JUNCKER; and JANE MCCUSKER. "A Randomized Controlled Study of a Home Health Care Team." *American Journal of Public Health,* 75:2, February 1985.

ZOOK, C. J., and F. D. MOORE. "High Cost of Medical Care." *New England Journal of Medicine,* 302:18, May 1, 1980.

INDEX